DR. HENRY LEE'S
forensic files

FIVE FAMOUS CASES

scott peterson,
elizabeth smart, and more . . .

DR. HENRY LEE'S
forensic files

DR. HENRY C. LEE and JERRY LABRIOLA, MD

Prometheus Books

59 John Glenn Drive
Amherst, New York 14228-2197

Published 2006 by Prometheus Books

Inquiries should be addressed to
Prometheus Books
59 John Glenn Drive
Amherst, New York 14228–2197
VOICE: 716–691–0133, ext. 207
FAX: 716–564–2711
WWW.PROMETHEUSBOOKS.COM

10 09 08 07 06   5 4 3 2 1

Library of Congress Cataloging-in-Publication Data

Lee, Henry C.
    Dr. Henry Lee's forensic files : five famous cases—Scott Peterson, Elizabeth Smart, and more / by Henry C. Lee and Jerry Labriola.
        p. cm.
    Includes bibliographical references and index.
    ISBN 1–59102–409–9 (hardcover : alk. paper)
    1. Criminal investigation—United States—Case studies. 2. Evidence, Criminal—United States—Cases. I. Labriola, Jerry. II. Title.

HV8073.L369 2006
363.25092—dc22

                                                                2006003365

Printed in the United States of America on acid-free paper

To our wives, Margaret and Lois;

to our friends;

and to all those who strive for justice

contents

prologue

As a group, the following five cases illustrate the changing nature of crime solving. Whereas homicide detectives and other law enforcement officials once relied heavily on the accounts of relatives, other witnesses, and—most important—on instinct, today's criminal justice system has the added advantage of modern forensic tools. Also, in earlier days, most serious crimes, like murder, were committed by close family members or by friends of the victim. Many police officials operated on such an assumption. Today, however—and this is a thread running through these cases—extended family members or complete strangers may also be scrutinized and must be completely exonerated, whenever possible. One of us (Dr. Lee) is widely known to counsel *against* tunnel vision and *for* an open mind with greater reliance on logic, a team approach, and on inspecting every shred of forensic evidence.

As in many endeavors, cooperation and teamwork are vital ingredients, and you will notice that we refer to them repeatedly. Some people are mentioned by name; others are not. But they are *all* important in any criminal investigation—hundreds, perhaps thousands, of them. Detectives, crime scene technicians, laboratory scientists, and many, many more—every one of them is a silent hero and deserves our thanks.

This book highlights how modern forensic technology is changing at a rapid rate. Ever-improving DNA analysis, for example, has opened up new opportunities for solving crimes. Included in the mix are image enhancement; expanding databases; and artificial intelligence with its components of crime mapping, crime scene reconstruction, geographical profiling, and expert systems in decision making. Furthermore, contemporary progress in chemistry, molecular biology, instrumentation, microcircuitry, computer technology, and electronics has virtually revolutionized the capabilities of criminal investigation and forensic science. Indeed, the "human" factor can never be replaced, but the definition of forensic investigation is fast approaching that of an exact science.

You are about to read five stories that reflect the emergent new face of crime detection—five cases for which I (Dr. Lee) was the forensic expert. Woven throughout the book—and from my unique perspective—are concise examinations of such forensic and related topics as crime scene reconstruction; bloodstain pattern analysis; search warrants; fingerprint, hair, and fiber analysis; cadaver dogs; consciousness of guilt; the human genome; motive, opportunity, and means; advanced electronic equipment; satanic cult theories; wiretapping; sociopathic behavior; the death penalty; underwater crime scene searches; fire scene investigations; shooting scene reconstruction; child abductions; and the Amber Alert System.

It should be noted that, although the book has dual authorship, when the pronoun "I" is used, it refers to Dr. Lee.

Finally, it is our desire that this book inspire the reader—as well as those in criminal justice—not only to look at all the pertinent evidence but also to view it in its totality, so that justice can best be served.

Dr. Henry C. Lee
Jerry Labriola, MD

chapter 1

the scott peterson case

Eagle, Colorado. Summer 2003. I was maneuvering my rented Dodge Intrepid along the curves of a spectacular mountainside. The air was thin; the sun, high noon. Kobe Bryant's rape investigation was fresh in my mind.

I well remember the call on my cell phone.

"Henry, you got a minute?"

We know each other's voice. The friendship between famed defense attorney Mark Geragos and me goes back some years—in and out of television studios.

"Mark, how are you doing?" I replied.

"Fine, fine. You're working on the Bryant case, right? Is he guilty?"

"Yes."

"He's guilty?"

"No. I mean, yes, I'm working on the case. You know forensic scientists. We don't prejudge anyone; we leave guilt or innocence to the courts. By the way, how's yours doing?"

Mark ignored the question. "I'd like your opinion on something," he said.

"Shoot."

"Can a single strand of hair split into two if it gets bounced around in an envelope?"

"What are you talking about?" I asked.

"Look, forget the question for now. How about joining our team?"

YEAR 2002: DISAPPEARANCE TO VIGIL

Modesto, California

Scott Peterson called his mother-in-law, Sharon Rocha, several times on a raw, dank Christmas Eve 2002. He said that she was missing. He explained that he had seen his wife, Laci, at 9:30 that morning prior to his traveling to Berkeley for a solo fishing trip, about a ninety-minute drive. He mentioned that Laci, who was eight months pregnant with their son, had plans to go grocery shopping and then walk their golden retriever, McKenzie, in nearby East La Loma Park. When he returned home later in the day, she wasn't there. Yet her Land Rover was, as were her purse and cell phone.

Thus began an odyssey that would transfix a nation.

The police were called at 6:30 PM and arrived shortly thereafter. They were joined by Scott and neighbors as they immediately fanned out across the neighborhood in search of Laci—into the park, down dead-end streets, along the banks of Dry Creek. Even a police helicopter beamed its search-light up and down the area. But she was nowhere to be found. Observers said Scott appeared frantic.

Sharon Rocha was terrified, later recalling, "I was scared to death because I knew she wouldn't just be missing. Laci just didn't disappear. I knew something had happened to her and it was cold that night and I had my friend Sandy take me back to my house and get blankets and coats for everyone and I got one for her [Laci] because I knew [she] would be freezing when we found her."[1] She told officers she had talked to her daughter the evening of December 23 and Laci seemed fine, was excited about the baby, and was looking forward to sharing Christmas Eve dinner with her and her husband, Ron Grantski.

Early on, Sharon and Ron, along with Scott's mother, Jacqueline, dismissed any suggestion that Scott was involved in his wife's disappearance, but the authorities were suspicious. The notion of a fishing trip in San Francisco Bay on Christmas Eve did not sit well with them. This in the face of a husband who appeared distraught—at least, initially—seemed odd.

Jacqueline stated that Scott and Laci doted on each other, each acting like a honeymooner even after being married five years.

That December 24 evening, Scott consented to allow the police to search his and Laci's vehicles, which were parked in the driveway. Det. Al Brocchini noticed a roll of chicken wire and four or five large umbrellas wrapped in a blue tarp in the bed of Scott's 2002 Ford pickup. Peterson said he placed the umbrellas there early on the morning of the twenty-fourth with the intention of storing them at his place of employment, a warehouse that contained work-related items and his boat. He explained that he was a California and Arizona sales representative for Tradecorp, a Madrid-based manufacturer of fertilizers. He described his boat as a 1991 fourteen-foot Sears Gamefisher aluminum model with a fifteen-horsepower outboard motor. He claimed that he was an avid fisherman and hunter, and had bought the boat two weeks before. Later it was learned through Big 5 Sporting Goods that on December 20 he had purchased a two-day fishing license for December 23 and 24. But during the earlier conversation with Detective Brocchini, Scott stated his decision to go fishing was made the day that he went: December 24. He handed over a Berkeley Marina launch receipt that indicated he had arrived at the marina at 12:54 that afternoon.

Several hours after Laci's reported disappearance—shortly before midnight—Scott agreed to drive with the detective to the warehouse. Brocchini's official report contained the following:

After searching the vehicles, I asked Scott if I could have our ID tech respond to his residence to take photos and look for evidence. I told Scott I would also like to see the boat he used to go fishing. Scott agreed to allow [our] evidence officer [to] check out the inside of the house, and he agreed to take Officer Evers and [me] to his shop.

I requested the watch commander have ID Officer Lovell respond to the scene. I had Officer Letsinger stand by at the house while we went to Scott's warehouse. I directed Officer Letsinger to have Lovell use an alternate light source in the house to look for any signs of blood. I also requested the wet towels and mop and mop bucket be recovered so they could be inspected for evidence.

The search of Scott's warehouse and the requested recovery of mop, buckets, and towels brings to mind a question I'm frequently asked: "When may investigators search for and seize physical evidence without an administrative or search warrant?" This is where the Fourth Amendment comes in.

It states, "The right of the people to be secure in their persons, houses, papers, and effects, against unreasonable searches and seizures, shall not be violated, and no warrants shall issue, but upon probable cause, supported by oath or affirmation, and particularly describing the place to be searched, and the persons or things to be seized."

The importance of knowing when the Fourth Amendment applies and when it does not cannot be overemphasized. When it does apply, investigators must either obtain a warrant or be certain they fall within one of the narrowly defined situations where they are excused from obtaining a warrant. The most common of these latter situations may be grouped under two broad headings: consent and emergency.

Consent, when voluntarily given, is one of the well-known exceptions to the warrant requirement, and, in the case under discussion, it must be stressed that Scott Peterson voluntarily consented to this initial search-and-seizure operation.

With respect to emergency searches, one of the most incontrovertible involves a fire scene. Another is in the case of police officers arriving on the scene of a homicide and they reasonably believe that a person within is in need of immediate aid. They may then make a prompt warrantless search of the area to see if there are other victims or if a killer is on the premises. (We addressed the issue in *Famous Crimes Revisited*,[2] in connection with the O. J. Simpson case. Detectives claimed their "going over the wall" and entering O. J.'s residence constituted an emergency.) But once police officers have determined that there is no suspect and have rendered any necessary aid, they are required to obtain a search warrant.

As you will see in the searches described on the following pages, seized items must be properly packaged and inventoried, and the chain of custody must be kept intact. The officer who seized the item and every officer who has custody or control of it must be specified in writing. It is also critical that a chain of custody document indicates whenever evidence leaves police custody—as, for example, when evidence is turned over to the laboratory. The investigator should be able to reconstruct at a later date to whom the evidence was given at the laboratory, as well as from whom it was retrieved, and the date on which all these activities were performed.

Detective Brocchini's report continued:

On Tuesday 12-24-02 about 2305 hours, I drove Scott to 1027 N. Emerald. Officer Evers followed us in his patrol car. Peterson identified this as his place of employment. This is a small warehouse [where] Peterson keeps his boat stored and work related items [*sic*]. Scott said he was the only employee that used the warehouse.

Peterson unlocked the door to the office, which we followed him into. Inside the office I could see a desk containing a computer and a fax machine on the ground. I noticed a fax on top of the desk dated 12-24-02 1428 hours indicating it was faxed at that time. Peterson told me that would have been New Jersey time making a three-hour difference, indicating the fax would have arrived in Modesto at 1128 hours. Peterson initially told me he received that fax when he arrived at the shop, before going fishing. I told Peterson it was cutting it kind of close by leaving Modesto at 11:28 and arriving in Berkeley at 12:54. Peterson said he possibly received it when he got back from fishing, but he seemed to think it was before, indicating he did not leave Modesto until after 11:28.

Scott said there was no electricity in the shop, so Scott opened the roll-up door so I could position my unmarked vehicle so the headlights illuminated the boat. I inspected the inside (of the) boat and saw there were two fishing poles. One was an ultra light type stream fishing pole and the second was heavier type [*sic*] fishing pole. There was a small plastic tackle box, which contained old fishing jigs and lures. There was a 6 foot red rope, possibly used to tie the boat to the dock and a pair of yellowish rubber gloves. The rope and gloves [were] wet. There was one piece of concrete, which appeared to have been homemade in a bucket or can. This concrete had a small-hooped piece of rebar on the top making it similar to a homemade anchor. There was no rope attached to this piece of concrete and I saw no other rope in the boat, so I don't know how it could be used as an anchor.

Scott pointed out the mortise he had built the morning before he went fishing. The mortise was on the back of a flatbed trailer, which was also in the shop. From looking at the mortise I couldn't tell if it was built that day or any other day. All of the screws on the mortise were loose, meaning it wasn't put together very well. I saw the warehouse had a forklift and pallets of products double stacked against both walls. I did not do a thorough search of the inside of the business. I only inspected the boat and took a few 35 mm photos.

While taking the photos Scott made an unusual comment to me. As I took photos from outside the shop which would have been a picture of the boat inside the shop, Scott commented, "Don't let my boss see that." That seemed like an unusual comment from a person whose pregnant wife was missing.

About 2345 hours, we left the warehouse and drove directly to the Modesto Police Department where Scott agreed to be interviewed. Once I arrived in front of the Police Department I realized I had placed my notebook inside the boat while I took pictures. I told Scott I needed to return to the shop to get my notebook. I followed Scott in through the office door into the shop area where I found my notebook sitting inside the boat. We then returned to the Modesto Police Department.

On Wednesday 12-25-02 about 0001 hours I met with Peterson in the upstairs interview room. My interview with Peterson was audio and videotaped. Peterson agreed to come to the station and be interviewed regarding his activities from the last time he saw Laci Peterson. I told Peterson I would transport him home at the conclusion of the interview.

On Tuesday 12-24-02 Peterson said he got out of bed about 0800 hours. Peterson said Laci got up a little before him, went out in the kitchen and had a bowl of cereal. Peterson said he got up at 0800, took a shower and then went out and had a bowl of cereal. Peterson said he and Laci watched a portion of Martha Stewart, which Peterson claimed was Laci's "favorite show." Peterson remembered Martha Stewart was baking something with "meringue."

During Scott's bowl of cereal, Scott decided it was too cold to go golfing so he was going to go fishing. Scott said he had recently purchased a 14-foot fishing boat and he was going to take it out for the first time. Laci told Scott she was going to clean up the kitchen area, go to the store and walk the dog. Laci asked Scott to bring in a bucket of water from outside so she could mop. Scott said Laci would not lift a bucket of water because of her pregnancy. Scott said Laci was mopping the tile area, kitchen area and dining area when he left to go fishing. Scott said Laci was last seen wearing black pants, a white long-sleeved top and she was barefoot. Scott doesn't know what type of jacket Laci would wear if she went out, stating she would [probably] wear one of his. Laci usually wears white tennis shoes when she goes out. Scott didn't know if Laci's shoes were missing.

Scott reported that he left the house midmorning, went first to the warehouse to drop off the umbrellas, and then left Modesto around 11:30 AM. He drove to the Berkeley Marina in his truck, with his trailer and boat behind, and arrived there about 1:00 PM. His intent was to fish for sturgeon. He said he had caught none and headed home in the late afternoon. On the way, he used his cell phone to call Laci. There was no answer.

Search for Evidence

The search for Laci intensified. A reward for her discovery grew to six figures while reports of her disappearance appeared on national television. Search parties included hundreds of volunteers, law enforcement personnel, and water rescue crews. On Christmas Day, a tip line was established; anyone with information about the disappearance could phone it in anonymously.

Over the next few days, several interviews of Scott and family members took place while police officers, detectives, and criminalists, armed with warrants, searched his home and warehouse. Chemical tests for blood were conducted on every reddish stain they could find. Swabs were taken from all suspected areas. They recovered Scott's pickup truck, the boat and its contents, the car trailer, a spool of soft aluminum, a spool of plastic wrap, a blue tarp, a gray boat cover, the roll of chicken wire, a pair of needle-nose pliers, a wire cutter, a dog leash, a comforter cover, a Simple Green container (clean wipes), a sponge mop, a string mop, a blue bucket, dirty towels, a Dirt Devil vacuum, a folding pocket knife, a Llama pistol, Donner boots, Timberland shoes, Levi's jeans, and C-20 blue jeans.

On the trailer, there was a circular plastic container into which the homemade cement anchor fit. There was dried cement in and around the container; loose cement rings were scattered about the surface of the trailer.

And all the while, the police were growing more suspicious. A dominant theory was that Scott killed his wife at home, used the towels and mops to clean the crime scene, and then used the truck to transfer her body to the warehouse. There, he wrapped the body in the blue tarp and then the chicken wire. Next, he placed her body in his boat and attached five cement anchors to the body. Subsequently, he threw her body and the anchors overboard in the bay.

Surprisingly, despite early suspicion of Scott by the police, it was later discovered that the Peterson home had never been dusted for fingerprints. Items removed were fingerprinted but not the home itself.

*   *   *

Before discussing the seized evidence, I must first comment on the lack of a thorough fingerprint sweep of the Peterson house itself. Fingerprints along with DNA analysis constitute the most important category of physical evidence at a crime scene. And make no mistake: if the police were suspicious of foul play at an early stage (and all indications are that this was the case), then the house had to be classified as a potential crime scene—as was the warehouse. Moreover, palm prints and footprints could also have been found. Although finding Scott's and Laci's fingerprints in their house would have had no direct forensic value in the investigation, the lack of their prints in their own home would have been a clear indication that the house had been recently cleaned. If their fingerprints or palm prints had been present, then the location, position, and estimated sequence of deposit of the prints could also have provided some investigative leads. Furthermore, prints other than those belonging to Scott and Laci might have provided exculpatory evidence.

Fingerprint evidence can be in latent, plastic, or visible forms. A latent print is an invisible one that requires physical or chemical techniques to develop into a visible form. Plastic prints are produced when the friction ridge on the finger or palm comes into contact with a soft surface (such as blood, butter, or a freshly painted surface) and makes a three-dimensional impression into the receiving surface. Visible prints are made within ink, grease, blood, or other substances. Each of these print types may require different searching, enhancement or visualization, and collection techniques.

Various lighting technologies are employed in visual searches for fingerprints.[3] Most common are side lighting or ALS forensic light source. Once fingerprints are found, the next step is photographic documentation before further processing or enhancement through chemical or physical visualization techniques. The preferred technique for enhancement or visualization depends on the type of fingerprint found and the surface upon which it was deposited. If the fingerprint is found on an immovable object, field processing

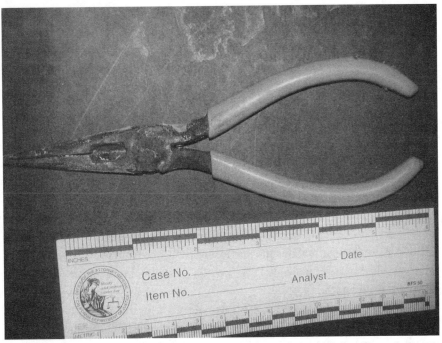

Rusty needle-nose pliers seized from Scott's boat.

is warranted and the print should be collected. This is what was *not* done in this case. If the print is found on a small movable object, then the object can be packaged for collection and examined in the laboratory. This *was* done.

*   *   *

The items taken from Scott's home and warehouse were later analyzed. They revealed the following.

There was no indication that the needle-nose pliers or wire cutters had been used recently, because the rust on them covered their cutting edges and no disruptions in the rust were observed on either of the tools. One hair was reportedly removed from the pliers. This hair was subsequently submitted to the FBI laboratory for analysis. The FBI reported that two hair fragments were found in the package that they received. Both fragments were tested for mitochondrial DNA and fell within the range of Laci's DNA profile. Each fragment had one mashed and splayed end, denoting physical action had possibly torn the two hair shafts. The hair created much confusion and discussion. It was believed that only one hair had been placed into the evidence envelope on December 27 since a picture taken of the pliers on that date showed only a single hair strand. But six weeks later, two detectives reported that, when they opened the envelope in the reception area of the Modesto Police Department building, two hairs were found. However, they did not make a big issue of it at the time. Later, during the trial, the prosecution suggested the hair broke in half while in the envelope, yet a criminalist testified that there were two separate hairs from the start. In any event, it was eventually determined that because Laci and Scott were a married couple, her hair could reasonably have been transferred to Scott, who, in turn, may have deposited the hair onto the pliers during their use by him. The pliers were swabbed for blood or tissue; the swabs tested negative.

Hair is produced by cells within the skin hair follicle and becomes a nonliving substance as it reaches the surface of the skin. Human hairs show great microscopic variation not only from person to person but even from one part of the body to another.

Two British forensic scientists, Angela Gallop and Russell Stockdale, have likened the structure of hair to that of a pencil. The inner core or medulla is the lead. The surrounding layer or cortex is the pencil's wood, and the covering cuticle is the paint.

By using a comparison microscope and relying on certain microscopic characteristics, analysts can determine whether a particular hair is human or animal, and, if human, they can also determine its broadly racial origin (Caucasian, Oriental, Negroid). Some of the properties for comparisons of human hair include its scale pattern, medulla pattern, diameter, length, color, reflectivity, tip, root, special configuration, cross section, pigment, cuticle, and damage.

Special mention should be made of various genetic markers in hairs. In the early days, forensic scientists attempted to type hair samples by ABO grouping and isoenzyme analysis. Well-known ABO blood group substances are present in hair, but their demonstration in hair *shaft* samples has had limited success. Such substances are more commonly used in identifying blood samples. Certain chemical entities called antigens reside on the surface of red blood cells, and it is these antigens that allow typing for identification purposes. Thus an individual may belong to blood type A, blood type B, blood type AB, or blood type O.

Hair *roots*, when present, give more reliable results. Isoenzymes (specific proteins found in the body) have also been detected in human hair roots.

The most valuable of the genetic markers for hair typing is DNA. Hair *roots* are required for the extraction of nuclear DNA from cell nuclei, but hair *shafts* may yield mitochondrial DNA for typing, hence identification. This kind of DNA is found within the cytoplasm outside the nucleus, and more of it is available for sample analysis. Other differences between nuclear and mitochondrial DNA will be considered later.

A few words about fibers, since they are often thought of in conjunction with hairs; both are referred to as trace/transfer evidence. Laboratory examination can identify the fiber type and determine the possible origin of the fiber from a fabric source. Where there is fiber evidence adhering to a movable object at the crime scene, that object should be wrapped and packaged intact. It is useful for the crime scene investigator to remember that fabrics are easily caught or torn by broken windows, edges of ripped screens, as well as other damaged or sharp materials or vehicles.

Other fiber evidence such as fabrics, thread, cordage, rope, or cloth may also turn up at a crime scene. They should be photographed, packaged in clean primary containers (druggist's folds), and placed in outer containers that are sealed and marked. Knotted cordage or ropes should never be untied; they should be photographed intact. In this particular case, when Baby Conner's body was later found, cordage was discovered looped around his neck, right arm, and chest. The condition of this cordage would later become one of the main focal points of the investigation. The police and the prosecution believed that such a piece of cordage was simply floating in the bay area and somehow became tangled around the baby's body. Meanwhile, the defense believed that the length of cordage—with three knots in it—was intentionally used by an unknown killer (or killers). If those knots had not been untied and disturbed and had been allowed to remain on the body, careful measurements and examination might have yielded more conclusive results with respect to this question. But we are getting ahead of our story.

As with hair evidence, known standards of possible sources of the fiber evidence must be collected and packaged for subsequent comparison in the laboratory. If possible, the entire known source should be collected. Cuttings from carpets, fabrics, or other materials can be used as the known sample of the possible source. The known control samples are packaged separately into primary containers, placed into outer containers, and preserved.

*   *   *

Let us return to the analysis of evidence in the Peterson case. The police removed the pistol from the glove compartment of Scott's truck on December 24. There was no indication it had been recently fired since it showed signs of neglect with numerous areas of surface rust and an overall dirty appearance. The analyst observed many types of small fibers, soil, and some vegetable matter on its exterior. Two reddish stains were swabbed for blood and tested negative. No blood, tissue, or similar evidence was seen on the muzzle.

The pocketknife seized from a guest bedroom in the Peterson house yielded no usable latent print impressions, nor did the knife reveal any blood. The blue tarp, boat cover, dog leash, clean wipes container, and Scott's clothing articles were all tested for blood and none was detected. Examination of the wipes container (found in the bed of Scott's truck) developed usable latent impressions. The prints were compared to both Scott's and Laci's and neither showed a match. No other identifications were established since it was felt the latent impressions were of insufficient value to warrant an AFIS (Automated Fingerprint Identification System) search.

When asked about the roll of chicken wire found in his truck, Scott said he had bought it to wrap around trees in his backyard because the cats were scratching them. Later, a detective testified he had indeed seen a cat scratching the trees. In addition, a check at Lowe's and Home Depot stores revealed that the wire was sold in twenty-five- and fifty-foot lengths. The wire seized was measured at twenty-four feet six inches. Furthermore, its cut ends were not consistent with being cut either by the pliers or by wire cutter taken from Scott's boat. The conclusion was that the finding of the chicken wire had no forensic value in this case.

Water that had been collected from inside the bow of the boat was later tested and identified as seawater. Several analysts familiar with fishing accessories opined that two rods and reels and fishing tackle found in the boat were designed for lake or stream fishing and were not adequate for ocean fishing. The prosecution used this information to discredit Scott's story about fishing. (The defense later failed to explain that he had just purchased the boat and that perhaps the fishing equipment came with it, or that it was equipment he had from previous trips.)

Christmas tree debris, feathers, pieces of glass, dried leaves, clumps of hair and fibers, and dirt debris were found inside the Dirt Devil vacuum, but there were no pieces attributable to the blue tarp. The tarp itself yielded thirteen hair fragments: eight possessed characteristics of cat hair, three of dog hair, and two were too small to provide a clear indication of origin. Finding human hairs in the vacuum or on the tarp would have had no direct forensic value unless certain conditions were met—and that was not the case here. A normal person usually sheds about fifty hairs a day. These hairs appear in the telogen phase, one of three in the life cycle of a hair. The first two are the anagen and catagen phases. Anagen refers to the initial growth period during which the hair follicle is actively producing hair. Catagen is a resting period between anagen and telogen, and telogen is the final period in which hair naturally falls out of the skin. Each phase can be microscopically identified by its root appearance. Thus, unless the vacuum and/or tarp hairs were human catagen or anagen hairs with blood or tissue adhering to them, then and only then would they have provided important investigative leads in the case.

In addition, considerable testing for blood was done. None was found on the steering wheel swab or six other swabs from Scott's truck, but four swabs taken from the interior driver-side door's panel did test positive. The DNA from one spot showed it to be Scott's. In a subsequent interview, Scott stated he had scraped his knuckle reaching into the side pocket of the door.

No blood was detected on numerous swabs of the house, warehouse, or roof liner and cargo cover of Laci's Land Rover.

I must emphasize that all these analyses were later examined and verified either by me or by other experts. Although I was not called into the case until May 2003, I followed it practically from its inception. Like everyone else, I was intrigued by the circumstances surrounding the case, the family pleas, and the innumerable theories that flooded national media outlets. They seemed to pour out on a daily basis; one couldn't help but take notice. I remember thinking how strange it was for Scott to go fishing—eighty miles away—just hours before a Christmas Eve dinner at his in-laws. He and Laci were expected to bring whipped cream. And also how strange that Laci's vehicle, cell phone, and purse had been left behind.

Key People

Perhaps this is the best time to introduce the key people in this case; some you have already met, one you will meet soon, and the others—members of the California legal establishment—you will meet before long.

Scott Peterson

Scott was born in San Diego on October 24, 1972. He was the youngest of Jacqueline and Lee Peterson's five sons. Both parents had three children from previous marriages. Scott enjoyed hunting, fishing, and golf at an early age. After graduating from the University of San Diego High School in 1990, he enrolled at Arizona State University on a partial golf scholarship. But in less than a year, he decided to leave and move back with his parents, who had just bought a new home in Morro Bay. Six months later he again moved, attended some classes at Cuesta College, then transferred to California Polytechnic State University, San Luis Obispo, and majored in business agriculture. He worked several jobs to pay for tuition, one of them as a waiter at the Pacific Café.

It was there that the handsome young man met Laci Rocha. They dated for two years and were married on August 9, 1997. Shortly thereafter, they opened a restaurant, the Shack, which they sold three years later before moving in with her parents for a short spell. Scott took a position as the California-Arizona salesman for Tradecorp, a fertilizer company, while Laci worked as a substitute teacher at the elementary school level. In October, they purchased their fifteen-hundred-square-foot, three-bedroom home in Modesto.

Laci Peterson

Laci Denise Rocha was born on May 4, 1975, and spent her early years on her family's dairy farm in Escalon, California. Her parents, Dennis and Sharon, divorced when she was seven, so she moved with her mother and older brother, Brent, to Modesto. After her mother married Ron Grantski, Laci grew up shuttling—without protest— between mother and stepfather in Modesto and her father in Escalon, the small farming community just a stone's throw north. She attended Sonoma Elementary School, La Loma Junior High, and Downey High, where she became a cheerleader and graduated in 1993. At California Polytech, she majored in ornamental horticulture, and, in 1995, this attractive young woman with a winning smile started dating Scott. They married two years later.

Conner Peterson

At the time of Laci's disappearance, she was more than eight months pregnant with a baby boy she had already named Conner. Her due date was February 10, 2003.

Amber Frey

Twenty-nine-year-old Amber began a passionate relationship with Scott in November 2002, five weeks before Laci disappeared. Never married, she was living in Madera County in a one-bedroom, eight-hundred-square-foot guest home. She later testified that Scott initially stated he was not married. Employed as a massage therapist in Fresno when they first met, she had a twenty-month-old daughter, Ayiana. In 2004 she gave birth to a son, Justin. She named the father as chiropractor David Markovich, forty-four.[4]

Judge Al Girolami

The original judge in the case, Stanislaus Superior Court Judge Girolami had served nineteen years on the bench. He had presided over hundreds of cases that ran the gamut of criminal conduct, including murder, rape, and child molestation. Prior to his election to the bench, the sixty-four-year-old jurist served thirteen years as a prosecutor. He is a graduate of Santa Clara University Law School.

Girolami transferred the Peterson trial to San Mateo County because of intense media coverage in Modesto. Later he opted not to continue on the case, stating he preferred remaining in his own community.

Judge Alfred Delucchi

On January 27, 2004, California's chief justice, Ronald George, replaced Girolami with retired judge Alfred Delucchi, seventy-three. Until 1998, Delucchi was an Alameda County Superior Court judge, who oversaw twenty-two capital cases in his three decades on the bench. Although retired, he remained active as an appointed judge, handling some of Oakland's most brutal felony cases. He earned the reputation of being fair-minded and decisive, and he was known for possessing the "human touch." Throughout the trial, he kept a coffee machine in his chambers; both prosecutors and defense attorneys would often drop by for coffee and conversation.

Rick Distaso

A senior deputy district attorney, Rick Distaso joined the Stanislaus County District Attorney's Office in 1996. He had been in the US Army Judge Advocate's Office for three years at the time. He graduated from Marymount Law School just prior to that position. In Modesto he prosecuted several murder cases and, at the time of the Peterson trial, was also on assignment for two other capital cases.

Birgit Fladager

Chief Deputy District Attorney Fladager, forty-three, worked on the Peterson case from the beginning, but at first she did not attend the trial regularly. That changed in mid-September 2004. Many feel the prosecution's case changed also and that she was instrumental in shifting its momentum. Bay Area defense attorney Daniel Horowitz said, "I call her Hurricane Birgit. She came into the courtroom and woke it right up."[5]

A 1986 graduate of McGeorge School of Law, she served as a navy lawyer for a spell and in 1990 joined the Stanislaus County District Attorney's Office.

Mark Geragos

Long before he took the Scott Peterson case, Los Angeles–based attorney Mark Geragos had achieved great fame by defending such big-name clients as Winona Ryder, Michael Jackson, rapper Nate Dogg, Whitewater figure Susan McDougal, and actor Robert Downey Jr. He also represented former congressman Gary Condit during the Chandra Levy disappearance. A frequent guest on the national talk show circuit, he is known for offering pithy legal analyses to pundits and celebrities alike.

Geragos, forty-five, graduated from Haverford College and Loyola University Law School.

The Search Intensifies

By Thursday, December 26, and into the weekend, thousands of volunteers posted flyers and organized search parties to comb drainage ditches, rivers, and farms several times over. Some joined officers in helicopters, on horseback, and in boats. Brad Salzman, a friend of the Petersons, contributed space and equipment to establish a command center at his hotel, the Red Lion. "When you just look at her picture and see her smile, you feel the warmth and want to do something," he told the *San Francisco Chronicle*. "Add to that the holidays and the fact she's eight months pregnant. Since Modesto has been through this twice before [in the cases of Chandra Levy and of three women found murdered in nearby Sonora], [people] really just come together."[6]

Modesto police and firefighters carried out another massive exploration along Dry Creek, then pushed ten miles west, to four thousand acres of wetlands along the Stanislaus, Tuolumne, and San Joaquin rivers. Still no sign of Laci. Many were uttering what no one wanted to hear: Laci Peterson had likely met with foul play. The faces of family, friends, and law enforcement officials grew long. But they would soon grow longer.

Members of the Search and Rescue Unit of the Contra Costa County Emergency Services began a bloodhound search beginning with the Peterson residence at Covena Avenue. The dogs had been "scented" to some of Laci's clothing items. Scott had told police that, when last seen, Laci appeared to be heading with their golden retriever north on Covena to its dead end and, he assumed, over the footpath into East La Loma Park. But the bloodhounds told a different story. They led officers out of the driveway, sniffing their way south toward Yosemite Boulevard. The dogs paused near a Dumpster in the vicinity. Police peered inside but saw no body.

The hounds then began a track in the area of Scott's warehouse on North Emerald Avenue and ran directly to his shop door, then eastward, and finally southbound toward Maze Boulevard.

The behavior of the bloodhounds—particularly running in the center of the streets—led their handlers to guess that Laci did not walk away from her home, but was transported by vehicle.

A subsequent search by bloodhounds at the Berkeley Marina resulted in one of them coursing down the ramp and dock in such a way that the handlers believed Laci's scent had left the location *and did not return*.

But there was also a stepped-up search for physical evidence. Friday, December 27, was an especially full day in that regard. The activities of the Modesto police personnel and others on that day display the diligence of most criminal investigators. Their numerous activities took place after issuance of search warrants for Scott's house at 523 Covena Avenue and his warehouse at 1027 North Emerald Avenue, Suite B-1. There was little doubt in their minds that if Laci indeed had been murdered, her husband, Scott, had to be considered the most likely suspect, if only by virtue of his "fishing tale." Some police officers labeled it "an outrageous alibi."

The team dispatched to Covena and North Emerald included, from the Modesto Police Department: Dets. Rudy Skultety, John Kanuck, Mike Hermosa, Rick House, Darren Ruskamp, Sebron Banks, Kirk Stockham, Al Brocchini, and Ray Coyle; Off. Horatio Ruiz; and ID Techs. Joy Smith and Denise Ducot. Those who took part from the Contra Costa Sheriff's Department were Chris Boyer and Eloise Anderson.

According to a Missing Person Supplement,[7] Dets. Dodge Hendee and Darren Ruskamp conducted an in-depth forensic examination of what was to be the baby's room—its crib, dresser, closet, and all items therein. These included a sonogram of what was believed to be Laci's and Scott's unborn child, two pairs of maternity stretch pants that appeared to be clean and possibly unused, and a canvas bag containing two pairs of boots, hiking gear, and clothing. The clothing was clean and the soles of the shoes were dirt free. ID Tech. Joy Smith photographed all items in place. A hallway closet was searched. Coats hanging there were tested for blood and examined for other forensic evidence. None was found. The household vacuum cleaner was located in the closet and was seized as evidence.

Detective Hendee turned next to the family room and specifically to an alcove that led out into the front yard. There he observed a large number of stains that might have been blood. The majority of them were located on the lower portion of a water heater closet door. There was one stain on the frame of the door (interior side) leading to the front yard. Two were located inside the doorjamb of that same door. Prior to collecting any of those samples, he conducted two presumptive tests on two different stains, both of which tested negative for blood. Despite the results and because of Hendee's belief in the seriousness of the investigation, he elected to collect the samples anyway. All were collected while wearing latex gloves, which were changed between each sample. Each sample was labeled, secured in a portable drying box, and carried to the Modesto Police Department's evidence van. ID Technician Smith transported the samples to the police department's evidence facility where Detective Skultety maintained control of them until Hendee's arrival. Hendee reassumed control of them and packaged them for long-term freezer storage in the department's evidence room. He documented the evidence items on the necessary standard forms.

*   *   *

The forensic investigation of the Peterson house, then, had both negative and positive features: no mention of searching for latent fingerprints in the house itself, but a very thorough search for the presence of blood.

Near the conclusion of activities at Covena Avenue, several members of the team, as well as other members of the Modesto Police Department, reassembled at North Emerald Avenue to process the warehouse pursuant to the search warrant.

The following is presented in an effort to convey the nature of a comprehensive, systematic search; that is, to show how the process works, in all its earnest attention to detail—but also in its tedium. Hence, very little has been left out. Parenthetically, I must add that this mundane but essential phase of an investigation lacks the glamour built into movies or a television series. It is part of the *real* work, however—the staple of good, solid police work. Furthermore, it is one thing to investigate an obvious murder scene—dead body, blood spatter, weapon, and so on—or to seize likely evidentiary items (e.g., a recently discharged gun, a spent shell casing, a bloody dagger). Yet it is quite another to collect items that do not cry out as evidentiary, or to deduce the commission of a murder in the absence of a body.

Detective Hendee continued as the team leader. He found the locked warehouse part of a multistorage/warehouse complex. Scott's storage area—Suite B-1—contained a main door and a roll-up metal garage door. Det. Rick House arrived shortly thereafter with keys to the main door. Hendee complied with the usual "knock and notice" protocol, announcing in a loud voice, "Modesto Police Department search warrant. Open the door." They entered after twenty to thirty seconds of no response. The lights were off and the warehouse was unoccupied.

The first thing observed was an obvious stain on the interior of the walk-in door. It was chemically tested for the presence of blood with negative results; however, Hendee still collected two samples and a control sample for laboratory testing.

The detective then entered the warehouse alone and conducted a walk-through to assess the scene and the work to be done. He came out and directed ID Tech. Joy Smith to enter and videotape the scene prior to any search and evidence gathering. Next, her associate, Denise Ducot, took broad still photographs of the warehouse.

That done, Detective Hendee asked Chris Boyer and Eloise Anderson from the Contra Costa Sheriff's Department to enter with their dog "Twist," a cadaver canine specifically trained to detect the odor of deceased or decomposing bodies. The dog "hit" on one area of the warehouse, along the wall adjacent to the roll-up bay. This was a location directly next to Scott's boat. There was no apparent indication, however, that any foul play took place in that area.

After the canine search, Hendee allowed teams to go in and conduct their investigations. Individual tasks were assigned. For example:

- Det. Rick House was to prepare a diagram of the warehouse and record the approximate location of the items collected.
- Det. Darren Ruskamp was to conduct a search of the boat.
- Det. John Kanuck was to search the rest of the warehouse for items of possible evidentiary value.
- Dets. Ray Coyle and Sebron Banks searched the office area, which was a small ten-by-seven-foot space containing a desk, a couch, and several filing cabinets and shelves with stacks of papers, documents, and binders. Items sought were dictated by the search warrant that had been prepared by Det. Craig Grogan and signed by the Honorable Nancy Ashley. Numerous items were collected. Potential bloodstains on the front door have already been cited. An IBM external floppy drive and an IBM Think Pad laptop computer, a Dell tower Dimension computer processor, and floppy disks were seized. Also collected was an Internet printout of San Francisco Bay fishing locations, financial records including bills, credit card documents, 2002 profit/loss statements, receipts, miscellaneous financially related documents, and a Big 5 plastic bag with a Big 5 receipt for the purchase of fishing lures. There was an unexposed roll of 35 mm Kodak film and several photographs collected off the wall of Scott, Laci, and family friends or possible employees.

- Det. Kirk Stockham was given the responsibility of transporting the computers and accessories separately to the police department and of beginning an immediate forensic analysis of the data files.

The large warehouse bay contained the flat pull trailer, the fourteen-foot fishing boat, a forklift machine, and numerous pallets of a fertilizer product in plastic bags. The pallets were spread out haphazardly throughout the middle to back portions of the bay.

An off-white powder entirely covered the shop's vacuum, which was positioned just outside the office door. A sample from the vacuum's interior and a pair of brown, stained work boots were taken as evidence.

There was a clear plastic water pitcher atop the trailer. The pitcher was partially full of dirty water and had a gray residue around its inside surface. The water was tested for blood, with a negative result. The pitcher was seized. Considerable amounts of the same gray powder were seen spread out around where the pitcher had been found. Small stones/pebbles and several wood screws were mixed in with the powder. The powder and stones appeared consistent with a cement mixture. Within the powdery area were five "voided" circles, each approximately six inches in diameter and consistent with the base of the pitcher. Photographs were taken to document the circles. Investigators speculated that the five circular areas represented spots where the pitcher was positioned when the cement mixture was poured into it, some of which either missed its mark or spilled out over the edge. Another possibility expressed was that additional weights or anchors were made and set there to dry.

The floor of the boat contained a single homemade cement weight, presumably used as an anchor. It was seized. Weighing approximately five pounds, it had a metal clasp cemented into its top, probably for purposes of a rope attachment. Its base was an off-white color similar to that of the powder mix found in the shop vacuum. The top half was gray, consistent with the color of the powder on top of the trailer and around the pitcher. Investigators placed the weight/anchor inside the pitcher and found it to be a perfect fit.

Detective Hendee was curious about a possible match between the color of the gray powder and the color of several small chunks of gray matter in Scott's pickup truck, which was still sequestered at the police department's parking compound. At the conclusion of the warehouse search, Hendee returned to the truck and, indeed, verified by looking that the colors were the same. However, this finding had no forensic value since almost every type of cement is gray in color.

Continuing with the search—a Craftsman sledgehammer was discovered on top of the flat trailer and taken. No hairs, fibers, or bloodstains were apparent on the hammer. Also seized were two large buckets: one red, one blue. Inside the red one were numerous items including black rubber boots, blue gloves, a pair of socks, and a black knit cap. The two containers appeared to have been used at one time or another to mix powder substances; this supposition would have been based on residue inside and around the edges. Whether the residue constituted cement was unknown at the time. In addition, a brown wooden-handled hammer was taken from the trailer. No trace evidence or bloodstains were evident on its surface. The trailer also yielded an unopened plastic bag containing a two-hundred-foot-long roll of 16-gauge metal wire.

A roll of plastic shrink-wrap was taken, as was a pair of black Nike tennis shoes. The shoes appeared to have an off-white powder on their tops and soles, similar to that found in the vacuum. A photo was snapped of a PVC plastic apparatus found on the trailer top. Several stains on it were presumptively tested for blood by Det. Darren Ruskamp and tested negative. Another evidence item was a sample of gray powder located near the roll-up door. The powder was spread over a four-by-six-foot area and was also believed to be a cement mixture.

A Delta hollow chisel mortise (often used in shaping wood or stone) was taken from the trailer. Scott had reportedly told Detective Grogan that he had assembled this item prior to his leaving for his fishing trip. It was a brand-new item that was found out of its box. Its cardboard flap, insert materials, and delivery-tracking sticker were all taken.

With respect to the highly important boat, the detectives seized a "Game Fisher" aluminum fourteen-footer. Its front portion contained one to two inches of water. Two samples were collected to determine if the water was of the fresh or salt variety. (It was found to be salt water.)

Earlier noted was a pair of needle-nose pliers found at the bottom of the boat. It was seized along with a single strand of black hair that was attached to it. The hair was approximately six inches in length. Subsequently, as noted, the FBI lab determined that there were *two* hairs and that they were microscopically linked to Laci's hair.

Other items taken as evidence were as follows: orange work gloves, a

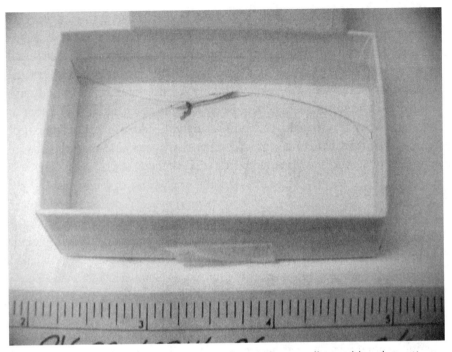

Hair from pliers collected by detectives.

piece of red nylon rope, a single orange-colored hair four inches long, a single brown shoestring, and a green nylon bag containing orange and black nylon rope, a blue hat, a pair of yellow gloves, a green glove, a camouflage jacket and rain pants, two fishing lures, a 1999 fishing license made out to Scott Peterson, and an unexpended Remington 20-gauge #8-shot shell. All these items did not exhibit any forensic value.

A paddle with a red fiber stuck to its tip was seized. Also taken were a brown tackle box, a Master Fish 650 GR rod and reel with a lure attached at its end, a Pro Guide fishing rod with reel, and a sample of liquid collected from the boat's engine, which was a pull-cord type. Detectives tried for at least ten minutes to start the engine, without success. Det. Ray Coyle transported the boat to the police department's auto shop. The four-hour warehouse search was completed at 6:30 PM. The roll-up door was resecured and the main door locked. Left on the desk were a copy of the search warrant and a copy of the property sheet that listed hundreds of items collected pursuant to the warrant.

All the other items were placed into the evidence technician van and transported to the Modesto Police Department where Detective Hendee reassumed control of them and secured them in the evidence room with the assistance of Joy Smith. Smith insured each package was properly sealed and then labeled them with her initials. All evidence with the exception of the boat and blood samples was secured in the evidence lockers. The blood samples were secured in the evidence freezer. As in the case of the search at Covena Avenue, each evidence item was documented. The exact number of items seized was unknown because several agencies and detectives were involved. In addition, each item generated subitems.

*   *   *

Police and volunteers pressed on in their search for Laci. The Red Lion command center bustled with activity, maps were dispensed, and the tip line had received nearly five hundred calls by Sunday, December 29.

Meanwhile, Scott refused to grant media interviews. Laci's brother, Brent Rocha, indicated Scott was too emotional for that. But Scott did appear at the hotel each day, manning the phones, thanking volunteers, and even posting a note near the main entrance: "As I see every person who comes through this door or out searching, I tell Laci about them, looking for her. Early this morning, I felt she could hear me. She thanks you."

And then, by the end of the week, police spokesman Doug Ridenour made this somber statement: "In investigating the circumstances of [Laci's] disappearance and in view of the timing of the holiday season, it becomes more apparent that the disappearance is the result of foul play. The investigation is progressing forward with that main focus."

By Monday, December 30, the scientific evidence had provided precious little of anything substantive. Put another way, the hundreds of pieces of evidence collected from Scott's house, warehouse, boat, and car did not yield any clues. But the human drama was about to receive an unexpected jolt.

The Frey Factor

At 1:43 AM, a lissome, blonde massage therapist from Fresno placed a call to the Modesto Police Department. She identified herself as Amber Frey and stated she was a single parent with a twenty-two-month-old daughter, Ayiana.

After dealing with two dispatchers and many delays, she was put through to a detective and claimed to have struck up a romantic relationship with Scott Peterson. She explained she had finally found out he had a pregnant wife who had disappeared. Eventually she was put in touch with Det. Al Brocchini. By then, it was New Year's Eve morning. At 11:00 AM Brocchini and fellow detective Jon Buehler arrived at Amber's home, where she agreed to allow them to record their conversation, and she proceeded to relate the details of a six-week relationship with Scott. They had met on a blind date on November 20, at the Elephant Bar in Fresno. She said that Scott told her he was not married. Her best friend, Shawn Sibley, had arranged the date. Later—December 9—Shawn told Amber she had learned that Scott might be married. When Amber confronted him, he said that he had "lost" his wife. Scott also said the current holiday season would be the first without her.

Police reports showed that Amber gave the following statement to the detectives:

> I told [the police] about the first time Scott called, and about our meeting at the Elephant Bar . . . and—much as it shamed me—about spending that first night with him at his room at the Radisson Hotel. I told them the day he met Ayiana, and . . . all the wonderful dates that followed, and how excited I was about the future. And then I told them about the afternoon he told me that he had lost his wife, which was precipitated by Shawn's discovery that he had lied to us both.

This, too, from the police report:

> . . . so I asked him, I said, you know, when you came to me later about being married . . . I didn't know Shawn is the reason you came to me on the 9th. I said . . . When were you going to come to me with this? And he said, well, I was going to come to you after I came back from Europe, was going to see . . . where things were going with us . . . but, you know, then [Shawn] confronted me. And I said . . . that just . . . that does bother me. And he goes, Amber, . . . I know, I'm sorry, but that was . . . it was wrong. He goes, Amber I just . . . I know you're an independent woman . . . and I just hope you can trust

me enough that—in a decision that would affect you and Ayiana—
that you would be able to say yes, and trust me in that. And I said, I
said . . . Can I trust you with my heart?

After lunch, the detectives suggested that phone calls between her and
Scott be taped. Amber agreed.

*   *   *

Here, I'm compelled to comment on this most controversial subject of wiretapping. In the United States, wiretapping and electronic eavesdropping have
become a confusing legal issue. There is considerable disagreement about
both the constitutionality of such procedures by law enforcement agencies
and the methods of controlling government eavesdropping.

Safeguarding an individual's privacy has always remained paramount in
developed democracies. Thus, in theory at least, wiretapping often requires
authorization by a court and is normally approved when evidence demonstrates it impossible to detect criminal or subversive activity in less intrusive
ways. In practice, however—depending on state law—permission for telephone tapping is easily obtained on a routine basis without further investigation by a court or other entity granting such permission. Some states, in
fact—Connecticut is an example—permit a finite number of wiretaps each
year.

According to the police reports, there were 340 calls exchanged between
Scott and Amber from November 2002 through April 18, 2003. Later, during
the trial, jurors would screen a total of forty-two phone conversations and
voice mail messages from December 16, 2002, to February 19, 2003—nearly
ten hours of recordings.

The following are more taped recordings, some taken from Amber's
book and others from transcripts introduced as evidence in the trial.

Scott: You don't deserve . . . the things that I've done to you, but . . .
there's no but. I'm sorry, hey, I agree with you. I want to explain
everything to you—
Amber: Yes . . .
Scott: —but I can't.
Amber: Why?

Scott: Um . . . primarily . . . well, there's lots of reasons. Primarily, protection, for everyone.
Amber: Protection of who?
Scott: Everyone.
Amber: Who is everyone?
Scott: Everyone is . . . is you, me, our families.
Amber: Everyone that would possibly look at you a little bit differently because who the hell am I? I . . . I . . . you know, you're telling me that we're . . . oh, I asked is there anybody else? "Oh, no, I'm monogamous as far as I'm concerned."
Scott: I never cheated on you.
Amber: Ha, ha, ha!
Scott: I never did.
Amber: You're *married*. How do you figure you never cheated on me? Explain that one to me?[8]

Amber: But isn't that ironic, Scott, when I first met you on our date, how you told me you were going to Maine with your family and you were going to Paris and Europe and all those things? And then you came to me after Shawn had found out you were married and you came and told me this elaborate lie about her missing and this tragedy and that . . .
Scott: No.
Amber: And that . . . that this will be the first holidays without her?
Scott: Sweetie, I never said . . . Amber, I . . .
Amber: Yes?
Scott: I . . . God, I don't want to fight with you. Um . . . you know that I . . . I never said tragedy or missing.
Amber: Oh, yes, you said you've lost your wife.
Scott: No . . . That—yes.
Amber: You said obviously without me saying much, but we were
. . .
Scott: I said that I lost my wife.
Amber: Yes, you did.[9]

Amber: I'm saying now, was Laci aware of the situation about me?
Scott: Yes.

Amber: She was?
Scott: Yeah.
Amber: Really? How did she respond to that?
Scott: Fine.
Amber: Fine?
Scott: Yeah.
Amber: An eight-month-pregnant woman fine about another woman?
Scott: You don't know all the facts, Amber. You don't know all the facts.[10]

Amber: Do I need to be afraid of you?
Scott: Absolutely not. I am not a monster.
Amber: Did you have anything to do with your wife's disappearance?
Scott: Ah, ah—no, but I know who did and I'll tell you when I see you.[11]

During the trial, more taped telephone transcripts were introduced by the prosecution. They became the most damaging evidence for the defense.

Consciousness of Guilt

On New Year's Eve 2002 more than twelve hundred people attended a candlelight vigil for Laci in East La Loma Park. Scott arrived late and didn't sit with the rest of the family on the stage. He told his brother-in-law he preferred to remain in the audience with a niece and some friends. At one point he allegedly was seen smiling and laughing.

This was but one instance of Scott's behavior that many described as suspicious, a characterization that is at the heart of a legal concept called "consciousness of guilt." Basically, a person to whom this concept is applied simply acts guilty. The appearance of guilt holds little sway in modern judicial circles, but in the early part of the last century, consciousness of guilt was regularly used against defendants. In the famous Sacco-Vanzetti case of the 1920s, for example, it figured prominently in the guilty verdict handed down in a double homicide.[12] Nevertheless, some experts hold that the concept is still alive, at least in the minds of the public and, of more importance, in the minds of jurors.

In Scott's case, his conduct during the early days following Laci's disappearance, throughout the months of the investigation, during the trial, and even at the conclusion of the penalty phase appeared odd, if not suspicious. It included a demeanor that remained his constant companion in and out of the courtroom and largely influenced, in the opinion of many, the ultimate verdict.

The interpretation of each item in the following litany may vary but, taken as a whole, they may be loosely categorized under the rubric of "consciousness of guilt." (We skip ahead in some instances):

1. When he first called his mother-in-law, Scott used the word "missing" to describe Laci, not "gone" or "not here."
2. Scott had volunteered to pick up a Christmas gift on December 24 from a nearby farm, but he never showed.
3. He claimed that a photograph of him and a blonde woman was a fake when, in fact, it showed him with Amber Frey.
4. Laci's mother asserted that the last time Scott had seen his wife, he said she "looked so cute" curling her hair, yet he told police that she was mopping the floor and he told Laci's cousin that she was watching Martha Stewart on television.
5. An avid fisherman, Scott maintained that he went fishing for sturgeon on Christmas Eve, but his fishing equipment was inadequate for catching that large a fish.
6. Two Modesto police officers said that Scott could not answer when asked what he had been fishing for on Christmas Eve; and then, immediately after, they saw him throw down a flashlight and curse under his breath for, what they considered, flubbing the answer.
7. At least a month before Laci disappeared, Scott's sister-in-law asked him if he was ready for fatherhood. She said that he replied, "I was hoping for infertility."
8. Scott declined early media interviews that would encourage the public to search for Laci.
9. Several people stated that he appeared unusually composed for one whose wife had vanished. Specifically, Laci's cousin alleged that he showed more emotion when he burned chicken at a summer barbecue than he did when his wife suddenly disappeared.

10. Scott traded in Laci's 1996 Land Rover to help pay for a 2002 Dodge Ram pickup truck; his Ford truck was still in police custody. Of this transaction, Laci's father, Dennis Rocha, said, "If he had any consideration for her, he would keep the car if he knew she was coming home." Scott's brother-in-law added, " . . . it just makes you question what is going on. His behavior is obviously not reflecting one that has a missing wife."

11. According to prosecutors, GPS (Global Positioning System) data indicated he drove to the bay three times in January 2003, possibly fearing someone would find the body (a "return to the scene" mentality).

12. There were reports he was contacting real estate agents about selling his house.

13. When he was arrested, Scott's hair was dyed reddish blond and he had grown a goatee. He was carrying fifteen thousand dollars in cash, his brother's ID, his sister-in-law's credit card, his mother's gasoline card, and four cell phones. In his car was a map showing directions to Amber Frey's workplace in Fresno plus camping and survival equipment. Since he was less then thirty miles from the border to Mexico, authorities speculated he might be about to flee the country.

14. But the best depiction of Scott's "guilty" behavior was that of Amber Frey's attorney, Gloria Allred, in an interview with CNN reporter Heidi Collins.[13] Allred said, "[W]hat kind of husband calls from the vigil that is being set up for his missing pregnant wife and is on the phone with his woman friend, Amber, and has this ebullient, man-about-town, bon vivant conversation with her, lighthearted, on New Year's Eve, where he's saying to her, 'I miss you,' and 'Hi, sweetheart.' And 'I'm at the Eiffel Tower,' and 'I'm in Paris.' Now, does that sound like a grieving husband who's missing his pregnant wife? I don't think so. And I think it was totally inappropriate, and I think the jury could find from that, that perhaps he wasn't a grieving husband at all."

YEAR 2003

Interviews

The new year began with an intensification of efforts to locate Laci. San Francisco Bay—particularly in and around the Berkeley Marina—was searched six times in January, nine times in February, and ten times in March. Most, if not all, searches were conducted with side-scan sonar devices, boats, and search-and-rescue diving teams—some of which were in cooperation with the US Geological Service. Experts had to juggle considerations of weather conditions, drift, and threshold velocity, and some used sophisticated-sounding equipment such as multibeam echo sounders. But no body was found during the three-month search period. At one point, a highly trained six-person FBI dive team arrived from New York and for nearly a week searched a theoretical target area, discovering no evidence. Other crews searched on a grid-by-grid basis. A special firm was summoned and, utilizing a state-of-the-art sonar device called REMUS, mapped the entire floor of the bay. The firm identified 260 targets and coordinated a diving effort with six boats and four dive teams from San Mateo, Contra Costa, and the US Coast Guard. They spent more than eight days recovering items— items that later proved of no evidentiary value: a tea bottle, a beer bottle, a fish net, some car tires, a rope, and several other assorted items. Again, the investigation reached a dead end.

In recent years, various types of advanced electronic equipment have been used to aid in underwater searches. A proton magnometer detects variations in the earth's magnetic field caused by ferrous metals. A side-scan sonar unit can be used to detect any objects that protrude above the bottom of the body of water. Sub-bottom profiler instruments generate high-resolution images of the bottom and some objects buried just beneath the bottom surface. If the surface can be searched by boat, then sonar devices, grappling hooks, or specially trained canines can aid in the process, particularly in the search for bodies. Experts agree that dogs can detect people underwater at depths as great as a hundred and fifty feet. If suspect areas or items are located, these areas must be marked for further diving and exploration by either placing buoys or identifying the location with a GPS unit. This system consists of twenty-seven satellites orbiting the earth at an altitude of about 12,500 miles. Through a process called triangulation, an exact position may be fixed. Highly sophisticated GPS units are accurate to within a few inches. As with land-based searches, it is important to identify perimeters and establish a search pattern or grid, thus ensuring that the entire area is searched. Searches for submerged bodies have further complications. As decomposition progresses, the body will fill with gas and float; any current or tide may remove it from the original site and deposit it elsewhere. For this reason, it is essential to attempt to determine if the location of the body is the primary crime scene.[14]

I have twice mentioned side-scan sonars. These are devices with a transducer (this converts a signal from one form of energy to another) that is housed in a tow vessel. The latter is dragged through the water ten to twenty feet above the bottom. The reflected sound waves are processed into an image similar to an aerial photo that is viewed real-time on a computer monitor. The side-scanner searches a swath sixty to one hundred feet wide at a speed of about two miles an hour, depending on the size of the object being sought. Despite the use of this sophisticated technology, no bodies were found.

At the time the bay was being combed, police, family, and friends were growing more pessimistic about finding Laci alive. Their misgivings about Scott's credibility mounted, and an ever-widening sense of distrust set in regarding his behavior. The whispers got louder. There was no letup. Laci's family was growing impatient with him, the news media hounded him, and the few local interviews he granted did little to change his image. Even his efforts to broaden the search 310 miles away to Los Angeles and as far as San Diego—430 miles away—were met with skepticism by the public and resistance by police officials. And there were collateral developments that were scrutinized and much publicized, too.

The number of tips received by the Modesto Police Department had ballooned to nearly three thousand. Scott's home was reportedly burglarized, but detectives concluded the incident was unrelated to the case at hand. The 1996 disappearance of a nineteen-year-old student from California Polytechnic University at San Luis Obispo was brought up. He and Laci had been students there at the time. But he was ruled out as a suspect. A submerged object located by sonar at the Berkeley Marina caused a brief stir, but it proved to be an old boat anchor.

One thing that was kept under wraps, however, was an authorization by Stanislaus County Superior Court Judge Wray Ladine to wiretap two of Scott's cell phones, allowing investigators to monitor and record every call he made and received. As I mentioned, the use of wiretaps is more prevalent than people commonly believe.

On January 24, Amber Frey held a press conference to confirm the affair that she had had with Scott. "I was told he was unmarried," she said. "Scott told me he was unmarried. We did have a romantic relationship. When I discovered he was involved in the Laci Peterson disappearance, I immediately called the Modesto Police Department."[15] After the conference, Scott flooded Amber with calls from his cellular phones, pleading with her to see him. But she refused.

Three days later, the police further expanded their surveillance. Upon learning that Scott had arranged to rent a truck from a rental car company, they in turn arranged to have a tracking device installed in the vehicle. Furthermore, the wiretaps revealed he had agreed to multiple interviews with members of the news media.

The next day, he was interviewed by Diane Sawyer of ABC News. He appeared alternately calm and teary-eyed during the ninety-minute television show. He indicated that he had decided to speak out after a month of relative silence because suspicion of him had distracted the public from helping find his wife. "I had absolutely nothing to do with her disappearance," he said. "And you use the word murder. Yeah, I mean, that is a possibility. It's not one we're ready to accept and it creeps into my mind late at night, and early in the morning." He denied that the revelation of his affair with Amber Frey led to a physical confrontation with Laci. "In the morning I've been taking the dog down to the park where she walked," Scott stated. "It was our time. It's a way to experience her now, for me. A lot of times I can't make it very far," he said, crying. He stressed that no anger or cruelty was ever expressed between him and his wife. "Violence towards women is unapproachable," he said. "It is the most disgusting act, to me."[16]

On January 29, Gloria Gomez of CBS affiliate KOVR in Sacramento interviewed him at his home.[17] He claimed he had told Amber a few days after Laci's disappearance that he was married, though, according to taped phone calls, he didn't inform her until two weeks later.

Scott allowed a third television interview, this time with local reporter Ted Rowlands.[18] It, along with the Sawyer and Gomez episodes, would be entered into evidence at the trial. A few revealing excerpts from the conversation with Rowlands include the following:

Scott: Obviously um, the relationship I had with Amber was inappropriate and unfair to a lot of people. And I owe a lot of people apologies for that and have no question that that's the case. I'm uh, I'm very glad that she came forward, Amber did, in the press conference. Um . . . I had told Laci about it in early December. Um, I also, uh, called Amber shortly after Laci's disappearance, a few days after. And told her that I was married and told her, you know, about Laci's disappearance so she knew. And then shortly after that she had a meeting with the police.

Rowlands: What's your level of cooperation in this?

Scott: Uh, it's complete, um, I know that Laci's family doesn't feel that and that's unfortunate . . .

Rowlands: Do you have some Christmas presents to open still? . . .

Scott: Yeah, no, no, they're in the corner. Luckily a friend who came up and you know, was helping, um, took down the tree and things like that, things that I wouldn't be able to do. And it was very kind of her to do that when I was gone one day. Just because it's a difficult reminder.

Rowlands: How about Conner, the approaching due date?

Scott: Yeah.

Rowlands: And then . . .

Scott: That's why these next couple of weeks are so critical, February 16th is the due date. That's why we need to get the flyers out there to all the medical offices that we can. Um, the nursery is really for him. That door is closed. I can't look, you know, in that door.

Rowlands: You worked on it. What sort of preparations did you do?

Scott: Yeah, it's a, it's completely outfitted. I mean the furniture is there, it's painted, it's ready. You know, all the little bitty clothes and all those wonderful things we have for him, it's ready for him.

Rowlands: You told Laci about the affair, explain what her reaction was to that. Was that something that really did put your marriage in jeopardy or not?

Scott: No. It did not definitely put our marriage in jeopardy. Um, obviously not a positive thing. Um, and you know. I think the real question that you're getting at and that everyone wants to know, is, you know, did that precipitate to me being involved with her disappearance. And, no, it did not. And I had absolutely nothing to do with Laci's disappearance.

Rowlands: Could it have precipitated in Laci leaving voluntarily?

Scott: No. No. No. Certainly not. You know, I mean when we get to the root of, you know, what the question is and that's did I have something to do with her disappearance and no, I had nothing to do with her disappearance. And please help all of our families, all the grieving families you've seen on TV, and help yourselves, more importantly help Laci because she's out there being held somewhere and she needs to be home with her family.

Reaction to Scott's interviews was hardly favorable. His in-laws, especially, were incensed, and his "performances" seemed to spark the removal of all subtlety from their remarks. Laci's mother, Sharon Rocha, for example, straight-out pooh-poohed the idea that Laci knew of the affair, but even if she had, Sharon added, she would never have accepted it as calmly as Scott had implied. She would later share with NBC's Katie Couric, "I don't believe that was true. I'd said that before. People close to Laci would have noticed a difference in her attitude. And in her personality."[19]

They also raised doubt he would have elected to go fishing just before their family dinner on Christmas Eve. "I had assumed he had gone golfing," Sharon told Couric, "because that's normally what he did was golfing. I'd never known him to go fishing by himself."

"That's what I was told," Laci's stepfather, Ron Grantski, chimed in. "I remember I think I said something about that to the police that night and still thinking that that's where he went, because everybody was running around. And then he told me, Scott said then, 'No, I didn't play golf. I went fishing.' So, that was the first I'd heard of it."[20]

Remarkably, the day he had spoken with Gloria Gomez was the same day he turned in Laci's Land Rover as a down payment on the new truck.

Before January's end, a few forensic findings were made public. One involved Scott's seized computer. Analysis revealed downloaded nautical charts and tidal information of San Francisco Bay. Another was the discovery that paint markings on Scott's boat matched the paint on some buoys at the Berkeley Marina. The latter simply supported Scott's contention he had gone fishing there, but authorities held it also supported their hunch that he may have dumped Laci's body in the bay.

Laci's due date—February 10, 2003—came and went as volunteer searchers streamed across a canal area west of Modesto. No sign of Laci or any relevant physical evidence materialized. That night, scores of family and friends held another candlelight vigil; just as many news reporters and camera people were also there—but not Scott.

His in-laws were making bolder insinuations. They and Scott's family were growing further apart. His mother, father, and siblings, however, refused to give up hope of finding their daughter-in-law and, on February 13, held a news conference in San Diego. Scott's sister, Susan Peterson-Caudillo, presided and opened with "Our families are once again asking for the public's help. It has been seven weeks since Laci and the baby were taken from us. With her due date being this month, we feel it is critical to continue our efforts in looking for Laci everywhere we can. Every day we post and deliver flyers. We meet people who are not aware that she is missing. We cannot ignore that Laci's pregnancy may have had something to do with her abduction. After seven weeks she could be anywhere. So please do not think you live too far from the situation to help." When a reporter asked her about Scott's whereabouts, she replied tersely, "He's in Modesto . . . 350 miles away. And we're here in San Diego. So we do what we can to help."[21]

On February 18 and 19, police conducted a second court-approved search of the Peterson house during which they (1) collected about fifty-four bags of potential evidence, ninety-five items in all; (2) observed that the nursery room had been turned into a storage area; and (3) impounded his new truck. *Larry King Live* had a special program on February 19. A panel of forensic and investigative experts was asked to participate. I was asked to comment on the meaning of the second search. I said that the many bags of material might indicate the police didn't have any solid evidence to use against Scott, although he still remained a suspect. So they were—to use one of my favorite phrases, "working the evidence"—hoping it would link Scott to the disappearance.[22] When asked what they were looking for, I responded that a missing person either walks away on his or her own or is a tragic victim. So, in addition to unusual trace evidence—that is, not belonging to Laci or Scott—no doubt the police were looking for bloodstains, broken objects, damaged walls, signs of disarray—anything suggesting a struggle. I pointed out that the police probably went through a crime scene reconstruction in the process, posing such questions as: Had the furniture been rearranged? The carpet shampooed? Anything missing from the house? I assured Larry that what the Modesto police had done was an excellent crime scene search. After all, I said, many of them had taken my courses on crime scene investigation. I don't remember, but I think I grinned, and the other panelists did, too. On that same show, we also touched on the polygraph—or lie detector—test. When asked about it, I explained that such a test is an investigative tool but not admissible in most courts as core scientific evidence; that people may react differently under stress. Larry pressed me on whether or not I understood why Scott would refuse to take one. I answered in the affirmative, expressing my opinion that if someone clears a polygraph test, he is still a suspect. But if someone fails it, he will be considered a liar. My final comment on the show dealt with a report I'd received that police had spotted some Viagra in the house.

February 19 was also the last day of taped conversations between Scott and Amber Frey. She asked him to discontinue calling her. He phoned her two more times after that, but she cut him short on both occasions.

Ostensibly, not much of any consequence happened for the rest of February, although the public and the media (including the Chinese and European press) clamored for information and swamped law enforcement officials with inquiries about any new leads in the case. Then on March 6, more than two months after Laci had disappeared, her case was reclassified as a homicide. Craig Grogan, the Modesto Police Department's lead investigator, issued the following statement: "As the investigation has progressed we have increasingly come to believe that Laci Peterson is the victim of a violent crime. This investigation began as a missing persons case and we all were hopeful Laci would return home safely. However we have come to consider this a homicide case."

On and off for the next few weeks, members of the Modesto Police Department, with assistance from their counterparts at the Tuolumne County Sheriff's Department and other law enforcement agencies, combed the waters north of the Berkeley Marina without success. They had focused primarily on that area because of information gleaned from the navigational charts downloaded from Scott's computer.

Discoveries and Arrest

April 13 and 14 marked sixteen weeks since Laci had vanished without a trace. The two days were bittersweet, depending on one's perspective. For law enforcement officials, they initiated a turning point in a criminal inves-

tigation filled with arduous, spare-no-pains work: identify, collect, and evaluate evidence; follow every lead; check all tips; monitor phone calls; and
scour endless neighborhoods, waters, and wastelands. For the Rocha family,
the days signaled the possibility that their grandchild, baby Conner, would
never be born and that his mom, their Laci, was dead. And as for the
inscrutable Scott Peterson—who knows where his mind was at that time? Or
he, himself, for that matter. He hadn't been seen in weeks since all surveillance had been put on hold.

At last a dramatic turn of events occurred. Two dogs discovered two
bodies on two consecutive days. They were neither bloodhounds nor cadaver
canines, but ordinary pets on a walk with their owners. On Sunday, the first
body, an intact, near-term male infant, was found along the shoreline bor-
dering the San Francisco Bay Trail, about seventy-five miles from Modesto.
A piece of ropelike material was wrapped around the baby's neck. It was
knotted at the back of the neck and circled around the arm and onto the chest.
On Monday, a woman's decomposed torso was discovered at the foot of a
sea wall, a mile away at the Point Isabel Regional Shoreline in Richmond.
She lacked a head, forearms, hands, an entire left leg, and both feet.

Police theorized that the bodies had washed ashore during a spell of
stormy weather over the weekend, but they were not certain of a connection
between the grisly finds, nor one to the Peterson mystery. It appeared that the
female body had been in the water a long time, no doubt months, although
the infant was remarkably well preserved, indicating that he had been in his
mother's womb well after her death or was deposited in the water at a much
later date. There was an unconfirmed report that a nursing bra usually worn
by women during late-term pregnancy was found on the woman's remains.
The Modesto police were notified. The bodies were taken to the Contra
Costa coroner's office for autopsies. An "eluviation" expert—one who
studies how water affects corpses—was consulted in an effort to determine
how long they had been submerged.

The autopsies did not reveal the cause or manner of death, but the
coroner's office did disclose that two of the woman's ribs were fractured and
most of her internal organs were missing. The womb, however, was present;
there was an "unnatural" opening at its upper portion and its cervix was
closed. If the bodies were related, this suggested that the baby left the
mother's body not through the birth canal but via the opening on top. As to
the condition of her body—the missing parts, specifically—the coroner

could only offer the likely explanation of decomposition, battering by tides, and feeding by creatures of the deep. The state crime lab acted swiftly in trying to analyze tissue samples to see if the bodies were, in fact, those of Laci and Conner. But, early on, there were thorny obstacles, both scientific and administrative. Was suitable DNA available? How long would it take to sort out the various problems of jurisdiction: territorial, police departments, crime labs? Yet, they were overcome with impressive speed and coordination, unlike that ever experienced by many officials. Such was the aura surrounding the case, the sudden public frenzy, and the barrage of national and international media coverage—not to mention high expectations for immediate action.

So, while the situation was still uncertain, some things were perhaps beginning to make sense. Here were two as yet unidentified bodies presumably washed ashore by a storm and found a mile from one another—a badly ravaged woman, possibly pregnant; the other, a near-term fetus, possibly hers. The possible husband of this woman, already under suspicion, had claimed to have gone fishing ninety minutes away from home—and finally we learn it was at a location *very near the discovery areas* where Scott had placed himself with the boat. This was a revelation that smacked of something greater than coincidence.

As mentioned before, the dog walkers' stumbling upon the bodies generated excitement for some and deep sorrow for others. Those excited, particularly police officials, had been influenced by a combination of factors: the families involved in the tragedy, the drudgery of the investigation, and the recent lull in its progress.

Larry King waxed poetic at the very end of an offhanded comment during one of his television shows: ". . . this extraordinary case which got so much attention and then seemed to be lost in the news. In fact, it had gone dead, as they say, right until, of course, this body recovery. And it happens almost right at the end of the Iraqi war. If you're looking at news timing, it's kind of weird, *like it waited*" (italics added).[23]

Defense attorney Mark Geragos, who, ironically, would later represent Scott at the trial, was a guest on that show. He followed with "It is. It's almost unbelievable, in terms of the news cycle . . . that all of a sudden, it washes—or the bodies wash ashore."

And now, there seemed to be a crack in the case. Thus, from the moment the bodies were discovered, identification teams focused entirely on Laci and

Conner. This despite a California database of one hundred DNA samples of other missing people. (The state has more than twenty-five thousand active missing persons cases.)

A positive identification of Laci and Conner Peterson was made on Friday, April 18. Scientists had used DNA samples from the baby's thighbone and muscle tissue, from the woman's shinbone and muscle tissue, from Laci's parents, and from a blood specimen obtained earlier from Scott.

But the day before, police were convinced of two things: (1) that the bodies were the "correct" ones and (2) that Scott had dumped his weighted-down and pregnant wife into the bay almost four months earlier. They didn't wait, therefore, for the testing to be completed. Instead, they opted to locate Scott and arrest him. Modesto Det. Craig Grogan, the lead investigator; Det. Phil Owen; and Stanislaus County prosecutors huddled with Superior Court Judge Wray Ladine. Shortly thereafter, Grogan, Dets. Al Brocchini and Jon Buehler, and Sgt. Al Carson left for San Diego, armed with a secured probable cause arrest warrant. The warrant, signed by the judge and addressed to the people of California, speaks for itself:

To any peace officer of said state:

Complaint upon oath having been this day made before me by Detective Craig Grogan, I find there is probable cause to believe that two counts of crime of 187 PC, homicide, committed on or about Monday December 23, 2002, or Tuesday December 24, 2002, in the county of Stanislaus by Scott Lee Peterson, date of birth 10/24/72.

You are therefore commanded forthwith to arrest the above-named defendant and bring him/her before any magistrate in Stanislaus County pursuant to Penal Code Section 187.

The within named defendant may be admitted to bail in the sum of: No Bail.

Scott was arrested without incident shortly before noon on the following day, Friday, and was to be arraigned on Monday. To repeat, it was an arrest made *before* test results confirmed the identities of the bodies. And it was made because authorities felt there was a good chance Scott was getting ready to flee the country. Remember, at the time, Scott's hair was dyed and he had fifteen thousand dollars in cash on him.

How did people react to the tumultuous news of that week? Perhaps there is no better way to illustrate the preponderant thinking of the law enforcement, forensic, and news communities than to select some opinions expressed on the TV show I cited earlier in quoting Mark Geragos. It was April 18, roughly six hours after Scott was apprehended. That night, *Larry King Live* featured, among others, Geragos; former prosecutor and Court TV anchor Nancy Grace; California attorney general Bill Lockyer; Modesto police chief Roy Wasden; and me. Lockyer and Wasden appeared as participants in hastily called press conferences in Richmond and Modesto respectively. The remarks of Mark Geragos, a good friend of mine, were singularly ironic. It seemed to me he spoke like a prosecutor at the time, yet, as we shall see, he came to be Scott Peterson's chief counsel later—only two weeks later in fact.

Geragos: . . . obviously, it's an awful time for everybody involved. But the one thing I would say has got [Scott] most up against it is the fact that the bodies and the remains are found within one mile or two miles of the very location that he provided to the police as his alibi. That is devastating, in terms of why they've arrested him so quickly. In fact, I—you know, my feeling was as soon as these bodies washed ashore, the fact that he—that it was a mile or two miles away meant to me that he was going to be arrested any moment.

. . . even though it's a circumstantial evidence case, the most damning circumstantial evidence comes out of his own mouth and his own hands, when he hands the police that receipt from the very location where two miles away, she's found. I mean, that is just a devastating thing. And if you believe that he's the one who, for whatever reason, got into it with her, killed her, put her in a tarp, put her in the boat, did all of that, I mean, in a sense, could they say, We're going to try . . . Oh, they're going to try him.

. . . if Scott Peterson did this crime—and everybody's, you know, innocent until proven guilty, and as I've said, it's a damning, circumstantial case—the man is a sociopath if he did this crime. I mean there's no other way to put it. This is his wife, his unborn baby boy. If he's the one who took the two of them up there and put concrete around them and threw them into the ocean and concocted this story and went out onto Diane Sawyer and gave that impassioned plea with the tears—I mean, that's not somebody that generally you're going to want to give manslaughter to.

Grace: . . . another thing that will aggravate a jury is that it just wasn't a murder, it was leading the family along for all these months, wondering what happened to the baby, what happened to Laci. And if he is responsible, not only [have] Laci and Conner been victims, but the family, every day wondering, looking out the window—and I know we all thought this was coming one day, but that family—I know, I've been there—held out hope that maybe, just maybe Laci would come home. That's all over, and he could be responsible for those moments of pain.

Lockyer (at the press conference and picked up by the show): Earlier this week . . . East Bay Park authorities discovered two bodies, an unidentified adult female and a full-term infant, in the Richmond Point waterway. After concluding that an identification could not be made using traditional coroner investigative techniques, the Contra Costa sheriff coroner, Warren Rupf, provided our DNA lab with samples from the unidentified bodies. And just to mention what we worked with—on Monday, we received these samples: from the unidentified female, a tibia bone—that is, a shin—and muscle tissue. From the unidentified fetus, a femur, or a thigh bone, and muscle tissue. On Tuesday, with the assistance of the Modesto Police Department, we received DNA reference samples from the regional lab in the Department of Justice in Stanislaus County. The reference samples are required in order to help make an identification of the unidentified bodies. Specifically, we received oral swabs from Laci Peterson's parents, Dennis and Sharon Rocha, a reference blood sample from Scott Peterson. Hair samples from a brush owned and used by Laci Peterson. . . . Over the last 24 hours, our criminalists have been working to compare the DNA from the remains with those reference samples. And tonight, we informed the Modesto police chief and Contra Costa sheriff coroner of our results. There is no question in our minds that the unidentified female is Laci Peterson. The unidentified fetus is the biological child of Laci and Scott Peterson. The Contra Costa coroner, of course, makes the final legal determination, but we are convinced that the match is one in billions. The family law code in California presumes paternity when the parental index exceeds 100, and in this instance, it's in the billions.

Wasden: They told us that it was 1.9 billion times on the identification of Laci to the hair and that it was 18 billion times on the identification of Conner to Laci and the identification of Conner to Scott.

I was asked to comment on the condition of Laci's body. I suggested that since she had no head or hands, there might have been a wire or rope around her neck and limbs plus a heavy weight anchoring her down. The combination of something sharp wrapped tightly around her neck, the decomposition process, and the waves in the bay might have caused the decapitation. I didn't believe she "jumped into the water" on her own for, if so, she should have been floating within a relatively short period of time instead of three months later.

In one of Mark Geragos's statements above, he used the word "sociopath." While I'm not an expert on psychiatric terminology, my countless investigative and courtroom experiences exposed me to forensic psychologists who are knowledgeable in that area. It might be worthwhile, therefore, to make a distinction here of the difference between sociopathic (another word for it is psychopathic) and true psychotic behavior. Psychotics are legally insane and, as such, are out of touch with reality. They often hear voices (e.g., "Son of Sam" would hear the voice of his dog, Sam, apparently advising him to kill) or they see visions, or both. They do not know right from wrong. Sociopaths (psychopaths), on the other hand, *do* know right from wrong. They are mentally ill for sure, but they are not legally insane. A sociopath lacks a conscience and essentially couldn't care less about the harm he might cause. They sashay through society experiencing little or no guilt over any evil deeds they leave behind. Most sociopaths lack any capacity to accept love.

Thus, on *Larry King Live*, representatives of those in law enforcement, the media, and forensic science weighed in with their opinions. But how about the reaction of Laci's family? At a press conference held immediately after Scott's arraignment, Laci's mother, Sharon, first took pains to thank everyone who played even the smallest part in the investigation. Then she delivered a poignant account of the family's ordeal, concluding with the words "I can only hope that the sound of Laci's voice begging for her life, begging for the life of her unborn child, is heard over and over and over again in the mind of that person every day for the rest of his life. The person responsible should be held accountable and punished for the tragedy and devastation forced upon so many."

And Scott's family? They spoke of a rush to judgment, of an unfair court of public opinion. Each member took turns lambasting the police and the prosecution. A spokesperson said, "[The Modesto police] worked strictly on a theory that was dreamt up by this lead detective within the first eight hours, and they've pursued it backward from there and they have neglected so many good leads." Scott's mother, Jackie, was vehement in her criticism: "[The police] were preening and patting themselves when the announcement [came] of who those bodies were. That's totally inappropriate. . . . You have a district attorney calling this a slam-dunk before there's even an arraignment. I'm feeling like I'm living in Nazi Germany or the Soviet Union. I'm sick of this." Wittingly or not, the Peterson family was tipping its hand to reveal a dominant defense argument during the trial.

Talk on the street? One person said, " Laci represented everything *good* about womanhood. And that cad? Everything *bad* about manhood." Some branded him "stupid" for dumping the body near where he went fishing. Others countered that it was clever of him to do so, calling it reverse psychology. A few felt a "public lynching" had taken place. Even fewer considered him innocent after the discoveries and arrest. But for the vast majority, sentiment slid rapidly from suspicion to hate to disgust. And those very few who considered him innocent wondered if he could get a fair trial.

At Monday's four-minute arraignment, Scott—handcuffed, shackled, and garbed in an orange prison jumpsuit—pleaded not guilty to two counts of capital murder. Public defender Tim Bazar was assigned to the case after Scott stated he couldn't afford a private attorney. He would later be assisted by Ken Faulkner. Kirk McAllister, who had previously represented him, refused to acknowledge whether or not Scott was able to afford his services. But after Scott's arrest, McAllister did say, "The police had to make an arrest in this case or they would have looked like *Mayberry RFD*. . . . The press wants instant truth. The police want self-serving truth. Hopefully, there will be a process to get to the whole truth about what happened."[24]

Two days later, during a taping for *The John Walsh Show*, District

Attorney James Brazelton hinted that his office might seek the death penalty and, within a day or two, the decision to do so was made official. It was a decision usually reserved until after a preliminary hearing—which was months away. Commentators surmised that a determination had been made that the crime was heinous, that it involved a double homicide, and that Scott's behavior evoked that old legal concept "consciousness of guilt." These factors, they said, no doubt influenced the penalty sought.

DNA and Other Physical Evidence

Have you ever noticed that stonewall masons periodically step back from their work in progress? So it should be during other endeavors. Let us pause to take stock of the meaningful physical evidence in this case thus far. It will not take long because, despite the commendable efforts of law enforcement and scientific personnel in accumulating and analyzing hundreds of possible evidentiary items, there were scant revelations; none, in fact, to link Scott Peterson to the crimes with certainty. Or to link anyone else for that matter.

Among the hundreds of items, perhaps the most potentially significant were the boat, the powdered cement, the pliers with adherent hair, the navigational charts from Scott's computer, the ligature around Conner's neck, the tapelike material on Conner's cheek, duct tape on Laci's body, and a blue plastic tarp that washed ashore the day after the bodies were found. Sources said the tape on Conner's cheek resembled audio or video tape rather than the sticky variety, which raised the possibility that his body came in contact with garbage in the bay. Subsequently, the medical examiner stated that it was not tape, but seaweedlike material—material that was not preserved for defense experts to examine.

It appeared that two other forensic issues were more important than the above-mentioned physical evidence, namely, the age of the fetus and whether or not the ligature around the baby's neck arrived there accidentally (from an artifact in the bay) or deliberately. It must be stressed, however, that all evidence was entirely circumstantial: there were no eyewitnesses, no fingerprints, no DNA incriminating Scott, not even a murder weapon or known cause of death. Speaking of DNA, we've seen how it identified the remains of Laci and Conner. But I must digress for a moment to share a comment recently made to me by a dear colleague. He said that whenever I speak about DNA, my eyes light up. I had never realized it, but I can understand

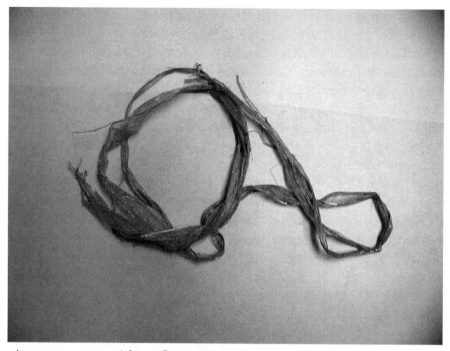

Ligature removed from Conner's neck and body by medical examiner.

why. For aside from my appreciation of this molecule as a valuable forensic tool, its role in the function of the human body—as the essential component of the human genome—has always intrigued me. Without getting too technical, let us consider the following discussion.

The human genome is the complete genetic code of an individual and, therefore, the blueprint of human life. It is established at conception and determines whether that individual has blue eyes or black hair as well as other inherited characteristics. The way to remember how the genetic code works is to divide it into parts. These parts include cells, cell nuclei, chromosomes, genes, and DNA (deoxyribonucleic acid). That's about it. Everything takes place within the cell and especially in its nucleus. The body has roughly one hundred trillion cells and most of them have a nucleus; red blood cells do not. A single chromosome is a long molecule of DNA. Genes (about seventy-five thousand in humans) are carried by the chromosomes (twenty-three pairs of rodlike structures in the cell nuclei) and mitochondria (the energy source of the cell). Mitochondria are located in the cytoplasm, which is within the cell but outside its nucleus. In humans, somatic (nonsex) cells have forty-six chromosomes, occurring as twenty-three pairs within the nuclei. Each pair consists of one chromosome from the mother and one from the father. One pair, the sex chromosomes, determines an individual's sex. Women have two X chromosomes, whereas men have one X and one Y. The very same DNA is in every nucleated cell of our body and is different from every other person's except in the case of identical twins. Basically, the cell, under instructions from the DNA, works like a miniature factory, pumping out proteins and enzymes, and carrying out other functions. As just mentioned, the identical DNA is in all nucleated cells, such as those of bone, the heart, the brain, and white blood cells. The thing that boggles my mind is how a heart cell can have the same DNA as a brain cell and, even so, knows enough to pump blood rather than to think.

I could go on and on about DNA, which has increasingly become the new identification tool in our forensic armamentarium, but I would become more technical, more laboratory oriented. For instance, what I was referring to in the above admittedly simplistic explanation was *nuclear* DNA. There is also *mitochondrial* DNA (mtDNA), as pointed out earlier. Both may be extracted from various body tissues (blood, semen, hair roots, organs, bone, etc.) and used to identify the origin of a particular sample. However, mtDNA is much less informative than nuclear DNA. The distinction to be made is that nuclear DNA usually degrades more easily, while mtDNA is less affected by exposure to most environmental elements. The type of DNA testing performed on Laci's and Conner's remains was nuclear DNA using the STR (Short Tandem Repeats) technique. This type of analysis allows for the extraction of DNA from small amounts of degraded tissue. The DNA can then be amplified in order to provide a sufficient quantity to determine the DNA profile.

The Preliminary Hearing

Two weeks after Mark Geragos pointed out the difficulties of defending Scott, he stood before Stanislaus County Superior Court Judge Al Girolami and spoke the words, "I was retained by Mr. Peterson's family." Geragos had thus just taken over from the public defender's office as Scott's defense attorney. Mark and I have been friends for many years. He is a very warm, personable individual and an excellent attorney with a long and distinguished track record. The next day, May 3, he contacted me.

*   *   *

The following are the most important 2003 dates of my role in the case. They represent just that—*dates*—and do not reflect the time consumed, the many meetings, the phone calls, the evidence examinations, the research, the conferences with other experts, and the effort put forth in pondering various analyses and directions in the investigation. Despite my behind-the-scenes consultations, I was never called to testify because the amount of forensic evidence was so meager. My findings were exactly the same as those of the forensic scientists from the California Department of Justice (DOJ) Laboratory.

May 3: First contacted by Mark Geragos as the defense expert in forensic science.

July 8: The start of my review of documents pertaining to the crime scene, autopsies, physical evidence, and overall investigation. Investigator William Pavelic provided me with additional information. (He and I had worked together on several cases before—a very experienced and thorough investigator.)

August 10–12: Flew to Modesto to inspect the Peterson house, the warehouse, the neighborhood, and the park; conducted a time line study and reviewed investigative leads.

August 11: Examined Laci's and Conner's bodies with my good friend and renowned forensic pathologist Dr. Cyril Wecht. Reautopsy performed (see below). Met with Mark Geragos, investigator Pavelic, and other attorneys to examine Peterson house.

August 12: Reviewed documents and examined physical evidence in DOJ crime lab.

October 23: Had conference call with Geragos's office: Review of DOJ fourteen-page report (discussed below, in conjunction with my analysis of the physical evidence).

October 25: Traveled with Dr. Wecht to Redwood City for meeting with Geragos and associates. Reviewed information given by pathologist Dr. Brian Peterson and various other forensic scientists. Reviewed all photographs.

With regard to Dr. Wecht's and my examination of the remains of Laci and Conner, the following are the particulars of that experience.

We found Laci's body to be in an advanced state of decomposition. Many barnacles were attached to her bones. Her head, neck, both arms, left leg, part of her right leg, and all her skin were missing. We did not find any of her internal organs except for a uterus (womb) that appeared to have a slit near the top. Its lower pole (cervix) was closed. We did not see any incision marks that would have suggested a cesarean section. These uterine findings led us to conclude that Conner must have been expelled, not through the normal birth canal, but through the abnormal upper opening. The reason for this continues to be somewhat of a mystery. My hunch, however, is that, because the baby appeared so well preserved, he had to have remained in Laci's uterus for some time before being released into the water and that this release occurred by virtue of the eventual tear in the uterus which, in turn, had been brought about by decay and marine creature activity.

We examined the body meticulously for evidence suggesting that any of Laci's external body parts may have been cut from her torso by a mechanical device (e.g., chain saw or hand saw). We found none. No bone fractures were evident either by visual inspection or by x-rays. It was our judgment that Laci had been weighted down in the bay and, as decomposition progressed, her head, neck, and extremities pulled away from the joints.

On the other hand, the baby's body was relatively intact. Conner's head, arms, and legs were all present. His internal organs had been removed during the original autopsy. There was no evidence of trauma. Plastic tape was wrapped around his neck and held in place by a knot. In terms of development, he weighed three and a half pounds (all his soft tissue was macerated owing to decomposition in the water); and he measured nineteen and a half inches in length. The latter statistic is within the range of a full-term baby. His remains were considerably less decomposed than Laci's. Our joint opinion was that the baby had been out of the uterus and in the water for approximately two to five days before washing ashore.

On March 18, 2004—just under three months before the trial—I exam-

> July 16, 2002
>
> Well, it's official. I am with child. Today Scott & I had our first sonogram. The baby looked like a peanut. So small, with a strong heart beat & active. She/He rolled over, kicked its arms & legs. I didn't realize a baby at 10 weeks would be so developed. My true feelings would be 'excitement & relief. I can't wait for the changes to come.

Page from Laci's diary.

ined and analyzed the important items of physical evidence. Most of this took place in a second-floor meeting room of the San Mateo County sheriff's and district attorney's office. (Examination of the fiber mass and of one pair of maternity pants occurred at the Modesto Police Department, while the boat was examined outside in its parking area.) There were sixteen items in all. Four have previously been discussed: gun, blue tarp, dog leash, and pliers. Regarding those four, my own findings and interpretations coincided with those expressed by various other analysts. My personal notes concerning the remaining twelve items are condensed as follows:

SUNGLASSES: Inside a carrying case. Ralph Lauren 125 model. Few scratches on lenses. No blood or trace evidence observed.

DIARY BOOK: 5 × 7 inches. Total of 12 written pages. First page dated July 16, 2002. No blood or trace evidence observed.

MEAD MEMO PAD: Red cover. Only one page has written notes. No blood or trace evidence observed.

MATERNITY PANTS: Size M. Woman's black stretch pants obtained from baby's room. Measures 27 inches long and 11 inches across. Relatively new but appears to have been worn. Numerous hairs on it. Most appear to be of animal origin. Some are soft body hair. Numerous fibers: multicolored. Grass, vegetation matter. No bloodstains seen.

IN DUE TIME MATERNITY PANTS: Black. Different style from previous pair. Measures 35 inches long and 14.5 inches across. Relatively new. Few hairs and fibers. No blood.

UMBRELLA: Large with white plastic evidence tape on it. 100 percent polyester. Made in China. Measures 110 inches long. Has some water marks and small tears. No blood.

BAG: A plastic bag with the logo and lettering of Target on it. Lettering is white, blue, and yellow. Some dirt but no blood.

TWINE: About 50 inches long with single knot at 11.5-inch location. Double strand from knot to short end, so entire twine is shaped like fork. Is polyethylene-like fiber. Clear in color. Has appearance of type of plastic film pulled and twisted into twine. Black/brown residue attached. Also algae, but no barnacles.

BRA: In small box. Bali brand. Large size, beige color. In good condition, nearly intact. Adipose tissue (fat) adhering to it. Some marine matter; many barnacles attached.

MATERNITY PANTS: Motherhood label. Size S. Made in Guatemala. Horizontal cut mark on right leg. One pinkish stain. Adipose tissue. Marine matter, many barnacles.

FIBER MASS: One large tangled fiber mass taken from Laci's right leg. Contains lump of materials: fibers, adipose tissue, algae, marine matter, barnacles. Also contains small piece of rope, one end with a knot; other end appears cut.

BOAT: Two seats on top, giving three compartments. No chemical or microscopic tests were conducted. Whitish residues were noticed in front compartment similar to aluminum oxidation residue. One 10-inch circular residue imprint pattern found in rear compartment. Residues were inconsistent with cement.

* * *

Public support for Scott continued to erode. Some predicted Geragos's familiarity with the media would be an asset, but others were not as sure. The defense attorney appeared to take the bull by the horns. Within twenty-four hours, he waived the right to a bail hearing and also gained permission from Judge Girolami for Scott to wear street clothes in court rather than an orange jumpsuit. The attorney had argued that images of his client in chains and prison attire were prejudicial. I remember thinking at the time that the most prejudicial image I ever had was that of accused killers Sacco and Vanzetti sitting in a Massachusetts courtroom every day in a metal cage! That was the custom in those days.[25] Geragos also claimed that reports by prosecutors indicated that the police used "voodoo" tactics including psychics, facial recognition programs, and voice stress analyzers during their investigation. The prosecution deflected the charge, taking the opportunity to stress that there were thirty thousand pages of evidence assembled in the case against the defendant.

At the same time, a "voodoo" or a satanic cult theory surfaced during those first two weeks—purportedly leaked by the defense and then openly advanced by Geragos. The theory was predicated on several points, not the least of which was a series of bizarre paintings on coastal rocks and wood slabs that lined the Bulb, a projection into San Francisco Bay. The Bulb is located one mile from where the bodies were discovered. In chilling colors, the paintings portray tortured figures, ghosts, flames of hell, and Satan himself. Other points raised were a mysterious brown van spotted in the Peterson neighborhood, an equally suspicious man with 666 tattooed on his arm, and the allegation that cults were operating in the Modesto area. Rumors circulated that Conner had been cut from Laci's womb during a satanic ritual and that her body was later found mutilated in a manner consistent with ritual sacrifice. Believers asked rhetorical questions: Why had Laci disappeared on Christmas Eve and reappeared on Good Friday? Why was her due date the same as Amber Frey's birthday?

Prof. Laurie Levenson of Loyola Law School gave the opinion: "There's been a concerted effort to try to change the hearts and minds of potential jurors. The strategy is to create questions now and hope that it will translate into reasonable doubt later."[26]

But Miami legal expert Sandy Marks, who was consulted by the defense in the William Kennedy Smith trial (I was the chief criminalist in that case), had a different take: "Jurors—and people in general—have a short memory. This will only be good for the next week or two. If he's got substantial stuff, why leak it now? Let's save it for right before the trial."[27] From time to time, though less so in recent years, the satanic cult theory has been dragged out by a criminal defense team, dusted off, and presented anew. Mark Geragos did it early in this case—and for good reason—but he eventually abandoned the tactic because his declaration that members of such a cult might have abducted Laci in a brown van could not be substantiated by investigators. He had also suggested a link between Laci's death and that of another eight-month-pregnant woman, Evelyn Hernandez, whose body had washed up in the bay several months before those of Laci and Conner. Geragos noted that the disappearance dates for both women marked holy days on the satanic calendar. But authorities, including the presiding judge, did not allow the defense access to the files of the Hernandez case, thus weakening its theory.

Moreover, satanic cults posed credibility problems among the public and within academia. These cults had been somewhat of a national obsession fifteen or twenty years earlier, when the public was flooded with reports of international Satan worshippers committing ritual murders: of supposedly fifty thousand people killed each year and then disposed of through cult-controlled hospitals and mobile crematoriums. At the time, remembrances of "Nightstalker" Richard Ramirez, "Helter Skelter" and the Manson family, the People's Temple, and even Count Dracula dominated conversations in coffee shops and on television.

In 1992 FBI agent Kenneth Lanning, a specialist in the agency's Behavioral Science Unit, stated he could find "little or no corroborative evidence" for the alleged widespread murders and abuse as promulgated by the media. "Until hard evidence is obtained and corroborated," he said, "the public should not be frightened into believing that babies are being bred and eaten, that 50,000 missing children are being murdered in human sacrifices, or that Satanists are taking over America's daycare centers or institutions."[28]

And with the Peterson case, all satanic references fizzled as more and more information was compiled and digested. Soon the news was dominated by other things. On Sunday, May 4, a day that would have been Laci's twenty-eighth birthday, three thousand people attended a memorial service for her at the First Baptist Church of Modesto. Neither a jailed Scott Peterson nor his parents were there. Nor was Amber Frey, who allegedly said her presence would only create a media circus.

The next six months resonated with continued press leaks, floated theories, police follow-ups of nine thousand tips, and constant legal one-upmanship. Judge Girolami sealed court papers containing evidence that the police had used to obtain a warrant to arrest Scott. The judge also issued a sweeping gag order, decided that Scott's taped phone calls to his former attorney and to news reporters should be given to Geragos, and banned cameras from the upcoming preliminary hearing. In such a hearing—often called a "mini-trial"—prosecutors must lay out their case so a judge can determine if sufficient evidence exists to hold a defendant for trial. The standard of proof is much lower than the reasonable doubt standard at the trial itself; the judge must simply rule that there is "reasonable cause" to believe the defendant committed the crime in question.

But there were no "bombshells," no new evidence—at least none that was made public. Divers conducted a week-long search of the bay for the express purpose of finding anchors that they believed had weighed down Laci's body—ones possibly matching the cement weights found in Scott's warehouse. They came up empty-handed.

Scott was still being hammered in the press, while, on the other hand, he was receiving hundreds of letters from female admirers. And the Peterson and Rocha families kept up their feud.

*   *   *

All eyes were on the preliminary hearing. After five postponements, it finally began on October 29, 2003, nearly a year after Laci's disappearance. It would be another six months before the actual trial would start.

In the weeks before the hearing, both the prosecution and the defense went to great lengths attempting to set its own stage. The prosecution appeared to be a bit more circumspect in its public pronouncements, simply hinting at blockbuster evidence while Scott's defense team promised it. Both sides also waged a paper war in court filings, regarding whether or not information obtained from DNA analyses, search dogs, police wiretaps, satellite tracking devices, and a hypnotized witness was worthy of consideration by the judge.

Mark Geragos maintained he had new evidence that "totally exonerates" his client. "The evidence which demonstrates Mr. Peterson's innocence," he wrote, "also provides evidence of the true killer or killers' modus operandi and provides clues as to the method and of circumstances surrounding the killings." He also referred to twenty thousand pages of witness statements, police reports, and phone tips—all of which constitute "discovery" materials—that prosecutors are required to hand over to the defense. "The recent discovery provided by the prosecution negates any possibility that Mr. Peterson committed this horrific crime," he stated.[29]

Court papers indicated that the prosecution would allude to the importance of black hair on the pliers found in Scott's boat and, through expert DNA testimony, would "prove" that the hair "matched" Laci's. The implication would be that a near-term woman would be unlikely to be on a boat. To help counter that argument, the defense was expected to label the hair fragment nothing more than secondary transfer evidence that originated from Scott himself—not unusual for a husband and wife living together. The defense would also dispute the reliability of so-called matched mitochondrial DNA in the case, for this type of DNA is maternally linked only; that is, it could yield information only pointing to the prosecution's contention that it derived from Laci or any of her maternal relatives, but does not, in and of itself, constitute a true "match."

Furthermore, legal analysts presumed that the prosecution would rely heavily on testimony from the handlers of the search dogs that tracked Laci's scent, the phone records revealing Scott's conversations with Amber Frey, and the prosecution's interpretation of his fishing trip. But the defense was planting seeds: implying that all the prosecution had was circumstantial in nature; that its evidence was theoretical; and that the preliminary hearing would lack facts of substance. District Attorney James Brazelton's comeback was that the defense had theories of its own.

Unexpectedly, three of the first four days of the hearing were spent on DNA issues. The first witness alone, an expert in the field, gave nine hours of testimony. And there was more time devoted to the subject later as both sides jockeyed back and forth, each side using its "own" expert witnesses—one extolling the value of mitochondrial DNA testing, the next denigrating it.

Detectives, scientists, relatives, even a cleaning lady were paraded onto the witness stand. The testimony of the medical examiner who performed the autopsies was especially riveting. Dr. Brian Peterson (no relation to the defendant) indicated that, in his opinion, Laci was dumped into the bay still carrying her baby. (The defense had publicly expressed the view that she had been abducted, held until she gave birth, and then killed.) The pathologist said that after weeks, perhaps months in the water, and because of massive decay, the baby's remains eventually separated from her womb. He said, in fact, that Laci's remains were so badly decomposed that he could determine neither the cause nor the time of death. He then spoke of the body's missing parts and his conclusion that the baby was much less decayed because he had been protected by his mother's womb. He stressed Laci had not delivered vaginally and that there were no incision marks indicating a Cesarean section. "With time, tidal action and animal feeding, the uterus was torn away and at that time, the fetus was released," he explained. However, Dr. Peterson also acknowledged he could not rule out live birth. (This was exactly the statement Mark Geragos wanted.)

The defense had suggested the ligature found around the baby's neck was proof that he had been born alive and then had become a victim in a kind of ritualistic killing. Dr. Peterson cast doubt on the significance of the ligature, however, when he opined that it represented "either flotsam or jetsam" (refuse floating in water). Geragos disagreed, maintaining that something, such as a bag, had been secured around the baby's body.

The estimated age of the fetus came up. It had been said earlier that Laci was thirty-two weeks pregnant when she disappeared. But the pathologist insisted the fetus was full-term, while another analyst placed the age at somewhere between thirty-three and thirty-eight weeks.

"Nobody estimated gestational age at 32 weeks," Geragos said, staring at the pathologist.

"Correct," the doctor said.

When all was said and done, on November 18, Judge Girolami ruled that prosecutors had enough evidence to try Scott Peterson for the murder of his pregnant wife and unborn son. He would face his second arraignment on December 3. The judge also ruled that mitochondrial DNA testing used to match the hair sample from the pliers to Laci's genetic profile was scientifically reliable and could be used as evidence in the trial. Observers partial to each side agreed that the hearing had considerable merit and would affect future strategies. One veteran crime reporter said shaky witnesses would not be called back at trial and "bombshells" that never exploded would be cast aside.

Some preliminary hearings for murder last only a morning or two, encompassing the testimony of a medical examiner and key police detectives. This one lasted eleven days, stretched out over nearly four weeks. DNA testimony alone took up almost a third of the time—perhaps a harbinger of things to come.

*   *   *

The next phase of the case lasted six months—from arraignment to trial—and included a number of crucial and hotly contested matters, most of which required ruling by the presiding judge.

1. In court papers, prosecutors contended that Scott killed his wife in their home, hauled her body to his warehouse, and placed it in his boat. From there, he drove the body ninety miles to San Francisco Bay and dumped it overboard. The body had been weighted down with cement anchors that he had made at the warehouse.

2. Judge Girolami acquiesced to Mark Geragos's written motion to change the venue of the case. The trial would be shifted from Modesto to Redwood City in San Mateo County, ninety-three miles away. Geragos had alleged that "daily, unremitting and inflammatory" local press coverage had created a "lynch mob atmosphere," making a fair trial impossible in Modesto.

3. Retired judge Alfred Delucchi replaced Judge Girolami as trial judge.

4. Delucchi ruled that cameras would be barred from the trial. "Jurors and witnesses get antsy," he said.

5. The fiercely debated issue of GPS evidence was ruled admissible, thus allowing jurors to hear about the electronic tracking of Scott after Laci's disappearance.
6. The judge ruled against the sequestration of the jury.
7. The judge ruled in favor of allowing jurors to hear wiretap evidence collected by investigators. During the first months of 2003 they monitored about three thousand of Scott's home and cell phone calls, including seventy-six between him and his first attorney. The defense held that investigators had violated his client's attorney-client privilege.
8. Judge Delucchi would allow evidence gathered by scent-sniffing police dogs at the marina, but not at the Peterson home.
9. In court documents, prosecutors outlined a motive for the murders, contending that Scott's affair with another woman (Amber Frey) drove him to the crime.
10. Jurors would be permitted to hear television interviews that Scott gave in the weeks after Laci's disappearance. Geragos had argued, "The prejudicial effect of admitting Mr. Peterson's media statements would far outweigh any probative value the statements would have." Prosecutors in turn said, "The defendant gives statements that conflict with those he told police, initially lies about his relationship with massage therapist Amber Frey, lies about his relationship with his wife . . . and makes admissions that evidence his guilt." And the judge declared that the interviews could "show consciousness of guilt" and the "defendant's state of mind. The court finds the probative value outweighs any prejudicial value."

Twelve jurors were finally selected: six women and six men. Six alternates were also chosen. The process took nine weeks.

THE TRIAL

If a preliminary hearing is sometimes called a "mini-trial," then maybe the Scott Peterson trial should be called a "maxi–preliminary hearing," for, in essence, that's what it was. Everything that took place at the hearing six months earlier was also raised at the full-blown trial, which began on June

1, 2004. Only, all of it was amplified. And much more was covered. At its outset, I fully expected to be called to testify, but, as the months dragged on, it became clear there was scarcely any forensic evidence beneficial to the defense—especially with regard to items seized at his house and warehouse. On the other side of the coin, the prosecution didn't have an eyewitness, a murder weapon, or even a single drop of blood linking Scott to the deaths. We shall see, however, what I believe the entire case boiled down to.

Opening Statements

Deputy District Attorney Rick Distaso delivered a four-hour opening statement featuring what he said were lies, caddishness, and suspicious behavior. He charged that, taken together, they represent dozens of small pieces of circumstantial but compelling evidence that prove the defendant's guilt. He focused on the affair with Amber Frey, flashing a series of photographs of the blonde masseuse on a giant screen before the jurors. He impugned Scott's fishing alibi and maintained that Laci never left her home alive on December 24, the day she vanished. Distaso pointed out the Martha Stewart television show on meringues aired the day *before* (the twenty-third) Scott claimed his wife watched it (the twenty-fourth).

The district attorney stated the prosecution would present expert testimony stating: that Laci's and Conner's remains were found just off Brooks Island, near where Scott said he had fished; that Scott, after the disappearance and long before the bodies were found, had repeatedly visited that same general area; that there was no chance he could have caught sturgeon fish with the rod and tackle he had taken to the bay and also in the improper boat for the job; and that he had bypassed many closer fishing spots in favor of the bay, eighty miles away.

Distaso indicated that a tarp which the prosecution believed was used during the fishing trip was found drenched in gasoline in Scott's shed, while another one lay under cover of fertilizer. Gasoline and fertilizer destroy DNA, he said, and, in addition, interfere with scents that tracking dogs would otherwise detect. One new revelation emerged: Scott had reportedly stated he stopped fishing because it began to rain; but the marina's harbor master said it had not rained that day.

The district attorney ended his opening statement to the jury with these words: "Ladies and gentlemen, this is a common sense case . . . at the end

. . . I'm going to ask you to find the defendant guilty of murder of Laci Peterson as well as the murder of his son, Conner."

Scott appeared relaxed for a person on trial for his life, and, while the prosecutor had been matter-of-fact and meticulous, defense attorney Mark Geragos was more animated and humorous. His opening statement was half as long as his counterpart's. Geragos agreed that Scott was a two-timing cad but pronounced that he was "stone cold innocent" of the murder charge.

"You want to say his behavior is boorish," the attorney said, "we are not going to dispute that. But the fact is that this is a murder case and there has to be evidence in a murder case." He set the value of the prosecution's body of evidence at "zero, nada, nothing" and announced that medical experts and eyewitnesses would support the view that Laci was abducted while her husband was fishing in the bay. He acknowledged his client had an affair but was quick to add, "He's not charged with having an affair."

Geragos made the distinction between the prosecution's *circumstantial* case and the defense's case, which, he said, contained *direct* evidence. In support of that, he would present evidence (1) that two men and a woman—three highly respected citizens—saw a woman resembling Laci walking her dog while his client was at the bay, (2) that a former police officer saw a woman resembling Laci being pulled into a van by some "homeless or scruffy men," and (3) that one of Scott's neighbors reported seeing a suspicious brown van in the neighborhood the day before Laci disappeared.

Of the Amber Frey affair, the defense attorney said Scott was not "going to chuck this entire life he had" for the mistress he took out on just four dates. Of baby Conner, he insisted he could have been born alive forty-five days after Laci disappeared. "If this baby was born alive," he said, "then clearly Scott Peterson had nothing to do with this murder." And of the meringue episode, he contradicted the prosecution's claim by playing a clip of Stewart's December 24 program. It showed her and a guest discussing various desserts including meringues.

Geragos went out of his way to upbraid detectives for failing to pursue other leads and offered "innocent" explanations for many of the prosecution's bits of circumstantial evidence. For example, he said Laci's hair was in the boat because she went to see the new purchase on December 20, four days before she disappeared.

Guilt Phase

The prosecution called on 174 witnesses during nineteen weeks of testimony. They included a cleaning lady, a manicurist, a supermarket manager, a salon owner, a mailman, jewelers, pawnbrokers, a yoga instructor, fertilizer conventioneers, a fish expert, a fireman, an accountant, dog walkers, a waterfront manager, a computer expert, a geologist, a hydrologist, a car salesman; endless numbers of detectives, police officers, doctors, scientists, technicians; and friends, relatives, and neighbors of the Petersons. Through such a list of witnesses, along with physical evidence, exhibits, recordings, photographs, and other visual effects, the prosecutors set out to toss a vast assortment of circumstantial evidence against the wall, hoping some would stick.

The prosecution hung its case on five main elements: motive, premeditation, alibi, timeline, and consciousness of guilt.

Motive

Scott's short-term girlfriend, Amber Frey, gave seven days of testimony that many said brought significant drama to the prosecution's case but little in the way of evidence. In anticipation of her appearance, a special lottery was held to accommodate media demand for extra seats in the courtroom. The massage therapist began her testimony on an early Tuesday after striding into the packed, hushed room in two-inch black stiletto heels.

She told the jury about her many taped conversations with Scott, the strip of unopened condoms he had left at her house, his promise of a future with her, and other lies about his marital status and alleged business trips abroad. Eventually, she said, she thought he was a pathological liar, and, when it became apparent he had a missing wife, she decided to cooperate with police in taping all phone calls with him. Many of them were played for the jury to hear: one reporter labeled the calls a "chess match of deceit."

The prosecution also cited several instances in which Scott admitted to relatives that he didn't look forward to his baby's birth and to Frey that he was considering a vasectomy. The district attorney, in effect, was saying that Scott wanted desperately to become unencumbered again, that he couldn't tolerate the thought of being trapped in a "dull, boring, married life with kids," and therefore he either strangled or smothered his wife. "He wants to live the rich, successful, free-wheeling bachelor life," Distaso said. "He didn't want to be tied to this kid the rest of his life. He didn't want to be tied to Laci for the rest of his life. So he killed her."

Scott's finances were discussed at one point, with evidence entered that "he wasn't doing good at his job"; he was in massive credit card debt; his parents had taken care of big-ticket expenditures in recent months; and he and Laci had been pawning jewelry that she had inherited.

Premeditation

The prosecution stated that the timing for the purchase of Scott's boat and fishing license was suspect. He had obtained the two-day ocean-fishing license days before Laci vanished, yet he said the fishing trip was a last-minute substitution for golf because of inclement weather. Also brought into question were the "anchor and cement" issue and Scott's computer research on tide and water current conditions in San Francisco Bay. Furthermore, the same day he bought the boat (two weeks before Laci's disappearance), he informed Amber that he had "lost" his wife and would be spending his first holiday alone. McGeorge School of Law professor Ruth Jones stated that of all the lies Scott told Amber, "that one is the strongest piece of evidence. It suggests that [he] knew that his wife would not be around for the holidays. The inference is that he knew it because he had something to do with it."[30]

Alibi

Scott's trip to the bay on Christmas Eve afternoon was portrayed more as a *fishy* story than a *fishing* story. The prosecution emphasized that he had never fished in the bay before; there were alternative fishing locations much closer; he chose an unpromising location at the bay to fish for sturgeon; he brought improper equipment for the job; and for a fisherman, he arrived unusually late at the marina and stayed for an unusually short time. But most important of all for the prosecution, the remains of Laci and baby Conner were found about a mile from the part of the bay where Scott claimed to be fishing.

Timeline

Scott told detectives Laci was mopping the floor when he last saw her and then she had planned to walk their dog after that. A neighbor, Karen Servas, testified that she saw the Peterson's golden retriever running loose, its leash dragging on the ground, at 10:18 AM. She based the exact time on receipts for store purchases she'd made that morning. Yet phone records indicated that Scott left his home at 10:08, providing only a ten-minute window for Laci to stop mopping, change clothes, leash the dog, leave the house, and be abducted, as the defense counsel had contended.

The prosecution said other discrepancies in this area were that Laci's near-term pregnancy precluded her mopping the floor; that, besides, a cleaning lady had done so the day before; that Scott was certain she wore a white top and black pants that morning whereas she was found wearing khaki pants; and that it was chilly in Modesto at that time (40 degrees), yet her coat and scarf were still hanging in their closet.

Consciousness of Guilt

I covered most of this before, but the trial brought out more detail and additional factors. For example, when Scott claimed he was distributing and posting flyers at a shopping mall, there was evidence that he went to his golf course instead. Some concluded that not only was he unconcerned with finding Laci but he also believed hanging posters was a fruitless effort because he knew that Laci wasn't coming home.

*   *   *

Overall, the prosecution's case was frowned upon as lackluster and boring with two exceptions. California defense attorney Steve Cron commented, "It does seem like the prosecution has maybe put the jury to sleep. They put on so much evidence, much of it of marginal relevance to the case, that I think strategically, they didn't handle it well. They anticipated what the defense would be in some areas and attempted to rebut it before the defense presented it to jurors. The textbook way of doing it is you put on your case, the defense puts on their case and then if there's something you like to challenge, you do it on rebuttal. But they [Peterson prosecutors] did this during their case in chief, perhaps to their disadvantage."[31]

The two exceptions were the contributions of Chief Deputy District Attorney Birgit Fladager and lead detective Craig Grogan. The momentum seemed to swing upon the arrival of the forceful DA. As for Grogan, he was perhaps the prosecution's strongest witness, the one who, one observer said, "connected the dots." To counter Geragos's much ballyhooed assertion that investigators had rushed to blame Scott for the murders, Grogan calmly recited what he maintained were forty-one clues leading police to suspect the defendant. "Mr. Peterson was the closest person to Laci Peterson," he stated. "He discovered her missing. He was the last to see her alive. It didn't appear that he had an alibi. He was by himself when she disappeared. He didn't call the police."

Sometimes somber, other times cracking jokes, Mark Geragos summoned only fourteen witnesses to the stand, less than 10 percent of the number called by the prosecution. He supplied alternative views for all the allegations and depicted Scott, on the one hand, as a loving, considerate husband, and, on the other, as one who had strayed into a romantic entanglement with an available Amber Frey. He also repeatedly assailed the Modesto Police Department as inept in their failure to investigate leads, much to the detriment of his client.

The defense's case revolved around (1) the assertion that someone else abducted and killed Laci, (2) the fact that no physical evidence linked Scott to the crimes, (3) the fact that Scott's adulterous ways did not make him a murderer, and (4) the fact that the prosecution was painting him as someone to be hated, a despicable lying scoundrel. Added to these were three other points. First, the defense insisted Conner remained within Laci's womb for about seven weeks after Christmas Eve and was full term when he died. The corollary to that theory was that Laci had been held captive during that period. Her abductors then removed the baby by a crude Cesarean section and killed both mother and baby. Finally, they framed Scott after learning of his highly publicized fishing alibi. Second, Geragos referred to a time-stamped receipt from a local store showing that the neighbor who spotted the wandering dog had actually returned home from the store later than the prosecution stated. That time line discovery lent credence to the scenario put forth earlier by the defense. Third—and it was stressed—Scott had had more affairs than the one with Amber, showing that he would not have killed his wife because of a desire to continue a relationship with the massage therapist.

Geragos attempted to deflate the prosecution by using *its* witnesses to bolster his own case. Three illustrations will suffice. Under cross-examination, hair expert Rodney Oswalt could not decisively determine if hair fragments taken from Scott's pliers were Laci's because the strands didn't have roots. (In any case, this is a moot point, for even if the hair belonged to Laci, it could have attached to the pliers after first being transferred to Scott.) Also, a prosecution criminalist from the DOJ lab conceded that no blood or other physical evidence was found on Scott's boat or in his house linking him to the murders. Finally, Det. Ray Coyle testified that the police tried to locate more than three hundred registered sex offenders and parolees living near the Peterson home. Geragos promptly disclosed that many interviews with them were incomplete, or the subjects were never located in the first place.

The attorney's tactical approach received both praise and criticism. "It's struck me how prosecutors have allowed themselves to be taken advantage of by Geragos, how [he] has used their own witnesses against them," said James Cohen, associate professor of law and director of clinical education at Fordham University.[32] But Court TV reporter and legal analyst Beth Karas offered a different assessment: "The initial criticism prosecutors faced was maybe unfair. They have a complicated circumstantial case and it is a case that has to be evaluated as a whole as opposed to its individual parts. These prosecutors are less experienced than Mark Geragos. Mark Geragos loves dealing with the press and is good at using [the opposition's] witnesses to his advantage."[33]

The prosecution gained some points when Amber Frey took the stand— and a few more when Detective Grogan tallied his forty-one clues. But in harping on Scott's deception, they may have overplayed their hand. To some court observers, his lies seemed not only implausible but also laughable: the fishing alibi, the explanation for his hair color change—swimming in the pool of a friend who later said he never did. Such apparent miscues seemed difficult to imagine, the thinking went, if the prosecution wanted the jurors to believe Scott was a conniving, "leave-no-trace" slayer. Attorney Cron put it another way: "He's either this mastermind murderer who has planned the crime without leaving any traces of evidence anywhere; and if that's the case, then why does he sound like such a dumb idiot when talking to his mistress on the phone, to police, to reporters? . . . It's hard to reconcile this perfectly planned crime with the Scott Peterson everyone's been exposed to."[34]

The battle for physical evidence was not particularly dramatic because there wasn't much of it. Furthermore, prosecution witnesses were concerned that there was no direct forensic evidence to prove that Scott was the killer. Whether the topic was tracking dogs, GPS technology, wiretaps, or mtDNA, the trial arguments amounted to the equivalent of a "he says, she says" fracas. Geragos spoke of devil worshippers, burglars, vagrants, predators, transients, and mistaken identity; he confronted the issues of cement, boat stability, and online activity. But it was the battle of medical experts that would skew the jury. It came down to (1) How old was the fetus? And (2) Was the ligature around his neck an artifact or was it deliberately applied? All the rest was background. Mark Geragos, of course, was well aware of this and therefore baby Conner became essential to the defense.

Accordingly, he called Dr. Charles March to the stand three weeks before the verdict was handed down. March, a Los Angeles infertility expert, stated that the unborn son lived at least five days after his mother disappeared. Since Scott had been under constant surveillance after the disappearance, testimony that the baby did not die with his mother on December 23 or 24 would have exonerated him. However, the doctor's opinion was severely undercut when he explained that he based his judgment on the "realistic" behavior of women at baby showers rather than on more scientific facts. The behavior entailed a home pregnancy test, the date Laci performed it, and her failure to mention—during a baby shower she had thrown for a friend—that it had registered positive. His assumption was that she was not pregnant at the time of the shower—otherwise, she would have mentioned it. That, he said, meant the baby's earliest time of death was almost a week after Laci disappeared.

When the prosecution challenged the validity of his assumption, Dr. March retorted, "I mean, women talk all the time. The chances that a woman hosting a baby shower would not announce on the day of a shower that she was pregnant and have everybody rejoice in two pregnancies—that's not realistic at all." Persistent cross-examination brought out his concession that he may have been "mistaken." Although the doctor later referred to an ultrasound of the baby that, in effect, substantiated his assumption, the damage had been done. It might have been the undoing of the defense's case.

Former San Francisco prosecutor Jim Hammer agreed. "This was supposed to be one of the high points," he said, "and this one sunk. If he had succeeded, it would've been like the glove in the O. J. Simpson case. The danger is not that he's neutralized. It's that some jurors might start wondering why [Geragos] is putting on an expert who is stretching the truth or twisting the facts."[35] The defense probably realized this, for there was an abrupt trimming of the witness list, suggesting Geragos had decided to reevaluate the potential negative impact of each person on it.

Closing Arguments

Prosecutor Rick Distaso had been roundly criticized early in the trial for presenting a lackluster, often disjointed case. In stark contrast, his three-hour summation received accolades. Variously described as compelling, brilliant, and cohesive, he threw down the gauntlet with great force in anticipation of a spirited closing by his rival on the opposite side of the courtroom. Former Alameda County prosecutor Jim Anderson said Distaso displayed the right amount of anger. "I call it controlled fury," he said. "His face is flushed, his voice is angry."

Distaso asserted that the defendant had maintained two lives: the "perfect husband" in public; an adulterous cad in private. "The reason he killed Laci was that Conner Peterson was on the way," he said. "If it was just Laci, he could do this two lives thing."

He deviated from some of his earlier theories of motive that included financial problems and the Amber Frey liaison. (Geragos later called it "waffling.") He described Scott's rising debt as a peripheral nuisance and termed Amber as not a motive, but a symbol. "Amber Frey represented to him freedom," he said. "Freedom is what he wanted."

The DA meticulously outlined the prosecution's views on the cause and manner of death—asphyxiation by Scott on either December 23 or 24—and on how he disposed of the body in San Francisco Bay. Normally mild-mannered, Distaso exclaimed that the location of the bodies near where Scott admitted he went fishing was "the one fact that cannot be refuted, no matter what anybody says. You can take that to the bank and you can convict that man of murder."

He ticked off examples of Scott's suspicious behavior and, assisted by audiovisuals and photos of a smiling, ebullient Laci, brought several jurors to tears. He characterized Scott as having "a betrayal aspect. . . . Laci Peterson had no idea what was coming. In fact, she probably trusted him more than anyone else," he said. At one point, Distaso ridiculed the defense's position that someone had framed Scott by placing Laci's body in nearly the same spot he supposedly fished. Who, the prosecutor asked, would want to frame "an unsuccessful fertilizer salesman from Modesto?" The framing concept received another hit by the DA: "Here's how you know without any doubt that [the framing concept is] not true. What possible reason would there be to weight down or even hide the bodies . . . if you're going to pin it on somebody? That's . . . ludicrous. . . . It didn't happen."

Part of Scott's interview with ABC's Diane Sawyer was played for the jurors. They heard him say that he had told police "immediately" about the affair with Amber. (But later he admitted that that was untrue.) Also, Scott, during the interview, stated that he informed Laci of the affair and "it wasn't anything that would break us apart."

"Do you really expect people to believe that an eight-and-a-half-month pregnant woman learns her husband has an affair and is saintly and casual about it?" Sawyer asked.

"Well. Yeah, you don't know—no one knows our relationship but us," Scott replied.

Distaso tore into the comment proclaiming, "I don't think there is a single person in this court who believes that." He stared and pointed at Scott. "Except maybe him. . . . 'Well yeah, I expect people to believe me . . . I'm Scott Peterson.'"

His voice edged with anger, the prosecutor fired off a series of occurrences: lying about the affair with Frey; lying about being in Paris near the Eiffel Tower; inquiring about selling the house within a week of Laci's disappearance; the fact that the remains were found near the place of Scott's alibi. Distaso paused to run his eyes across the jury box: "How many of these coincidences does the defendant want you to swallow and still call yourselves reasonable people?" he queried.

When Mark Geragos had his chance to cross-examine Amber Frey three months before, he had deadpanned, "No questions." Now at the start of his closing arguments, he again startled a packed courtroom by asking the jury, "Do you all hate him?" He accused the prosecution of painting Scott as a "jerk and a liar," but not a guilty man. "But if you hate him," he went on, "then maybe what they're asking you to do is just convict him . . . don't bother with the fact that the evidence shows clearly he didn't do this and had absolutely no motive to do this." He scoffed at the prosecution's changing theories of motive for the murders: "First it is Amber, then it is financial, then it is 'Because I want to be free,' then it's 'Because I don't want a kid.'"

He dwelled on the mistress angle and his client's overall behavior. "I think it is a fair statement," he said: "[Scott] thought he was going to get some sex and it was not going to be any heavy-duty commitment." People, Geragos continued, offer their opinions—that Peterson "just doesn't act right, just doesn't look right, acts arrogant, doesn't act concerned. . . . I'm not asking you to nominate Scott Peterson as husband of the year. . . . But I tell you, on most accounts, he treated Laci with respect . . . he cheated on her, and he's a 14-carat a-hole for doing it . . . but I've known lots of people in relationships that work."

Geragos launched a frontal attack on every aspect of the government's case against his client with particular emphasis on its version of what happened to Laci's body. He held that if the body had been dumped in the bay in the same location where Scott had fished, the fifty-one searches by police dive teams would have detected the remains. "We are talking about an area that is two feet deep. If the body was there, you'd be able to see it," he said, as if ending the sentence with an exclamation point.

Also high on the defense counsel's summation agenda was the matter of a rush to judgment. He stressed that from the moment investigators assumed Scott was the perpetrator (within an hour of the missing person report), every interview they conducted, every report they wrote, the *entire* investigation itself, was clouded by that assumption. "If you presume this guy is guilty," he said, "I suppose you can put a sinister spin on anything." Geragos used his words and body language in an effort to convince the jurors that his client didn't stand a chance.

Resolute in his demeanor, the defense attorney argued that Laci was alive on Christmas Eve morning and not the victim of a "soft kill," referring to the prosecution's claim that Scott had strangled or suffocated his wife the previous night or early the next morning. The police had overlooked evidence related to that morning, he stated: someone had surfed the Peterson's computer at 8:40 for a fleece scarf and a sunflower-motif umbrella stand. (Laci often wore scarves and had a sunflower tattoo on her leg.) It was Laci who was at the computer, Geragos said, and then he extended his reasoning: umbrellas were on her mind so she asked her husband to put the patio umbrellas in storage. And that was why, he contended, they ended up in his truck—not for the purpose of covering a body, as the police had theorized.

He chided authorities still again when he brought up the question of whether or not Scott's fourteen-foot boat would capsize if a man tried to push a weighted body overboard. Geragos said they never tested for it. "You know why they never did it?" he asked. "Because under the rules of law, if they do a demonstration, they must turn it over to the defense. If they do a demonstration and it doesn't work, case over." It was an excellent argument.

The defense attorney urged the jurors to set aside their hatred of his client: "This case basically comes down to evidence versus emotion. . . . If you do

what you're sworn to do, and don't engage in speculation, passion or prejudice
. . . you have only one conclusion—that is that Scott Peterson is not guilty."

The prosecution was entitled to a rebuttal. In a twenty-minute presenta-
tion, Distaso declared that Scott's guilt was predicated on the locations of the
bodies. To believe the defendant innocent, he said, jurors would have to
believe Peterson was framed—thus, (1) the real killers knew exactly where
to dump the bodies, and (2) they did so even as diving teams were scouring
the bay for Laci. He pointed to early news releases that Scott had been in the
bay area the day his wife vanished.

"How are these nameless, faceless people to know he went fishing out of
the Berkeley Marina off Brooks Island. . . . It's not reasonable [for] anyone
[to] put those bodies in the bay to frame him."

Deliberations and Verdict

After the rebuttal, Judge Delucchi issued instructions to the jurors about several legal concepts including reasonable doubt and circumstantial evidence.
They then filed out of the courtroom to begin their deliberations; it was
exactly noon, November 3. Several items are noteworthy here:

The panel elected as its foreman a lawyer who also had a medical
degree. He practiced medicine for two years before entering law school. A
prodigious note taker, he was seen carrying a stack of a dozen spiral-bound
memo pads into the deliberations room each day, but three days before the
verdict was announced, he was dismissed by Delucchi for undisclosed reasons. Reportedly the foreman had requested the dismissal. It marked the
third time in the trial that a juror had been replaced. The day before, one was
removed after it was revealed she was doing her own research on the case, a
violation of court rules. The first replacement occurred in June when a juror
was spotted speaking to Laci's brother.

Jurors apparently struggled in reaching the verdict, on one day alone
asking to review eighty-nine pieces of evidence. Among them, the trial judge
later revealed, were transcripts of the phone calls between Scott and Amber
Frey, tidal charts, a large plastic bag found near Laci's remains, and Scott's
homemade anchor. Earlier that morning, Scott's boat had been brought into
the courthouse for the panel to inspect, and the prior week, they asked to see
various videos, maps, and phone records.

The jurors sent many messages to Delucchi during the course of their deliberations, evidently about matters of clarification. Midway, the judge summoned them into open court and reread the instructions he had given the week before. Then he added the admonition: "Do not hesitate to change an opinion if you are convinced it is wrong. However, do not decide any question in particular because a majority of the jurors, or any of them, favor that decision." The weary jurors listened attentively as if asking for more. The judge went on: "Now this is important for you to know." And reading from California's official jury instructions, he followed with, "The attitude and conduct of jurors at all times are very important. It is rarely helpful for a juror at the beginning of deliberations to express an emphatic opinion on the case or to announce a determination to stand for a certain verdict. When one does that at the outset, a sense of pride may be aroused, and one may hesitate to change a position even if shown it is wrong." Delucchi looked up and concluded, "Remember that you are not partisans or advocates in this matter. You are impartial judges of the facts."

Outside the deliberation room, there were obvious discussions about the new foreman, a firefighter-paramedic, as well as his predecessor. Jury consultant Paul Lisnek said the defense no doubt opposed the dismissal of the first one because his education and disposition made him "the perfect defense juror. . . . This was somebody who was going to put the burden to the prosecution by being meticulous. With this guy as foreman, Mark Geragos might have believed he was guiding the jury toward a not-guilty verdict or perhaps a hang."[36] Another jury consultant, Richard Matthews, stated it would be wrong for anyone to fault the new foreman simply because he earned less money or filled fewer notebooks. Matthews noted that the skills required in the new foreman's job would serve him well in the deliberation room. "A firefighter-paramedic is used to dealing with very complex scenes and putting things quickly in order in terms of importance," he said.[37] Lisnek concurred: "As a paramedic arriving on the scene, you have to be quick, you have to be calm, you have to control panic in others. They may have seen these parts of this guy's personality coming through and may have liked what they saw."[38]

At 11:20 AM on November 12 the courtroom was jammed with reporters. Judge Delucchi casually took the bench and, after spending a minute on relatively trivial procedural matters, suddenly turned to address the press corps: "Ladies and gentlemen of the media, the jury has arrived at a verdict. One o'clock. We'll expect a verdict at one o'clock."

I cannot improve on the reporting of Court TV's Harriet Ryan:

11:21 AM: There was an immediate gasp and then reporters began rushing for the courtroom door. None of the victim's family members, nor relatives of Scott Peterson were in court. All are staying nearby, however, and are expected in court for the verdict.

Peterson, dressed in a navy suit, showed no reaction. A moment before Delucchi took the bench, he laughed and smiled with defense attorney Pat Harris. Afterward, he was expressionless. . . . His high-profile attorney Mark Geragos was not in court for the announcement. . . .

1:10 PM: Clerk Marylin Morton announces the jury's verdict in front of a packed courtroom: guilty of first-degree murder for Laci Peterson, and of second-degree murder for baby Conner. . . . Sharon Rocha's mouth falls open. She gasps, leans forward and then begins weeping. . . . (Scott Peterson looks straight ahead with no show of emotion, although he stared down each juror as they were polled to confirm their decisions.) Lee Peterson, the defendant's father, was absent. . . . Jackie Peterson was initially [there] but moments after her son entered before the verdict was read, she rushed out of the room with a court officer. The judge announces the penalty phase will begin on Nov. 22. The jury files out . . . not one juror looks at Scott Peterson.

1:39 PM: A crowd of at least a dozen clapping citizens send off the jurors as their bus pulls away en route to the hotel. Jurors . . . will no longer be sequestered, but are still under the gag order.

1:56 PM: The dour-looking defense team leaves through an underground parking lot. Mark Geragos's assistant appears to be crying. When asked for a comment, defense lawyer Pat Harris responds that they "are bound by a gag order."

2:05 PM: Judge Alfred Delucchi, escorted by two sheriff's deputies, walks toward the garage. "Here's a scoop for you," the veteran judge says. He points to his mouth. "I broke my tooth eating on an apple this morning. I'm going to the dentist's right now."[39]

The court's official deliberation time was recorded as "30 hours total—and 7 hours and 14 minutes for the final sitting panel."

Penalty Phase

The next decision to be reached was whether Scott should be imprisoned for life without parole or be sent to death row at San Quentin State Prison outside San Francisco. In attendance is the same jury panel of six women and six men, the same judge, and the same defense and prosecution teams.

There were seven days of wrenching testimony: the defense called thirty-nine witnesses to vouch for Scott's character; the prosecution called just four witnesses, all relatives of the victim. Sharon Rocha, Laci's mother, provided the most poignant moment when, screaming at Scott, she asked why he killed her only daughter instead of settling for a divorce. Later, juror Greg Beratlis was to say: "That comment that she made—'Divorce was an option'—struck me deeply."[40]

As in the guilt phase of the trial, both the prosecution and the defense gave summations. Scott showed no emotion at the defense table when prosecutor Dave Harris displayed large photographs of the badly decomposed remains of Laci and Conner. "Leaving his wife's body to rot in the bottom of the ocean, leaving his son's body to be found as trash in debris—that's not something that should be rewarded by sparing his life," he stated. At another point he referred to Scott as "the great manipulator, the great fraud,"whose only goal was getting free of his marriage and fatherhood. "Laci Peterson was an anchor around his neck . . . so he put one around hers," he said.

Mark Geragos countered by asking the jurors, "How does the idea of sticking a needle in his arm, how is that going to help? There is nothing that killing him is going to do but cause more death." He urged them to recommend a sentence of life in prison without parole, explaining that it would be harsh enough—"no picnic"—and that Scott would be sharing a cell the size of four jurors' chairs with another convict. "Someday, some guard is going to knock on his cell," he said, slamming his fist three times on the rail of the jury box, "and say, 'Peterson, your mom's dead.' And someday, six months, a year after that, some guard is going to knock on the cell again and say, 'Peterson, your dad's dead.'" A few jurors flinched when he banged on the rail.

Deliberations lasted more than eleven hours spread over three days. At 1:48 PM on December 13, the court clerk read the jury's decision: "We the jury in the above-entitled cause fix the penalty at death."

Scott sat stone-faced. The cheers of a large crowd that had gathered outside the courthouse were more subdued than those following the guilty announcement. Most of the Rocha family cried—but more quietly than before. Scott's parents appeared worn out but showed no emotion. District Attorney James Brazelton thanked prosecutors Distaso, Harris, and Fladager along with the Modesto Police Department for their efforts. Mark Geragos said that he was "very disappointed" and vowed to pursue all appeals and motions for a new trial.

Shortly afterward, three of the jurors participated in a news conference. When asked what helped influence their decisions, the responses were firm.

"I still would have liked to see, I don't know if remorse is the right word," jury foreman Steve Cardosi said. "He lost his wife and his child—it didn't seem to faze him. While that was going on—he is romancing a girlfriend."

Juror Beratlis said, "Those bodies were found in the one place he went prior to her being missing. . . . Was somebody trying to set up Scott? Was someone after Laci? It didn't add up."

"There are so many things, so many things," juror Richelle Nice said. "Scott Peterson was Laci's husband, Conner's daddy—the one that should have protected them. . . . For me, a big part of it was at the end—the verdict—no emotion. No anything. That spoke a thousand words—loud and clear."

Their thoughts may have reflected those of the entire jury panel.

*   *   *

On March 16, 2005, Judge Delucchi upheld the jury's recommendation and formally sentenced Scott to death. "The court is satisfied beyond a reasonable doubt that the defendant, Scott Lee Peterson, is guilty of first-degree murder" and second degree, the judge said. He added that he believed the killing to be "cruel, uncaring, heartless and callous." Moments earlier he had denied the defense's request for a new trial.

The courtroom scene was marked by near-violent confrontation and emotional outbursts as Delucchi allowed Laci's family members to deliver so-called victim-impact statements.

Laci's mother, Sharon, stared directly at her son-in-law as she spoke from a podium. "You decided to throw Laci and Conner away, dispose of them like they were a piece of garbage," she sobbed, trembling. "We had to bury Laci without her arms to hold her baby and without her head."

Laci's father warned Scott: "You're going to burn in hell for this."

And her brother, Brent, after admitting he had bought a gun during the investigation with the intention of killing Scott, said, "I chose not to kill you myself for one reason . . . so you would have to sweat it out and not take the easy way out."

Scott, shackled at the waist and wearing a dark business suit, was invited to make a statement, but he conferred with his attorneys and declined. At 3:10 the following morning, he was transferred from San Mateo County jail to San Quentin and became the 644th person awaiting lethal injection in California. Ironically, the infamous lockup overlooks the very bay where Laci's body had been discarded.

Once again Scott's expression was severely blunted, prompting some psychological and legal experts to describe him as having a sociopathic personality disorder. One such authority felt Scott should have made a statement when he had the chance: "He didn't have to express remorse but at least he could have declared his innocence and expressed sympathy toward the Rochas."

Some court observers believed that his attorneys barred a statement fearing that any miscue might work against their client during years and years of expected appeals.

POSTSCRIPT

Some random thoughts as we conclude the first of five notorious cases:

- Many have asked why Scott never testified in order to profess his innocence. The simple answer is that he probably would have been destroyed on cross-examination. Former prosecutor James Hammer expressed it a different way: "If he's on the stand and just once got caught lying in front of the jury, the case is over."
- Scott's demeanor was widely criticized throughout the investigation and trial. In essence, his stoicism spoke for itself, but prosecutors drew it out, played it to a fare-thee-well. On the FOX News talk show *On The Record*, host Greta Van Susteren said that so many prejudicial things were brought up about the defendant (e.g., his lack of expressed concern, bizarre behavior patterns, and

pornographic TV subscriptions after Laci disappeared) that the jurors grew to hate him. "They might have convicted him of killing Lincoln!" she quipped.[41]

The Associated Press reported that "there may be little difference between a death sentence and life in prison" for Scott. "In California, the chances are greater that a condemned inmate will die in prison than be executed by lethal injection."[42] It might take four or five years, for example, before even the first phase of the appeals process begins. Statistics tell the story. Currently, the state has 644 men and women on death row. Since the state restored capital punishment in 1978, only ten executions have been carried out. The last one was in 2002 for a murder that was committed twenty-two years earlier. In the same twenty-seven-year period (1978 to 2005), thirty-eight death row inmates have died of other causes: a dozen committed suicide, three were killed by other inmates, and the remainder died of natural causes.

Speaking of the appeals process, the consensus among legal analysts is that the defense will focus on three main issues: Scott's fishing boat, the dismissal of the two jurors during deliberations, and Mark Geragos himself.

Just before the guilty verdict was rendered, jurors were seen standing in the fishing boat, rocking it back and forth in the courthouse garage. Geragos complained that the defense wasn't given the same opportunity (i.e., to test for stability and buoyancy), nor were they allowed to show jurors a video of a test boat capsizing under conditions put forth by the prosecution. He asked for a mistrial at the time but was turned down.

Many of those who favored the defense questioned whether or not the two jurors had been dismissed because "they didn't go with the flow" to convict. The term "stealth jurors" also arose during the trial. This referred to a few men and women on the panel who allegedly lied during the voir dire selection process in order to make it onto the jury—because their belief in Scott's guilt was so strong. It might also include anyone who wanted to publish a book or otherwise profit financially from participation in the high-profile case.[43]

Mark Geragos is a good friend of mine and I respect him very much as an attorney, but, being a stickler for objectivity, I would be remiss were I not to mention the following. I bring it up only as it might impact on the appeals process.

Some pundits on talk shows said that Mark "lost" the case because (1) during his opening statement, he promised he would not only prove his client was "stone-cold innocent" but also identify the real killer; (2) he suggested conspiracy theory after conspiracy theory but never settled on a credible one; and (3) his fertility expert was a flop as a witness. The doctor wasn't able to convince the jury—as Geragos had promised—that baby Conner could have been born alive sometime *after* Laci was reported missing.

Some members of the legal profession and the media were not hesitant in criticizing the defense's case for acquittal and were quick to add that it might carry considerable weight during the appeals process: "Geragos is going to take a hit on the defense appeal. I don't think he will handle [it]," said ABC News Supreme Court reporter and legal analyst Manuel Medrano. "He made a few critical errors. For example, I was astounded when, during closing arguments in the penalty phase, he essentially admitted he hadn't prepared for this part of the trial because he didn't expect a conviction. The question is whether that can be brought up on appeal as an argument that he [Geragos] provided ineffective counsel."[44]

Attorney Michael Bachner said on *ABC News Now*, "Unfortunately Mark is going to become a pincushion not only for legal analysts but for people working for Scott Peterson on his appeal. And they're going to be dissecting every one of his decisions. Look, the bottom line is, no lawyer can guarantee results."[45] I would add that, while Mark took the blame for losing the case, I feel strongly that Scott's laid-back attitude, his lies, and his demeanor influenced the jury's decisions. In essence, he convicted himself.

And Bill Bickel, from All Info about Crime, made an interesting (and prophetic) observation even before the verdict was handed down. He was alluding to the fundamental concept of innocent until proven guilty: "What Geragos did was redefine the contest . . . [rather] than a trial in which the prosecution can only win by proving Scott's guilt beyond a reasonable doubt, the verdict could now depend on whether Geragos can prove his claim . . . no defense lawyer should ever put himself in the position of having to prove something to win his case. And make no mistake, even jurors reluctant to convict without strong evidence will side with the prosecution when they're reminded that Geragos promised something he didn't deliver."[46]

My involvement in the case (and that of my colleague and longtime friend Dr. Cyril Wecht, coroner of Pittsburgh's Allegheny County) was largely low-key. We were poised to testify for the defense right up to the final days of the trial, but the determination was made that there was insufficient forensic evidence to talk about—that this was a circumstantial case, after all. In addition, the forensic experts on the prosecution's side were fair and objective, and they conceded on issues during Geragos's cross-examinations. Hence, our testimony was not required.

I firmly believe that if the jury's decision had been based on logical forensic evidence, we would have seen either a hung jury or a verdict of "acquittal"; if based on instinct and emotion, then the verdict would have been "guilty." As we all know by now, the latter is what happened. In a nutshell, it was a contest between scientific facts and passion. And passion won.

My thoughts regarding the death penalty have always depended on the nature of the crime—or more specifically, on the category of the murder. Arbitrarily, I have my own two categories. As a kind of preamble, I must admit that the decision to put *any* individual to death has never sat well in my mind. Nevertheless, in the first category, I include such examples as serial killing, mass murder, rape/murder, and the killing of a police officer. Other examples in this group would best be described as heinous in nature. Again, although I'm somewhat ambivalent about the death penalty per se, and have compassion for the families of both the victim *and* the murderer, I believe that giving the ultimate penalty is justified in this category. My rationalization is that, in the long run, society is protected. It, of course, goes without saying that in these instances convincing evidence must have been presented. In the second category, I place all crimes of passion that result in murder, particularly if it is determined that the crime in question was a single-episode crime—that is, that it would be highly unlikely the perpetrator would ever strike again.

In this Scott Peterson case, I have struggled between the two categories, if he indeed had committed the crime. A jury of his peers sided with the state in both the guilt and the penalty phases. They apparently saw it as premeditated murder. I have great sympathy for both of the involved families. And certainly a double homicide is a heinous crime, but my mind would be more at ease if some compelling physical evidence had existed. There was none, however. In my view, neither forensic science nor the investigation played a significant role. Ultimately, it was Scott himself that did him in.

chapter 2
the elizabeth smart case

If you can hear us, we love you, Elizabeth. We haven't forgotten about you. We won't stop until you come home.

—Lois Smart

On Wednesday, June 5, 2002, a fourteen-year-old girl was abducted from her Salt Lake City, Utah, home, and what followed was a national media frenzy of massive proportions. Her name is Elizabeth Smart. There may have been numerous reasons why the media picked up on Elizabeth's story so assiduously—the videos on television displayed a blue-eyed, shy beauty; she came from an affluent family; her uncle had ties with the press; and the 2002 Winter Olympic Games in Utah had ended just months before—but the fact remains that the twenty-four-hour television news networks had discovered that horror sells and that millions of people reached by talk show radio, the cable systems, and the Internet are fascinated by such stories. The press asserts that when they latch onto such cases—one hundred or so stranger-abductions each year—they are performing a public service by utilizing publicity to generate information and possible witnesses. Also, they say, they are helping other families avoid similar nightmares. Yet many believe that excessive broadcast coverage helps foster a false reality. In truth, there was not in 2002, nor is there now, an epidemic of child abductions. It is the sheer *volume* of reporting that creates the perception. The

National Crime Information Center (NCIC) stated that immediately prior to Elizabeth's kidnapping, the number of "involuntary" missing-child reports, in which the victim was known to have been taken away against his or her will, was down nearly 10 percent, the lowest level since 1993.

Yet such encouraging statistics do not seem to be highlighted by news organizations. If we were to refer to a related category, juvenile homicides—keeping in mind that 98 percent of children abducted by strangers do not survive beyond the first thirty days—former attorney general Janet Reno indicated that in 1997 such homicides had declined 30 percent over a three-year period, and no one even noticed. It wasn't even reported in the *Washington Post*, not far from her offices.

Another factor that made the Elizabeth Smart case so captivating but, at the same time, disturbing was addressed by the Associated Press shortly after she was missing. It made a distinction between abductions carried out by relatives (including a parent) and those by strangers: "Most of the more than 350,000 children abducted in America each year are taken by relatives. Random abductions by strangers are rare but (more) *terrifying*."[1]

The *Waterbury Republican-American* reported in an editorial: "The TV news blitz on behalf of Elizabeth Smart . . . gives us the illusion of a 'trend' or a 'problem,' that might respond to public-policy tinkering. It's true that all of us can do a better job of looking out for each other. . . . But no amount of news coverage will change the fact there is evil in the world, some of it in human form, and perfect safety—as opposed to sensibly managed risk—is unattainable."[2]

The above-mentioned "public-policy tinkering" has turned out to be beneficial for society in this case. Elizabeth Smart's story fueled the drive toward a nationwide Amber Alert law.

BACKGROUND

Salt Lake City is the capital of and largest city in Utah, with a population of approximately 180,000. Set in the Salt Lake Valley at the foot of the Wasatch Range of the Rocky Mountains, its skyline is uninterrupted by even a single giant skyscraper so dominant in other major cities.

It is home to the world headquarters of the Church of Latter-day Saints (LDS), more commonly called the Mormon Church. Half of Salt Lake City's citizens practice the Mormon religion. The Mormon Temple with its majestic six spires occupies the heart of the downtown area. Next to it is the Mormon Tabernacle, famous for its 325-voice choir and imposing organ of eleven thousand pipes. The choir, founded more than a hundred years ago, regularly tours the world and has been heard on US radio networks since 1929.

The LDS church has eleven million members around the globe with holdings estimated at twenty-five billion dollars. Its members believe that their church was established by Christ and that the church did not survive in its original form, but was restored in modern times through a living prophet, Joseph Smith. Mormon teachings are derived from modern revelations as found in the Bible, the Book of Mormons, and an array of other scriptures. The church's leader is considered a "living prophet" and is also the president of the church.

Some Mormons practiced polygamy as a religious principle in the mid-1800s. But it was outlawed in 1890 after the US Supreme Court ruled it illegal. Such plural marriages continue to dot the state of Utah, however, since the religion holds that polygamy is part of the afterlife. As will be seen, the concept of polygamy apparently played a powerful role in the kidnapping of Elizabeth Smart. From the start, many asked whether or not it was the work of a polygamist or a sexual predator, or a combination of both.

A hardworking, upper-class Mormon family, the Smarts were perceived as distinctly unique in their comportment throughout the ordeal of a missing child. They survived the whispers that suggested complicity by a family member in the abduction. They withstood open dissension with police authorities, as well as the nine-month-long anguish of a beloved child stolen from their midst. Focused on finding and recovering one of their own, some members of the extended family suffered near nervous breakdowns; most battled exhaustion and prolonged periods of insomnia.

Elizabeth's parents, Ed and Lois, expressed the experience in their book, *Bringing Elizabeth Home*: "Until the morning of June 5, our lives felt blessed in every way. . . . But losing Elizabeth brought one point painfully home: *Nothing* is more important in this world than our family. Not money. Not work. Not a fancy new car or an expensive big house."[3]

Their seven-thousand-square-foot house was indeed expensive—and beautiful. Valued at over one million dollars, it was situated on Kristianna Circle at the end of a cul-de-sac. The upscale neighborhood, Arlington Hills, overlooks the Salt Lake City skyline. Behind the circle are two other streets, and directly behind them, the mountain begins its slope.

Ed Smart was devoted to his work as a mortgage broker and owner of two real estate companies. An integral part of his business was buying and then selling houses after refurbishing them. Lois applied the same devotion to tending to her children and home. They have six children. Besides Elizabeth and Mary Katherine, the younger daughter, there are Charles, William, Andrew, and Edward. Elizabeth, an accomplished harpist and horseback rider, was regarded as obedient, innocent, and sweet. She didn't have an e-mail address or use the computer.

Her parents came from large families, too. Ed is one of six children; Lois one of nine. Elizabeth's aunts and uncles in turn provided her with seventy-six first cousins. Her uncle Tom, a longtime photojournalist with the local newspaper, the *Deseret Morning News*, has considerable clout with state and national media outlets and was most instrumental in generating valuable publicity about his niece's abduction. He has five brothers and sisters; in addition to Ed, there are Chris, Angela, Cynthia, and David. Upon learning of the abduction, they all immediately pitched in—notifying other family members, searching on foot, galvanizing whatever resources they could find.

FACTS AND INVESTIGATION

Abduction and Search

Elizabeth was taken from her bedroom—reportedly at gunpoint—in the middle of a Wednesday night. As was her custom, she was sleeping in the same queen-size bed with her nine-year-old sister, Mary Katherine. Reports vary as to the exact time of the abduction, but the younger girl, frightened into silence by the male intruder, didn't run to the nearby bedroom to alert her parents until an hour or two later, around 4:00 AM. Her father, Ed, and mother, Lois, bolted from their room and searched their house frantically before calling 911 three minutes later. Ed then notified numerous friends and family members. Police arrived at 4:13 AM; the first friends at 4:15.

Mary Katherine indicated that the man appeared to be wearing a cap and light-colored clothes and was carrying a backpack. From what she could make out in the dimly lit room—and in her terrified state—she believed that he was of medium height and that the backs of his hands bore hair that was either brown or black. He was soft-spoken, she said, and his voice might have been familiar but she couldn't be sure. He commanded the pajama-clad girl to put on some sneakers and to be quiet or he would kill her and her family.

Both parents and police noticed that the screen of a kitchen window had been cut. (This finding will be examined later, as well as a malfunctioning security alarm system, the probable escape route, and other crime scene particulars.)

Keenly aware of the chilling statistic that the first three hours are the most important in recovering a live child, the family, friends, and police sprang into action. Some employed tracking dogs as they fanned out before dawn over the streets and steep foothills searching for the child. For the first time, Utah's Emergency Alert System, known as the Rachel Alert, was initiated. It had been established two months earlier to broadcast information about an abducted child. Named after a Utah girl who was kidnapped and murdered in 1982, the system was modeled after the Amber Alert, named for nine-year-old Amber Hagerman who also had been abducted and killed.

Police authorities stated that there was no indication that the man knew Elizabeth, yet they checked the family computer for clues and, within hours, even interviewed her eighth-grade classmates at Bryant Intermediate School. The consensus was that authorities were not dealing with a purely random act and that the perpetrator had to have known where the victim lived and which bedroom was hers.

Twelve hours into the case, Ed appeared before the media in the first of the twice-daily press conferences that he and his family would hold. He pleaded with the abductor to let his daughter go and offered reassurance to her that everyone was doing everything they could to help find her.

Various national response teams volunteered their services; each had vast experience in organizing searches for missing children, distributing educational material, and setting up phone banks. Key among them were the Laura Recovery Center based in Friendswood, Texas, and the Abby and Jennifer Recovery Foundation from Grand Junction, Colorado. An Elizabeth Smart Web page was also set up, and it soon was receiving up to two million hits every twenty-four hours.

On Thursday, despite more than one thousand tips, a reward of $250,000, the use of state helicopters, and the dogged efforts of twelve hundred volunteer searchers, no sign of Elizabeth materialized. Police Chief Rick Dinse stated that nobody had been eliminated as a suspect, including family members. Ed Smart appeared on NBC's *Today* show, appealing once more to the kidnapper. Lois tried to make a similar appeal but could hardly speak. Having experienced her father's death the week before, Lois's brother, Mark Francom, indicated she barely had had time to mourn and wondered aloud why anyone would target her home. Investigators also knocked on neighbors' doors trying to determine whether any of them had surveillance cameras that might throw some light on the baffling case.

Hundreds of police officers from neighboring cities joined in the investigation. Soon the number of volunteers had swollen to over two thousand per day, and the consensus was that the case had become the most publicized kidnapping since that of the Lindbergh baby who was murdered in 1932.[4] The police revealed another statistic: most children abducted by strangers are taken by pedophiles, some of whom also seek a ransom. If they do, they usually contact the family within the first twenty-four hours. No contact had taken place—then or later.

Elizabeth's father was particularly diligent in the search. Some labeled his actions frenetic—so much so that he was hospitalized on Friday morning after collapsing from exhaustion. Two days later he was given a lie detector test; police stated it was not uncommon for such tests to be administered to parents of missing children. After the FBI reviewed his test, it was reported that he had passed it. Subsequently, Elizabeth's uncle Tom Smart was also tested. Reeling from sleep deprivation and the emotional toll that the abduction had exacted, the results came back "inconclusive."

On Sunday evening, more than five hundred people gathered in Salt Lake's Liberty Park for an emotional candlelight vigil. Ed fought back tears as he offered a prayer for his daughter; his wife, Lois, told the throng that the family was confident Elizabeth would be returned. (It was a scene played again six months later in the Laci Peterson disappearance.)

Meanwhile, twenty-five volunteer pilots flew their planes over rugged mountain terrain, but they were unable to add anything useful to the investigation. Pictures of Elizabeth were posted throughout Salt Lake City and on the Internet. Massive numbers of light-blue ribbons—those of her favorite color— were widely distributed. Half the population could be seen wearing them; many hung them on car antennas, lampposts, and trees. While some police officers were ferreting out six thousand leads, others eliminated the possibility that the girl had staged her own disappearance and was, in fact, a runaway.

The hunt expanded geographically. The following day Tom spearheaded a drive to have forty or fifty all-terrain vehicles (ATVs) assemble just west of the city to help search the West Desert region of Utah. Fifty-five ATV owners showed up and each explored a twenty-five-square-mile area.

As searches continued and the Smarts continued their appeals—and news of the kidnapping branched out across the country, even into foreign lands—tensions between the family and law enforcement officials reached a boiling point. Some family members were openly critical of what they believed was an inefficient investigation; the police in turn were dismissive of the charges, indicating that proper procedures were being strictly followed.

Then, about a week into the case, the *Salt Lake Tribune* ran a front-page story with the headline: "Police Eye Relatives in Probe."[5] The article indicated that some authorities believed that a member of the victim's extended family might have been involved in the crime. Their speculation was predicated, the newspaper stated, on the inability of detectives to explain, (1) how an intruder could have squeezed through the opening of a small kitchen window, and (2) why the window's screen appeared to have been cut from the inside out. If that were the case, the thinking went, had it been cut to make it look like a break-in? Was it staged? The paper stated its information was obtained from four different sources, all of whom had requested anonymity. It went on to claim that detectives, operating on the theory that Elizabeth knew her abductor, decided to ask for lie detector tests for certain family members. For countless people around the country who were both concerned and intrigued, this immediately harked back to the 1996 JonBenet Ramsey case. JonBenet, a six-year-old beauty queen, had been murdered in her home in Boulder, Colorado, and some members of the task force considered her parents to be among the early suspects.

The Smarts were outraged over the story even though most tried to act composed before the media; each one gave variations on the theme that responsible law enforcement officials must be thorough in their investigation. They also issued a statement saying that, while they were disappointed by the story, they were continuing to cooperate fully in every aspect of the investigation and urged the public and the media to avoid distraction from what was most important. Translation? "Find Elizabeth."

Police were also busy on another front. The preceding day, they had launched an intense manhunt for a twenty-six-year-old transient whose car had been seen driving slowly up and down Kristianna Circle two days before the abduction. The eyewitness was the neighborhood's milkman. The transient, Bret Michael Edmunds, was identified through a partial license plate number provided by the milkman. Further checking revealed that Edmunds was already being sought for assault on a police officer and violation of parole. Eventually he was found in a West Virginia hospital after being admitted for an apparent drug overdose. He survived and was later cleared as a suspect in the kidnapping. But a man named Ricci would replace him.

At the two-week point in the investigation, there was still no sign of Elizabeth and no solid leads. Police Chief Dinse released updated statistics: they had eight thousand to ten thousand leads; thirteen hundred warranted follow up; nine hundred were cleared; and four hundred remained to be evaluated.

On June 24—nearly three weeks after the crime—police began questioning Richard Albert Ricci about Elizabeth's abduction. The forty-eight-year-old handyman with a twenty-nine-year criminal record had been arrested a week before on an unrelated parole violation. When it was learned that he once had access to the Smarts' home, the police began taking a closer look at his whereabouts and activities during the first week in June. About a year before, he had done some painting, basic carpentry, and yard work at the Smart home over a period of three months, and it was known that he became friendly with the children. With a criminal history dating back to 1973, he had been in and out of prison most of his life, based on such convictions as burglary, aggravated robbery, attempted homicide, and prison escape. Ed Smart said publicly that the man had been friendly and competent enough but that if he had known of Ricci's background, he never would have hired him. What Ed didn't know at the time was that Ricci had been stealing odds and ends from his home. This had apparently been a pattern for him: burglarizing the homes where he worked in order to help fund his alcohol and drug addictions. Sadly, the career felon's own nine-year-old son had been killed by a drunk driver in 1985.

The police were skeptical of Ricci's alibi but didn't elaborate further, which fueled more mystery concerning the handyman's potential role in Elizabeth's kidnapping. Chief Dinse explained simply that he was not currently a charged suspect, even though he was "a person of interest." Eventually Ricci's wife, Angela, claimed that her husband was asleep next to her on the night of the abduction, but the police still viewed him as their primary suspect.

Another twist concerned a 1990 Jeep Cherokee given to Ricci by Ed as payment for work. A federal grand jury had convened to question potential witnesses. Among them were Angela Ricci and auto mechanic Neth Moul. What followed was a paradigm of "he-says-she-says" confusion. Moul said Ricci had taken the Jeep from his shop on May 30 and returned it for more work on June 8. The mechanic said that the vehicle was covered with mud and its floor was strewn with newspapers. In an apparently angry mood, Ricci allegedly removed two seat covers and a post-hole digger from the Jeep and took off across the street. There he greeted a friend and they drove away.

Moul made several other allegations, including: (1) Ricci took the vehicle on May 30 without notifying anyone at the shop; (2) earlier that same day, a woman claiming to be Ricci's wife had called about the Jeep; and (3) when the vehicle was returned on June 8, its odometer registered one thousand new miles.

When grilled, Ricci could not explain the added miles, denying he'd taken the car in the first place. Furthermore, Angela said the Jeep never had seat covers and she had never phoned the shop.[6]

On July 11 Ricci was charged with a wide range of theft and breaking-and-entering violations. But there was no reference to Elizabeth's disappearance.

The daily press briefings continued as did international media coverage and massive search efforts by devoted volunteers. But no one seemed comfortable with the way the investigation was going: not the police, not the media, and certainly not the Smarts. Theories about the disappearance were rampant. Some even held that white-slave traders had kidnapped Elizabeth. The family issued another statement, this time expanding its reach to the entire globe. It reaffirmed its belief that Elizabeth was still alive and that keeping everyone aware of their plight might somehow save other children and their families from a similar fate.

To the holder(s) of Elizabeth Ann Smart and Friends Throughout the World: It has been several weeks since our daughter Elizabeth was awakened during the night and taken from her home by force. Every minute of the day we continue to search for her, pray for her, and yearn for her to come home. So many of you have joined us in our search and prayers. Since we last saw Elizabeth on the evening of

June 4, we have not received any communication from the person who took her. We continue to eagerly await information about her location. We believe that through awareness of this terrible tragedy in our family many children throughout the world will be saved. As the authorities continue to piece together a puzzle, we still are only interested in one thing—finding Elizabeth. We believe that she is still alive and wants desperately to be returned to us. Whether or not you are the person who took her, we are pleading with you to do the right thing and let her come home.

Anxiously awaiting,

Ed and Lois Smart[7]

The Richard Albert Ricci chapter ended with a thunderclap. While in prison, he developed a ruptured cerebral aneurysm and died suddenly on August 30, 2002. In *Bringing Elizabeth Home*, Ed Smart remarks, "To some degree, we felt at peace when Ricci died. At the very least, there would be no trial. We would not be forced to relive Elizabeth's nightmare if he was in fact the kidnapper. If he didn't abduct our daughter, what was it that he was hiding right up to the day he died? Who picked Ricci up at Neth Moul's shop? Where did Ricci go from May 30 [*sic*] to June 5? What about those unexplained miles on the Jeep?"[8]

Feuds

Even as the insinuations of the *Tribune* article smoldered among the Smart clan, another much-ballyhooed flap arose, one involving nationally known personalities: child protection advocate Marc Klaas; FOX News Channel's Bill O'Reilly, host of *The O'Reilly Factor*; and forensic artist Jeanne Boylan. Klaas took up his cause as a spokesman for missing children shortly after his twelve-year-old daughter, Polly, was abducted and later found murdered in 1993. Boylan earned her reputation through her sketches of Polly Klaas's abductor, the Unabomber, and others.

When Klaas offered to help the Smart family, they were initially appreciative but soon maintained he hadn't told them he was working on behalf of FOX News. Tom Smart was particularly critical: "He came here under the guise of helping us," he said. "But his sole intention was to get an 'inside' story. What he did was duplicitous, sick and completely unethical."[9]

Klaas was livid and retorted, "I was never deceptive with them at all. The first thing out of my mouth was not always 'Hello, I am working for FOX.' It was 'Hello, I am Polly Klaas's father.'"[10]

And that was the beginning of the rancor they shared for each other. It became worse when Klaas suggested that Boylan meet with Mary Katherine for purposes of creating a sketch of the person based on the child's description. Tom opposed the idea, stating the family was cooperating with the FBI and local police on that score.

O'Reilly entered the fray when Tom was scheduled to appear on his program. Tom canceled, however, citing extreme exhaustion. His daughters, Sierra, twenty-one, and Amanda, seventeen, appeared in his stead. But Klaas appeared. The show was rife with sarcasm, thinly veiled accusations, and indirect criticism of the young women's father. At the heart of much of it was a back-and-forth of the Jeanne Boylan issue.

During one exchange, O'Reilly said to Klaas, "There does seem to be a bit of a problem. Can you define it for us as you see it?"

"Well," Klaas replied, "it's almost interference. We've encouraged Ed and Lois to talk to everybody at every possible opportunity. And once we think we're getting towards that direction, Tom then will come in and sort of play things around a little bit so that might not occur. . . . Tom made sure [the meeting with Boylan] didn't happen, and I just find that extremely frustrating."[11]

At the conclusion of the program, Tom's daughters left in tears. Tom, in turn, reacted angrily, stating O'Reilly used his show to accuse him through his daughters.

Boylan's services as a sketch artist were never utilized but, eventually, those of a person recommended by the police, Dalene Nelson, were. Her sketch, based on Mary Katherine's recollection, was made public several months later.

And there were other feuds. One involved the tabloid the *National Enquirer*, which printed a story alleging that Ed, Tom, and David Smart were involved in a homosexual sex ring. The day before the story ran, the police had returned the family computers after examining them. Reaction in Salt Lake was swift, as everybody from the authorities to citizens on the streets flew into a rage. A month later, the tabloid retracted its claims, stating they were based on false information provided by unnamed sources.

Another was the ongoing feud between the Smarts and the police. The family contended that leaks and misinformation were hurting the investigation by diverting attention away from finding Elizabeth. "It started the very first day," Tom said. "When they said Ed called family and neighbors before he called 911. When they said family and friends were at Ed's house before police and ruined the crime scene. When they said the screen was cut from the inside. The investigation started with those lies thrown on the family."[12]

Salt Lake's mayor, Ross "Rocky" Anderson, a friend of the Smart family, made his feelings known in a memo to Police Chief Dinse a month into the case: "I have significant concerns about the numerous apparent leaks of information . . . by the Salt Lake City Police Department (SLCPD) during the course of the investigation in the Elizabeth Smart case. . . . In this case it appears that unauthorized disclosures of information have either (1) compromised the investigation . . . or (2) inflicted tremendous damage on members of the Smart family, who are already undergoing the most tragic situation any family could experience."[13]

If, in the eyes of the Smarts, all this controversy was counterproductive and demoralizing, so was the attempted abduction of another young family member on July 24, seven weeks after Elizabeth had vanished. Jessica Wright, Elizabeth's favorite cousin, was asleep when she was awakened in the middle of the night by the crash of picture frames near one of her windows. She sat up and saw what appeared to be an arm retracting from the window. Jessica bolted from the room and bumped into her father, Steven, who had rushed in after also hearing the noise. A superficial search of the grounds by Steven and a more thorough one by the police revealed no sign of an intruder. But there were eerie similarities to Elizabeth's abduction: roughly the same-aged child, a cut screen, and a chair propped against the side of the house directly below a window.

(It would later be determined that Elizabeth's captor was indeed the perpetrator in the Jessica Wright case. His plan was to kidnap one of Steven's daughters, just as he had her cousin.)

The Jesus Guy

By now, the whole world knows that Elizabeth Smart was eventually found alive and well. Her abductor turned out to be one Brian David Mitchell, who was assisted in holding the girl against her will by his wife, Wanda Barzee.

Brian—drifter, panhandler, and self-proclaimed prophet—talked about his work as "God's messenger" to anyone who would listen. He had a dark beard and long hair, and, among his homeless friends, he was known as "the Jesus guy." He spent countless hours on the street corners of Salt Lake City, where he stood seeking handouts, draped in robes that were usually purple, sometimes white. His wife stood by his side and hardly uttered a word. People throughout the city, even the downtrodden, tended to avoid him because of his nonstop, often incoherent preaching. Some called him sick; others viewed him as evil.

Brian's family history, his troubled past, and the many transformations in his life are beyond the scope of this book. Suffice it to say he was born in 1953, may have had a learning disability, and, even in his preteens, appeared to have an abnormal interest in sex. He did manage to receive a high school diploma and, for a time, took some college courses. Brian developed a drug habit that lasted for several years. When he kicked it, he purportedly found religion and became a devout Mormon. He married his third wife, Wanda, in 1985. Eight years older than Brian, she was shy but intelligent. She loved playing the piano and, in some quarters, was judged to be of concert caliber. Her first husband was abusive. In 1985 she welcomed Brian in marriage as the man of her dreams. Although most observers felt one was odder than the other, the couple worked diligently for the Salt Lake Temple. But their marriage soon grew stormy. At first Wanda would hold her own during their many violent outbursts, but eventually she sank deeper into isolation, more into the role of a follower.

For Brian's part, he slid further away from reality, became increasingly critical of the LDS church, and maintained it wasn't doing enough to help the homeless. After several name changes, the sloughing off of most material possessions, and severing ties with the church, the couple took to the road, wandering throughout the country: Idaho, Massachusetts, Pennsylvania, Florida, California, even Hawaii and Alaska. They returned to Salt Lake a few years later, in 1997, and lived in a teepee set up in the Wasatch Mountains. They shed their street clothes in favor of robes and assumed the names Immanuel and Eladah. Brian claimed he'd had a revelation, was about to initiate a new religion, and would soon draft its "essential doctrine" for his followers. (See below.)

In 2000 Wanda confided in a friend that she, too, had a revelation and that her husband's full name was Immanuel David Isaiah and hers was Hephzibah Eladah Isaiah. Wanda added that they would secure forty-nine new brides for Brian (who by then had declared an allegiance to polygamy), but they would have to be very young so as not to be set in their ways. She proudly maintained that the girls would be her sister-wives.

Interestingly, after 9/11, some people who approached Brian at street corners stated his beard made him look like Osama bin Laden. He shaved off the beard for a short spell.

*   *   *

The twenty-seven-page *The Book of Immanuel David Isaiah*, dated April 6, 2002, contained a rambling three-page introduction. Excerpts are provided here to illustrate the depths of irrationality to which he had plunged:

> Hearken! Oh ye inhabitants of the earth. Listen together and open your ears, for it is I, the Lord God of all the earth, the creator of all things that speaketh unto you. Yea, even Jesus Christ speaking by the voice of my servant whom I have called and chosen to be a light and a covenant to the world in these last days. I have called him and given him a name to be had in remembrance before me, even the name Immanuel David Isaiah, which name being interpreted means: God be with us—Beloved of God—The Lord is salvation—signi-fying the deliverance that shall come to my people by my mighty hand in these last few days.
>
> . . . And I, the Lord God hold in reserve a swift judgment against every worker of iniquity who will not repent while the day lasts; and lo, lo, I am even at the door. Yea, great and marvelous shall be the destruction of the wicked. Yea, great and marvelous shall be the deliverance of my people. For I, the Lord God will deliver my people with a mighty hand. Yea, I will bring to pass my strange act, my unwonted act, to make all glorying in the flesh a reproach. Yea, I will bring to utter shame and execration all those who exalt them-selves. And all those who humble themselves before me, and who are not ashamed of me, and who glorify me in their flesh, will I lift up and clothe them in mine own power and in mine own glory, even that of the Father and the Son and the Holy Ghost. Amen.[14]

The preceding two passages were part of the *introduction*. Selected excerpts from the *body* of the text—including misspellings—seem to bear on the abduction of Elizabeth, the first of the forty-nine "sisters." Jessica no doubt was the anticipated second one:

> And my prophets sought with great diligence to restore the law unto them but the people and the church would not receive it. And in consequence of their continued disobedience, I, the Lord God took away from my church the fullness [*sic*] of the new and everlasting covenant of marriage, and I commanded them to have one wife only. Wherefore, they received a lesser law and a lesser blessing. Nevertheless, I the Lord God am merciful and just and I know the hearts of my children, and I restore every blessing lost to them so long as they sin not against the Holy Ghost.
>
> Therefore, Hephzibah Eladah Isaiah, thou art called and chosen to be a helpmeet unto my servant Immanuel David Isaiah, and to be his wise counselor and best friend, and to be submissive and obedient unto thy husband in all righteousness, and to be a comfort and a strength and a companion to thy husband in every time of trial and affliction unto the end.
>
> . . .Wherefore, Hephzibah, my most cherished angel, thou will take into my heart and home seven sisters, and thou wilt recognize them through the spirit as thy dearest and choicest friends from all eternity. . . . And thou shalt take into my heart and home seven times seven sisters, to love and to care for forty-nine precious jewels in thy crown, and thou art the jubilee of them all, first and last, for all are given unto thee for thy glory and honor and exaltation, even as thou art given unto them, for thou art a Queen, Oh Hephzibah! . . .[15]

* * *

Seven months before Elizabeth's abduction, Brian Mitchell approached her mother, who was walking with all six of her children near Salt Lake's Crossroads Mall. Lois remembered him as thin, clean shaven, and neatly dressed. They struck up a brief conversation. Speaking softly, he asked if she might offer him some financial help, and she handed him a five-dollar bill. She learned he was in need of work. Like many of their affluent neighbors, the Smarts had often hired the homeless to do odd jobs around their house. Lois provided him with their telephone number and, through Ed, Brian ended up spending the following day working at the house, mostly on roof repairs. Ed joined him, and, as they kneeled in work, Brian pointed out that his "real" name was Immanuel and that his "real" work was spreading the word of Jesus to the homeless. The man then raked the lawn. He stayed working at the house for about five hours. Ed paid him fifty dollars and invited him to return the next day for additional work, but he never showed up.

Not until Elizabeth returned home did investigators piece together exactly what had happened in the early morning hours of June 5. It was Brian who had entered the house through the kitchen window after slashing its screen with a hunting knife, the same knife he used as a threatening weapon minutes later. Thus, Brian had wielded a knife and not a gun as Mary Katherine had initially thought. (A description of events in the upstairs bedroom has already been provided.)

Brian and his victim had left the house through a kitchen door that was located a few feet from the entry window. Strangely, it was one of only three doors in the house that by mistake had not been connected to the alarm system during installation.

Elizabeth was forced to walk along a footpath in the backyard, through a vacant lot and upward to Tomahawk Drive; they moved onto a steep dirt trail that led them past some old lime kilns, through the Bonneville Shoreline Trail, and directly up the steep mountainside. Brian slashed underbrush with his knife as they plodded onward. Elizabeth was petrified. Periodically she managed to mouth questions about the man's intent, but they went unanswered. In their place were ranting utterances about fulfilling the work of the Lord and saving her from all the evil of the world.

Near daybreak—after an ascent of three thousand feet and a journey totaling four miles—they arrived at a makeshift lean-to surrounded by tall, dense trees. Wanda was there to greet them. The twenty-foot-long lean-to covered a narrow excavation in the ground and was made of logs, tree branches, soil, plastic bags, nails, and duct tape. To one side, a tent was pitched in a flat area. Brian called it their campsite, and it was there, not far from Dry Creek Canyon, that Brian kept his victim for the better part of the next two months. Elizabeth was immediately tethered to a tree with a cable running from her leg. It was also there—according to court papers—that Wanda, using the threat of Brian's murdering the young girl, removed Elizabeth's pajamas.

To this date, specific details of what Elizabeth was forced to endure at the concealed campsite have been kept confidential. Yet much can be interpreted from a probable-cause statement filed by Salt Lake City authorities on March 18, 2003 (reprinted at the end of this chapter). What is clear, however, is that, from the beginning, the two captors attempted to use physical and mental methods to alter Elizabeth psychologically so that she took on a new self-identity. They even renamed her Augustine.

In *Bringing Elizabeth Home*, Ed and Lois summed up their daughter's plight and forced compliance:

> People ask us all the time why Elizabeth didn't try to escape—why she didn't try to break free. The answer is simple. She did try, and she couldn't get away. She was never left alone. . . . She told us later that she could not live in fear, because to her if she did, her worst fears would come to fruition. She chose to survive. . . . Brian Mitchell thought he could force his beliefs onto Elizabeth until she was, in a sense reprogrammed. . . . Many people have asked if Elizabeth suffered from Stockholm Syndrome, which is a phenomenon where victims begin to identify with their captors as they fear for their own lives. . . . [She] exhibited some of the traits . . . but unlike most victims she never bonded with her kidnappers.[16]

Consultation

Before tracing the events of Elizabeth's nine-month-long ordeal, we skip ahead to August 2002, two months into the case. I received a request from Ed Smart for my assistance in the investigation of his daughter's disappearance. We had several subsequent phone conversations. It was a time when I was extremely busy with my Court TV program, *Trace Evidence: The Case Files of Dr. Henry Lee*. I hadn't realized how much time, effort, and energy went into a television show like that—on the part of producers, directors, detectives, researchers, camera crews, and, in this case, yours truly. But I was deeply moved by Ed's sincerity and his profound love for Elizabeth. I informed him that in the US judicial system, there are jurisdiction issues that must always be considered and that, unless a formal request were made by a law enforcement agency or a district attorney's office, it would be difficult for me to (1) obtain direct information about the case, and (2) examine any forensic evidence that had been collected by the police. A month later, I received an official written request from Chief Dinse to assist in "reviewing evidence, evidence collection and forensic analysis" in the case. The request was made with the concurrence of the district attorney for Salt Lake County. Former captain Cory Lyman of the SLCPD, commander of the detective division, was also instrumental in securing my assistance.

We spoke on the phone several times, reviewing the case's most current information, including forensic laboratory results. I learned that only about a dozen pieces of evidence had been collected and that none of that evidence had paid any real dividends. We agreed that the case was a much more difficult one than the public realized and that the Salt Lake City police and other state and federal law enforcement agencies had put enormous amounts of time and effort into trying to solve the case. I was told that hundreds of police officers and detectives had already given up weekends and holidays to help find Elizabeth. There was no question in my mind at that point: I must fly to Utah to study the crime scene and to examine physical evidence firsthand.

I had just retired for the third time as Connecticut's commissioner for the Departments of Public Safety and State Police. I was hoping to spend some quiet time with my wife, Margaret, and to catch up on my research, writing, and teaching. The governor had twisted my arm to accept a position as Chief Emeritus of the department's Division of Scientific Services. That would relieve me of any administrative duties so that I could work on difficult criminal cases and on matters concerning criminal investigations. The arrangement would also allow more time for me to devote to police training and case consultations. Although the annual salary was only one dollar, the work appeared very attractive—so I accepted the offer. From that point on, I became known as the most valuable "One-Dollar-Man" in Connecticut!

As for the Utah case, two issues that arose were my consultation fee and travel costs. Most police departments in this country operate on a shoestring budget. I therefore decided to waive my consultation fee. The Smart family, meanwhile, would cover a portion of my travel expenses. Captain Lyman and I then made preliminary plans to review the case in its entirety.

Right around that time, I had to be in Alaska to deliver a two-day lecture to a conference of police officials, attorneys, and criminal investigators. The subject would deal with the newest technologies in criminal investigations. I altered my travel plans and, on the way to the conference, made a stopover at Salt Lake City's airport. Dets. Mark Sharman and Bill Henry were there to greet me. We have known each other for years. They are hardworking individuals and excellent detectives. Both have taken my training courses. I should point out that every year a portion of my time—perhaps a quarter—is allocated to law enforcement training. I travel extensively around the country and the world to conduct courses on forensic science and criminal investigation. At the same time, I'm able to share my experiences with students, police officers, and attorneys. Many of them have become good friends of mine. In this connection, I've visited Utah several times in the past and have been impressed by the warmth of its people and the natural beauty of the state itself. My lectures there have been well received by members of its law enforcement community; and they always seem to go out of their way to extend me every courtesy.

Anyway, Mark, Bill, and I had a two-hour meeting during which they updated me on the case at the airport. They then handed me a complete casebook, which included the crime scene photographs, laboratory results, and all other information on forensic evidence. It was meant to brief me on the current status of the case. I left Salt Lake City with more work to do.

Later—and after a detailed study of the material—I made plans to return in order to conduct a personal crime scene analysis.

Accordingly, I arrived in Salt Lake on Tuesday, October 15. Mark, Bill, and Juan Becerra from the FBI met me at the airport. We avoided a media mob as they took me directly to police headquarters. I met Chief Dinse and had a very informative conversation about the case and its investigative issues. We then retired to a conference room so I could meet the task force members and be briefed on any new developments. Captain Lyman, a tall, handsome fellow, chaired the meeting. We exchanged ideas and leads, and, during the give-and-take, I realized that the team had indeed been laboring very long and hard on the case. As the meeting wound down, I made known the tasks that I envisioned for myself during my two-day visit:

- meet Ed and Lois Smart and the rest of the family
- study the crime scene photos and investigative reports
- visit the crime scene at the Smart residence
- canvass the neighborhood and surrounding areas
- meet the forensic team assigned to the case
- reexamine the physical evidence
- listen to Mary Katherine's recollection of the suspect who had taken her sister away
- meet again with the task force to present my findings

This was quite a list, especially since I was pressed for time; I would have to start work immediately. At the conclusion of the meeting, I was told that a large media contingent had gathered for a news conference concerning my visit. I faced the journalists and was asked: "What kind of new clue do you expect to find?" I replied: "That is an excellent question. When I find one, I'll let you know."

That afternoon, we went to the Children's Justice Center to listen to an interview with Mary Katherine. Mark, Juan, and another detective, Cathy Schoney, were there in an adjacent room. We had already supplied the interviewer with some questions that I hoped the young child might answer.

After the interview, we motored to the Smarts' home, a thirty- to forty-five-minute drive up a winding road. Their house sat on a hill at the end of a dead-end street—a beautiful house in a very nice neighborhood. Ed and Lois greeted us at the door. This was the first time we had met, but I could tell on the spot that I could trust them. They exuded honesty and goodness. I was shown around the house and was introduced to Mary Katherine and her four brothers. Each was polite and appeared to be well educated.

Corner view of family room area.

Initially, I checked every window, door, skylight, chimney, and every aspect of every room in order to formulate a mental picture of the suspect's possible movements on the night of the kidnapping. Then we focused on a likely point of entry. Generally, we use a process of elimination: when the impossible sites have been ruled out, whatever remains becomes more probable. A kitchen window looked more and more like what we were looking for, but there were two major problems with this hypothesis: (1) Had the screen been cut from the outside in or, as some investigation members believed, from the inside out? And (2) the original crime scene photos taken the night of the crime showed a green metal chair propped against the house's exterior wall, below that window. But only its two front legs rested on a red stone step below, while the back pair was suspended in air. The question was raised as to whether or not the chair, in such a position, could support a person's weight.

We decided to conduct a set of experiments. The green chair had been seized for evidence. Taking a similar one from the common set, we placed it on the same red stone step beneath the window. Next, we used the original crime scene measurements of the kitchen screen to mark the cut areas. The highest cut point was 105 inches from the bottom of the step stone.

We conferred briefly about who was going to stand on the chair, which would have only two front legs resting on a stone step. Since I've retired three times and have no young children, I volunteered. Now I'm five feet eight inches tall, and, try as I might, I couldn't reach the top of the cut point. Then I asked Captain Corey, who is six feet two, if he would give it a try. He easily reached *above* the point. Thus we determined that the suspect could have made the cut from the outside in; that the propped chair could have supported his weight; and that he was taller than five feet eight, and much shorter than six feet two.

We also measured the width of the window; it was eleven inches at its maximum opening. Tongue in cheek, I indicated that neither Cory Lyman nor Mark Sharman could ever squeeze through the window. There was no disagreement. So we figured that the suspect was a tall slender man. We further deduced that he most likely had worked in and about the house before and was familiar with the kitchen area and the red slate walkway out back. He knew, we believed, the exact location of Elizabeth's bedroom.

Next we studied the footpath in the backyard and climbed up a steep dirt trail to the top of the hill overlooking the home. We agreed that this was the probable route that the suspect and his captive had taken.

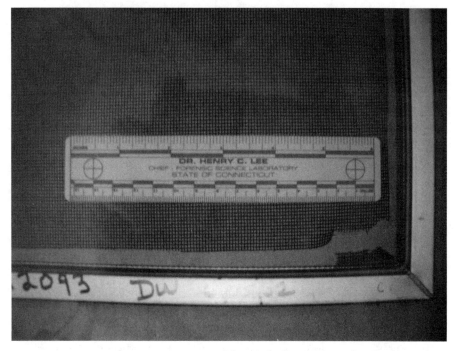

View of sharp cut in kitchen screen.

We departed the scene at about 6:00 PM. I was taken to a very old but elegant hotel. At seven, I had dinner with Ed and Lois Smart, Chief Dinse, Captain Corey, and the FBI regional chief. Of course, our conversation centered on the case, and I shared some of my initial observations with them. As we prepared to leave, I turned to Elizabeth's parents and emphasized that criminal investigations rarely yield absolutes and that crime scenes are filled with gray areas. I tried to offer encouragement. "Also, you have to be patient," I said. "You never know when that lucky break will occur." During that interlude, I had the strangest feeling that Elizabeth was still alive and that she would eventually be reunited with her family.

I got back to my room at about eleven. I still had tons of material to read, analyze, and absorb: crime scene reports, laboratory work sheets and reports, photographs, and more. I knew that the following day would find me meeting with laboratory scientists, reexamining physical evidence, ascertaining what testing had been done, and deciding which results could be utilized to develop investigative leads. I finished my study at 3:00 AM, at which time I walked out onto the balcony. The view overlooking the city was magnificent—so beautiful and peaceful. But I was preoccupied: Where is Elizabeth?

The next day, I attended a meeting with Salt Lake City Crime Lab and Utah State Crime Lab scientists, including Jay Henry, Kevin Patrick, Karen Elliott, and Larry Marx—a group of true professionals. They are all competent and experienced forensic scientists who are a pleasure to work with. We examined each piece of physical evidence. I paid particular attention to the green metal chair and the kitchen screen. We noticed a few fingerprint ridges concentrated in a small area on the right side of the screen. We knew this was not a large enough pattern area for an AFIS search (Automated Fingerprint Identification System), but we decided to swab the spot for trace DNA analysis. We then examined the cuts in the screen, both macroscopically and microscopically, and reached a joint opinion that the screen had been cut with a sharp knife, in a direction running from the left top down to the bottom, then laterally to the right, and then upward from there—an overall cut that was U-shaped. We also believed it was most likely cut from the outside (in contrast to numerous media reports that the cuts were made from the inside out).

Later, there was another meeting with Cory, Mark, and Juan. I elaborated on my findings concerning the forensic evidence to date.

It is generally accepted that the Smart house had not been secured quickly enough, allowing people into a crime scene that forensic investigators had not yet searched for physical evidence. In fact, on September 7 the *Deseret News* printed a story headlined "Smart Scene Unsealed for Hours." In it Chief Dinse conceded that some evidence could have thus been compromised. Ed Smart estimated that fifty family and church members milled around the house in the first few hours. Later I read one of the district attorney's explanations for the police officers' early inaction. He said that this is how the members of that church functioned—with everyone trying to help each other. So after the police got there, they had to undo the chaos before they could begin reasonable forensic procedures. Another law enforcement official's comments caught my eye: Captain Lyman refused to characterize his officers' conduct as a blunder—as some had done. Instead, he chose to stress the first obligation of initial officers on a crime scene: the preservation of life. They had a greater responsibility than to seal that scene, the captain maintained. Naturally, it was to see if Elizabeth was nearby and, hopefully, alive and well.

Still, during the meeting, I stated that the investigators had done an excellent job collecting evidence and following up on thousands of leads. I knew that there were differences of opinion with regard to the kitchen screen. However, I pointed out that it was still the key evidentiary item related to the probable point of entry. Associated with that was the green patio chair propped up against the stucco wall directly below the window. Thus, my expressed conclusion was that a tall, thin intruder could have slipped through the cranked-open window after first cutting its screen vertically down from the outside, then reaching inside to make another cut horizontally across to the other vertical cut.

I shared with them the notes I had made concerning my observations and preliminary conclusions:

1. Smart residence located at East Kristianna Circle. House situated at east end of Circle. The Circle runs east and west and dead-ends at east end. House is on north side of Circle. Large amount of scrub oak on west side and in backyard. Red rock walkway starts on west side of house—goes to back, then east along back of house to back door patio. Walking south along east side of house, we find another red rock walkway that leads to front porch. This walkway is directly under Eliz.'s bedroom (front of house on east side). There is window on east, south, and west walls of the room. The south window overlooks the street. Walkway then continues on west side of the front porch and down to the driveway. Front, including a deck area, is heavily covered with trees and foliage. East side of a front yard so covered as well. Walkway is right next to the house. Eliz.'s and parents' room are at upper level. No blinds. Eliz.'s window open—not unusual. Other children's windows are at ground level. They do have blinds. Two doors on upstairs level lead to an atrium, one from Charles' room, the other from Edward II's room. Door from Charles' room had no handle, so not able to open door. Other OK, so could access atrium from there. Door to atrium from outside was locked. Garage overhead door was down. There is walk-through door from garage that exits out to west side of house. Door [did] not have handle but was secured by board that was horizontal at chest level and attached at each side by single screw. Sliding glass doors of family room alarmed and sounded when I tested. French doors of living room reportedly not

alarmed. I tested anyway—no sound. Back door not alarmed. Also tested front doors and door leading from basement to garage—all sounded. I checked contacts on front door and found it had screw at top that made contact with door frame thus sounding alarm system. No such screw on back door. Detective walked me through backyard through wooded area east of house, up cul-de-sac later identified as Tomahawk Drive. After four months, no relevant footwear impression evidence or other probative items could be found. Returning to areas around exterior windows and doors for closer examination I saw no obvious tool marks or signs of forced entry.

2. Kitchen window and outside area around it: window is casement style with large center section and narrow sections on each side. Narrow sections with crank out (north-south). Original window had been replaced since incident, but replacement is the exact size as original. Informed that green cast-iron patio chair found propped against stucco wall below said window. Topography of area permits only two legs of chair to be in direct contact with step. We did experiment with similar chair and found that it could be placed in balance with its back resting against wall of house. Three matching chairs on patio. No indentation marks on wall above where chair had been propped, but at probable contact area, transfer pattern observed.

3. Power outlet just east and above chair. Two scrape marks on stucco wall west of kitchen window and one on ledge.

4. Informed that ladder found on ground east of back door. Had been used by crime lab tech to reach window so that it could be processed for latent prints. Marks on wall no doubt made by ladder. Told that same tech had processed back screen door on both sides, the back door itself on both sides, the point of entry window and screen, Eliz.'s bedroom door upstairs and also a crooked corner post of her bed.

5. Informed that white cloth material found on patio table.

6. Informed that razor blade with cardboard wrapper found on rock steps just west of front porch. On step above it, bloodlike stain found.

7. Informed that at front of driveway, few bloodlike stains found.

8. Informed that some glass particles found on driveway and cement steps from driveway to house. Told that while someone brought groceries in house, jar of jam was dropped.

9. Inside, observed that entry window is located above counter near sink. Was told there was some question about location of bag of flour, flower vase, box of crackers, and soap dish—different versions. Was told that kitchen scene thoroughly processed for latent prints and shoe impressions on the counter top. Moveable items were taken as evidence. Scene had been diagrammed and photographed.

10. I walked through rest of the first floor and observed nothing out of the ordinary. Particularly struck by beauty of Eliz.'s harp near piano.

11. Upstairs in Eliz.'s bedroom, nothing remarkable on initial run through except crooked bedpost. Informed room received usual processing and that many of Eliz.'s personal items were taken by forensic team. Processing included examination for seminal fluid—none detected.

Back in Connecticut, I pondered the case during every free moment. Finally, my Crime Scene Reconstruction Report was completed. Among its particulars:

Item #1 – Metal Chair:

This item is a cast-iron type of metal chair, which was found outside of the Smart residence against the stucco wall, below the kitchen window. Investigators and forensic laboratory personnel in Utah had previously examined the chair. The following observations were noted on October 16, 2002:

1. The chair has a cast-iron construction with a diagonal grid design. No visible footwear imprints were observed on the chair. However, dust, soil, and other trace material were noticed on the metal surface. The majority of these materials were located on the joint areas of the grill. A small piece of adhesive tape was observed on the front left portion of the seat.

View of living-room area showing Elizabeth's harp near the piano.

2. There is static abrasion type damage on the back of the chair. This static transfer pattern was similar to the observed pattern associated with placing a similar metal chair against the stucco wall on 10/15/02.

Item #2 – Kitchen Window:

1. On the left side of the exterior surface of the window, partial fingerprints were detected at a location of approximately 11 inches from the bottom edge of the window.
2. About 4 inches above these partial prints, there were finger smear type marks. There were only a few ridge details. The marks were subsequently removed for DNA analysis.

Item #3 – Window Screen:

This screen was removed from the kitchen window at the Smart residence on June 26, 2002. The overall dimensions of the screen are 61 inches × 17 inches.

1. There is a "U" shaped cut in the screen. Macroscopic examination of the cut areas revealed a series of cuttings in subgroupings.
2. On the right side of the screen, the cut consists of several sub-groups of cuttings. A few of these cuts clearly originate from the bottom and progress in an upward direction. Other cuts appear to travel in a downward direction. These cuts were made from the outside. Several areas of hesitation marks in cutting can be noted.
3. The measured distance from the top of right cut to the bottom of the screen is 38½ inches. It appears that the cutting motion is in a downward direction from this point.
4. Along the bottom of the screen, there are a number of cutting motions that produced the observed pattern. There is a continued vertical cut along the right edge of the screen that extends to the bottom edge. Zigzag type cuts follow for approximately 1 inch from right to left. A longer more continuous cut then follows toward the left side of the screen along the bottom edge.
5. At the lower left portion of the screen, there are more zigzag cuts that lead to an oblique cut, left and upward for a short distance, and finally straight up. The total vertical cut on the left measures 30½ inches from its top end to the bottom edge of the screen.[17]

My *conclusions* submitted to the task force authorities were, in part:

1. The Smart residence is located in an exclusive community of homes. The house is located on the left side of the street, toward the end of a dead end. The driveway winds uphill toward the house. The location of the residence would suggest that this was not a randomly selected target.
2. The site is located on rugged, sloped terrain. The pathway that leads around and behind the house is uneven and disjointed in areas. Lighting and visibility were poor during the evening. These facts suggest that any perpetrator using the pathways around the house as a means of entrance or egress must be familiar with the Smart residence and the immediate area.
3. The screen was cut by a sharp cutting instrument from the outside. The majority of the cuts were clearly initiated from the outside. Some of the cuts were from an up to downward direction, while

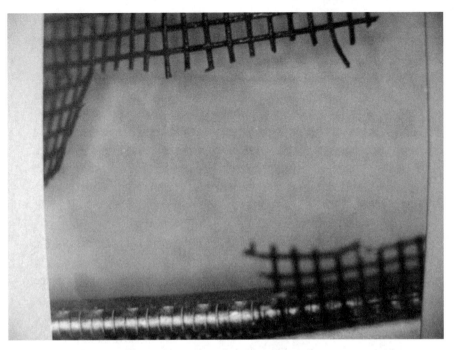

Close-up view of the screen showing outside-in cut.

others were from the bottom upward or sideways. The height from the ground to the window frame is approximately 64 inches. The height from the ground to the lower edge of the screen is approximately 67 inches. The height from the ground to the highest cut point on the right side of the screen is approximately 105 inches. Given these measurements, the height of the perpetrator could be 6 feet tall with a long arm reach.

4. The metal chair was lifted from the patio area and placed against the stucco wall under the window to gain entrance. Based on the Utah laboratory report, shoe print types of patterns were found.

5. Macroscopic and microscopic examinations of the cuts on the screen indicate a majority of the cuts were initiated from outside the window.

6. The location of Elizabeth Smart's bedroom and the fact she was sharing a room with her sister suggest that the victim was a selected and planned target.

7. Additional analysis and reconstruction are dependent upon the

submission of remaining crime scene photographs, laboratory testing results of physical evidence, and other relevant investigative reports.

My *suggestions* were:

1. Trace evidence collected from the metal chair (item #1) should be compared with the trace evidence collected from the known metal chair. Any foreign particles not from the Smart residence should be used to be compared with trace material collected from any suspected vehicles or shoes.
2. Fingerprints found on the screen and window should be digitally enhanced and placed in AFIS for further comparison and searching.
3. Although the chair and screen have been handled and processed previously, the metal chair (item #1) and the area adjacent to the fingerprint on the screen should be swabbed and tested for DNA.
4. Upon submission of all laboratory testing results and worksheets, complete inventory lists of physical evidence, and other relevant investigative reports, further analysis may be possible.[18]

NINE-MONTH-LONG NIGHTMARE

Whereas some of Elizabeth's story remains closely guarded by her relatives; whereas some of the members of law enforcement, the media, and the Smart family openly clash; whereas medical and psychological professionals must be protective of a teenager's mental health—an accurate time line and description of her captivity is bound to contain gaps.

The period between her abduction and rescue was filled with moments of stress on everybody related to the case and with huge voids in determining what exactly was going on—in regard to both the treatment of Elizabeth and the course of the investigation. What is now fairly well established is that she and her captors spent the first two months living at the campsite. Brian would sporadically wander down to the city to panhandle and gather up provisions for the three of them. He was particular in keeping plenty of beer available for his own consumption. And, of course, he worked on his young victim psychologically, beginning with a steady barrage of what can only be described as brainwashing—until she apparently became as compliant as he wished.

By August, Elizabeth had no doubt settled into a closed world of misery and probable cruelty; she must have remained submissive to survive. This was the time when there were reports of sightings of the trio around the city: roaming around food fairs, strip malls, and health-food stores; riding buses or hitchhiking here and there. They would walk in a tight file; one resident called them "Joseph and Mary and that young girl in white robes and a veil."

In retrospect, many question why Elizabeth never tried to get the attention of a passerby—a word, a sigh, a rolling of the eyes. A favorite deduction among cult experts is that she had long before been stripped of her identity. They point to the robes that she was forced to wear as contributing to the transformation.

In 1973 publishing heiress Patty Hearst was kidnapped by members of the Symbionese Liberation Army, an extreme radical group. She was kept locked in a closet and repeatedly raped for the first two months of a yearlong captivity—and even participated in a bank robbery with her abductors. Hearst, in a *Larry King Live* interview, said: "Because you have been so abused and so robbed of your free will, you . . . believe any lie your abductor has told you . . . you don't feel safe. You think that either you will be killed, or if you reach out to get help, you believe that your family will be killed. . . . You have absorbed this new identity that they've given you. You're just surviving."[19]

On the home front in August, the number of press advisories and appeals from the Smart family had dwindled. Differences of opinion continued to surface regarding the police's handling of the investigation versus the expectations of the Smart family.

Ed decided to redirect some of his energies to encourage Congress to pass a national Amber Alert system. The system, mentioned previously, was not only named after a child who was abducted and murdered but also, as an acronym, stood for **A**merica's **M**issing: **B**roadcast **E**mergency **R**esponse. If ever the title of something described its mission, that was it. Elizabeth's father also used the occasion of the 9/11 anniversary to call attention to the importance of homeland and individual family security.

Richard Ricci, as noted, died in late August, taking to his grave many unanswered questions, most important of which was whether or not he had kidnapped Elizabeth. The theory held that she had either been murdered or, after his death, was being restrained by accomplices. Most of the Smart family felt that he was innocent of the crime; some police authorities still felt he was guilty. In its September 1 edition, the *Salt Lake Tribune* ran another front-page story: "Why Ricci Topped Cop List." Reporters Michael Vigh and Kevin Cantera, using unidentified police sources, argued the case against Ricci, then concluded, "Among the inner circle of investigators there remains scant doubt that the career criminal, who died Friday, somehow managed to snatch the girl without a trace."[20]

In actuality, during early fall, Brian orchestrated some brazen moves. The three, as mentioned, would parade boldly through the streets (most thought they were religious "weirdos") and would stand together on corners as Brian begged for money. On one occasion, they crashed a house party. On another, they holed up for a week in the apartment of a man named Daniel Trotta, the cashier at a market that they often frequented. Certainly, these constituted missed opportunities for the family and law enforcement.

Aside from my Salt Lake visit in October, the other key development in that month involved Mary Katherine. It would be a turning point in the case. She was browsing through the *Guinness Book of World Records* when something triggered a memory and she said to her parents, "I think it might be Immanuel." She was referring to the man who once briefly worked on their roof. Adding that revelation to her insistence that Richard Ricci was not the kidnapper encouraged the entire Smart family. But some of the investigators were not convinced. Lois Smart believed that her young daughter's sudden announcement of the name Immanuel was the result of "divine inspiration." She asked Captain Lyman when the police would go public with the news. "Probably never," was the answer she recalls. According to Lois, the captain said, "What do we have to go on? An alias name? Three sketches from your family that don't look alike? And Mary Katherine isn't exactly sure."[21] The investigators still believed Ricci was the most likely perpetrator. And there was confusion over the fact that Mary Katherine's description was that of a long-haired man, not the clean-shaven Immanuel who, a year before, had shown up to make repairs at the Smart home. After once again disparaging the sketches that other family children had provided, the police wanted to enlist the aid of a professional artist.

It was then that Dalene Nelson entered the picture. She worked with Ed and eventually produced a sketch that wasn't totally acceptable at the time, but which the police circulated among several homeless shelters in and around Salt Lake City. They didn't want to take it any further than that for fear of scaring Immanuel away—if he was, in fact, the man in the first place, as they purportedly put it.

Ed and Lois interpreted this as relative inaction among the police, which seemed to reinforce confusion and disappointment among family members. The parents lumped these negative emotions and others together as challenges. They voiced concerns about dealing with the investigation and the investigators, handling the media, and facing the deluge of theories. They declared in their book that the assumptions were: "Ricci did it. The father was involved. Elizabeth was a runaway. None of it was right, none of it helped find Elizabeth."[22]

Immanuel's sketch wasn't released for several months. And that was lucky, for, as we shall see, Brian, Wanda, and Elizabeth had moved to California. The police were right after all, because if the sketch had come out in October, perhaps they might not have returned to Salt Lake City. Ed and Lois were certain that this was another instance of divine intervention.

November 3 marked Elizabeth's fifteenth birthday and approximately the fifth month of her abduction. By then the task force assigned to the case numbered five: three detectives from the SLCPD and two FBI investigators. There was no unanimity among them as to the identity of the culprit, much less the how and why of the crime. The three most plausible theories were that she was taken by a sexual predator, abducted in a bungled burglary, or kidnapped for ransom. They even postulated that a kidnapping for ransom could have been bungled. And even after Ricci's death, they continued to target the handyman as the abductor. Before his death, he had admitted to knowing the layout of the house and, according to court documents, admitted to stealing jewelry, perfume, and a collection of seashells from the house. The documents also state that he had broken into another house in the Arlington Hills neighborhood, making off with jewelry and cash. Earlier, he had done some remodeling at the house. Captain Lyman offered a bleak assessment of the situation: although the case did not die with Ricci, the unexpected turn of events set back some of the theories of the case. The police leader believed that the deceased career criminal had information, either culpable or exculpable, that only he knew. Up until then, the police had devoted more than 4,250 man-hours to the investigation and logged ten thousand miles in running down sixteen thousand leads.

The Associated Press reported that search efforts had decentralized by then and that individuals having information to share did so through the dedicated Web site.[23] One such person used the Internet trying to extort three million dollars for Elizabeth's safe return. It was obviously a hoax and the man was later apprehended. His note was not the only one of its kind. The family received batches of letters from around the world, all demanding ransom money. And the number of psychics claiming to have the definitive word on Elizabeth's whereabouts was staggering. Many—six hundred of them—disclosed that they were informed of important information through their dreams. Each had to be investigated, however, because even the National Center for Missing and Exploited Children maintains that such dreams may be the result of a truth revealed by someone unwilling to become directly involved with a crime; that is, some psychics may have valuable information given to them by people who do not wish to be identified. The psychics, in turn, may or may not have had a dream about the information. But while these communications exacted an emotional toll on the family, the majority of communications received were heartwarming.

The wire service gave examples of what authorities were up against: A man fled after he was seen digging a gravelike hole in Sanpete County on June 9. His description matched the one given by Mary Katherine. The background of a California man who was in Utah around the time of the crime was intensely scrutinized and then he was cleared. The sighting of a Lincoln, Nebraska, girl in a van who was a dead ringer for Elizabeth proved to be a false alarm. Police search-and-rescue units descended on many of Utah's twenty thousand dangerous and open mine shafts after having received tips related to the disappearance. None of the inspections proved fruitful.

The Associated Press also hinted at what the Smart family was up against. "Every day is a struggle," Lois confessed in an interview. "It would be very easy for me to stay in bed, never leave." She referred to her other five children, however, when she said they needed their parents to figure out how to live without Elizabeth so that they could, too. "They take their cues directly from us," she said. "As long as we are able to function, so are they." In the same interview, she choked back tears as she recounted how Mary Katherine came into the master bedroom in the middle of that June 5 night and what immediately followed.

"She wasn't hysterical," Lois said. "She came to my side. She had her blanket around her. She just said, 'Elizabeth is gone.' Ed got up and checked the other kids' rooms. He and I went downstairs to look for Elizabeth. [I] saw the window screen near the back door had been cut, and became hysterical. Ed called 911." Lois stated she didn't remember how many police officers arrived at their home, or when. "It [seemed] like they were there fast. Everyone got there fast."[24]

"There have been false sightings all over, in several states," Tom Smart said. "There are clues but there are no traces. It's crazier than any fiction. I still believe they'll solve it."[25] His comments were more charitable than the words on the dust jacket of the book he penned with reporter, Lee Benson: ". . . the first comprehensive look into how the police botched the investigation, the media's manipulation of the family, and the eyewitness testimony of nine-year-old Mary Katherine Smart, which went largely ignored by investigators."[26]

Around the time of Elizabeth's birthday, Ed and Lois said they still weren't sure what the kidnapper had said in their daughter's bedroom. Bowing to the request of investigators, they hadn't questioned Mary Katherine about what she had told police. Children have malleable memories, they reasoned, and they didn't want to taint her as a witness. But the parents did talk to her if she initiated the conversation. They were led to conclude that, as their younger daughter feigned sleep, Elizabeth stubbed her toe and was about to scream. The man then said either "If you don't scream, I won't hurt you" or "Be quiet or I'll hurt you." The nine-year-old slipped out of bed to follow them, but when she saw them looking into her brother's room, she rushed back to bed. "Mary Katherine was brave, courageous and strong that night," Lois said. "She did the right thing. I want the world to know that."[27]

Shortly before Christmas, the airing of two television shows had an impact on the case—one positive, the other not so positive, although the latter one helped keep the abduction story alive. Ed and Lois appeared on John Walsh's *America's Most Wanted*. After the show, Ed confided to Walsh about Mary Katherine and the Immanuel revelation. He also told Walsh about the sketch and remarked that the police didn't want to go public with it quite yet. The victim's advocate disagreed with that approach, hailing television's valuable role in solving cases. But he indicated he would abide by the wishes of the Smarts if they decided to follow the advice of the police.

Nevertheless, on December 23, Walsh appeared on *Larry King Live* and, when queried about his take on the case, he responded, "Their daughter has now said that she believes that Ricci wasn't the guy in there that night, that it may have been another guy that did some work on their roof, an itinerant guy that worked at a homeless shelter, and he may be a suspect, and I don't want to give away a lot of breaking information here, but *America's Most Wanted* is going to take a look at the Smart case."[28] The family was initially indignant but later stated that John Walsh's making the announcement so quickly—and without informing them in advance—was really another blessing. He would subsequently feature Elizabeth's kidnapping on two additional shows: February 15 and March 1.

Brian, Wanda, and Elizabeth had moved west in October, traveling by way of Las Vegas and San Diego and eventually settling in Lakeside, California. The town, twenty-five miles east of San Diego and about an hour's drive to the Mexican border, was a throwback to the cowboy days of the Old West. They remained there for about four months after setting up campsites in two locations. They also lived in a rundown abandoned trailer for a time. But their main quarters were unevenly divided between an area dubbed by local residents as the "river bottoms" and a camp Brian constructed on a hill about a half mile away. It was not unlike the one they had occupied in Salt Lake City.

The river bottoms provided a ready supply of water and bridges under which to take shelter during storms. Many of the area's homeless were there, so the three would fit in and be camouflaged. But there was also a perceived liability weighing on Brian's mind: county sheriffs periodically scouted the region. They therefore used their higher-ground camp most of the time, reserving the lower site to hide supplies in holes that they dug in the earth.

It didn't take long for them to become regulars around town, where they even developed some guarded friendships. People stared at the robed trio as they carried on a daily routine of walking into town to preach, hand out religious pamphlets, and panhandle. They apparently felt safe in Lakeside despite the fact that most in the "cowboy" town thought they were "creepy" and avoided them. Yet they circulated about freely, purchased food, used the Laundromat, and sat at picnic tables together. Brian would always do the talking, giving terse responses to predictable questions: "We're from heaven"; "Please don't call them costumes"; and "God is with us." A grocery clerk remembered them in insightful terms: "He weirded me out. He used to ask the women 'Do you want a drink?' They'd nod. They never talked. I figured he converted them. I didn't like to wait on him. When it was his turn, I'd turn to [the storeowner] and say, 'You take him.' It was so weird, a man who looked like Jesus, buying beer. He bought one almost every day. That Steel Reserve that he bought, it's really a strong beer. Only heavy drinkers buy that."[29]

In mid-February, Brian was arrested for breaking into a preschool classroom of the Lakeside Presbyterian Church. It was around five in the morning. He had intended to loot the church, but he was so drunk that he passed out instead. When the police arrived later, he was sleeping on the floor. They booked him and he was jailed for six days. He gave his name as Michael Jenson, but when authorities checked on his fingerprints, the name that turned up was Brian David Mitchell.

Ironically, three days after the arrest—February 15—was the date of the second story about him on *America's Most Wanted*. And Brian was sitting in a jail cell. The segment mentioned that police officials were trying to locate the man in connection with Elizabeth's disappearance, that his name was Brian David Mitchell, but that he preferred the name Immanuel. There was no nationwide alert about him, however, and apparently none of Lakeside's law enforcement authorities had seen the program, so no one there—from police officers to the judge who later released him from custody—was aware of the person they had in their hands.

February 15 was significant for another reason. That day Ed Smart held a news conference during which he spoke about Brian and his alias, "Immanuel," and about Mary Katherine's near certainty that he was her sister's kidnapper. Ed also released the sketch they had.

The sketch did it. Brian's sister came forward and identified the man who was portrayed. And days later, after the Walsh show was telecast, police officials dismissed the new developments and refused to remove Ricci's name from the top of their suspect list. An annoyed Mayor Rocky Anderson swung into action. He issued a memo to Police Chief Dinse, indicating that he had tried not to interfere in the investigation but had become increasingly concerned about the attention still being given to Richard Ricci. In that connection, he listed the following:

1. The only witness, Mary Katherine Smart, has maintained from the beginning that she did not think Richard Ricci was the abductor.

2. There is no physical evidence tying Richard Ricci to the abduction.

3. Richard Ricci has no history of sexual abuse or abduction.

4. Mary Katherine independently suggested that the abductor may have been "Immanuel."

5. Immanuel was somewhat familiar with the Smart home.

6. Immanuel has a history of child sexual abuse.

7. Immanuel was seen nearby, at a Kinko's on First South Street, near the University of Utah, on the afternoon Elizabeth was abducted.

8. Immanuel was known to camp out near the Bonneville Shoreline Trail, above the Smart home.

9. Perhaps the most telling, Immanuel has left the area since information about his possible involvement was revealed.[30]

Things began to happen. Wanda Barzee's adult sons provided new photographs of Brian—with and without a beard—and they were shown on the March 1 episode of *America's Most Wanted*. Tips poured in as a result of the show. Rumors swirled that he and his female companions had been spotted everywhere. The print media—from the *Deseret News* to *Time* magazine—ran fresh stories of the case. Particularly reports that implicated Immanuel. There were recent sightings at a Lakeside library, at a nearby roadside (they were hitchhiking), at a McDonald's, and, on March 11, at a Las Vegas Burger King.

*   *   *

It was 12:52 PM, March 12, when police—through 911—were called in Sandy, Utah, twenty miles south of Salt Lake City. Rudy and Nancy Montoya reported seeing three people walking along the street carrying shabby bedrolls and Wal-Mart bags. A minute later, a similar call was placed by Anita and Alvin Dickerson. The first caller said that she had seen the bearded man's image on television—on the John Walsh show. Another of the callers, Anita, got close enough to the man to make eye contact. She swore he looked just like Immanuel. Both calls revealed the youngest in the group wore baggy jeans, a wig, and sunglasses.

Karen Jones was the first police officer to arrive on the scene. When asked, the bearded man stated his name was "Peter Marshall," his wife was "Juliette," and his daughter was "Augustine." A second officer arrived, backup was summoned, and the Salt Lake police were alerted.

The girl in the veil denied that she was Elizabeth. "I know you think I'm that Elizabeth Smart girl who ran away, but I'm not," she insisted. One officer later said he could see her heart beating through her shirt. In their book, Lois and Ed Smart cite such behavior—and their daughter's reluctance to accuse her captors and ask for help—as evidence of psychological bondage. "She was frightened," they wrote. "She was confused, tired and emotionally battered. . . . The hold that Brian David Mitchell had over Elizabeth was excruciatingly strong. . . . When asked [by the officers] about her identity one last time, she finally admitted who she was by proclaiming, 'If thou sayeth, I sayeth,' and then she began to cry."[31]

Brian and Wanda were handcuffed and placed in a patrol car. The officers were stunned when Elizabeth asked, "What's going to happen to them? Are they in trouble?"[32]

Ed Smart was called by the Sandy police and told to hurry to the station-house. Both caller and recipient were cautious. The police believed that if they had divulged the reason for their request, the father might never have been able to make the twenty-mile drive. On the other hand, Ed was just as satisfied not to know the particulars, to remain unaware of what was in store. He had been disappointed so many times before: promising leads, false alarms, and the like. He had simply grown immune to wild goose chases. He had a vague hunch they might have wanted him to identify someone they had in custody, someone who might fit the description of the roofer. But that was the extent of it.

When Ed looked down at Elizabeth sitting on a couch, arms folded over her chest, he froze, then burst into tears. He slid beside her and pulled her in tightly. Seconds later, he pulled back and said, "Is it really you?"

"Yes," she said.[33]

*   *   *

After nine months of captivity, Elizabeth had defied the odds. She had been found bewildered and grungy, but largely unharmed. And she was assured, from the moment of her rescue, that the pillars of her life—her parents, her real home, her real family, her real friends—would eventually help in obliterating her emotional scars.

The immediate postrescue period became a time for jubilation, celebration, and cautious handling of what might be called "Elizabeth's debriefing." The Smart family showed a fierce determination in helping her to reclaim her life, insisting, for example, that prosecutors be considerate of their teenager's psyche during any questioning. Indications were that Elizabeth adjusted very well in the early recovery phase, yet psychological counselors urged that the process unfold slowly.

It was also a time for reflection and analysis, particularly of what went wrong—if anything—with the criminal investigation and with responsible journalism. Heavy doses of praise and gratitude were heaped on the throngs of volunteers who had pitched in during the entire ordeal. The Smarts and their LDS friends thanked the faceless many across Utah and beyond who had offered daily prayers and support.

But it was hard to comprehend why so many sightings of Elizabeth and her captors had never registered with those who had seen them. "Right under our eyes" was a favorite comment. As published photos of her in robes and veil began to circulate, the predominant feeling was "If only I'd known."

KSL News media director Russell Banz said he knew that feeling. The day after the rescue he said, "I feel really stupid now, looking back, you know, how could you be so close and not have done anything, you know?" He added he felt sick to his stomach the night before, when he saw Elizabeth's photo. Banz thought back six months ago when he and his family were having dinner at a restaurant. He recalled that a veiled Elizabeth walked past their table three times to get food and that she kept making eye contact with him. "I don't know if she recognized me," he said, "but she definitely made some distinct eye contact for quite some time . . . sort of made some eye gestures . . . maybe I'm reading more into it, but it seemed she was trying to do something with her eyes." Banz believes such behavior made sense because he is in the same LDS congregation as the Smarts and had seen Elizabeth many times before. "You can see how they went for quite some time being undetected," he explained, "because, I mean two feet, literally two feet away from me as she walked by . . . her outfit would brush against our chairs as she walked by."[34]

And in the San Diego area, where the trio lived for five months, the reactions were just as striking. Residents of Lakeside recalled the bearded man who wore a long tunic and walked the streets preaching the Gospel—and the two mute women who tagged behind.

"We never associated them with the missing girl in Utah," said Terri Sparks, who operates a recycling center in a store parking lot. She indicated that they had frequently walked by the center. Transients near Lido Park, in the center of Lakeside, recalled that they had first noticed the trio the past fall.

"Hey," exclaimed a homeless man to a group of friends. "Did you hear about Immanuel? He . . . kidnapped that girl."

"They were always very pleasant," said another. "She didn't seem like she was kidnapped. She acted like she was part of the family."

A merchant stated they were regular visitors to his store and that he was disturbed that he hadn't made the connection. "I could have done something, you know," he said. "The next time someone raises my suspicion, I'm going to think twice."[35]

*   *   *

Brian and Wanda were taken from their separate cells in the Sandy police station to the Salt Lake County Adult Detention Center. When quizzed by police about his address and emergency contact person, Brian replied, "Heaven on earth" and "God."

On March 18 they were charged with aggravated kidnapping, aggravated sexual assault, and aggravated burglary. Bail was set at ten million dollars for each individual.

"We do believe that these defendants, particularly Mitchell, should be prosecuted as a predatory sexual offender," said Salt Lake County district attorney David Yocom. "If he ever hits the streets, [he should] carry that label for the rest of his life. We are not dealing with just a religious zealot, we are dealing with a predatory sexual offender." Yocom revealed that the charges stemmed from about twenty thousand pages of material amassed in the case.[36]

On both March 24 and August 11, 2004, Wanda Barzee was found to be incompetent to stand trial and is a patient at the Utah State Hospital. Brian David Mitchell was subjected to several mental competency evaluations over a seven-month period and, on August 15, 2005, a Utah judge ruled that he, too, was mentally incompetent to stand trial. The judge ordered that he be institutionalized until he is deemed capable of standing trial—if ever.

POSTSCRIPT

Much might be gleaned from the Probable Cause Statement filed by Salt Lake City law enforcement authorities on March 18, 2003—not the least of which is a summary of the case. Herewith is the statement in its entirety:

THIS INFORMATION IS BASED ON EVIDENCE OBTAINED FROM THE FOLLOWING WITNESSES:

Detective C. Parks, Detective M. Sharman, Detective C. Nelson, Steven Wright, Deputy T. Stocking, Chief Investigator M. George, Lois Smart, Elizabeth Smart, Special Agent G. Dougherty, Special Agent S. Sorenson, Special Agent J. Ross, Detective C. Schoney, Detective K. Moreno, Detective R. Moser.

PROBABLE CAUSE STATEMENT:

1. In the early morning hours of June 5, 2002, Elizabeth Smart, a minor child under the age of 18 years of age, was awakened and abducted at knifepoint by an individual she came to know as "Immanuel," later identified as BRIAN DAVID MITCHELL, who entered her home located in Salt Lake County, Utah, by using a knife or other sharp instrument to cut the screen to a first-floor window.

2. MITCHELL forced Elizabeth Smart to leave her home, against her will, at knifepoint. MITCHELL had neither permission nor consent from Elizabeth Smart's parents to take her or have custody of her. MITCHELL had neither permission nor consent from Elizabeth Smart's parents to enter their home.

3. Your affiant received information that sometime after June 5, 2002, WANDA EILEEN BARZEE told Elizabeth Smart that she knew BRIAN DAVID MITCHELL was going to kidnap her and bring her to a camp in the mountains to be held against her will.

4. After being abducted from her home, Elizabeth Smart was compelled at knifepoint to walk in her pajamas up a mountain trail to a concealed campsite approximately four (4) miles from her home. Elizabeth Smart stated that from the time she was confronted by MITCHELL in her home and throughout her forced

march to the camp, MITCHELL threatened to harm or kill her family if she did not comply with his directions.

5. At the campsite, BARZEE attempted to remove Elizabeth Smart's pajamas. When she resisted, BARZEE threatened to have MITCHELL forcibly remove Elizabeth Smart's clothing, at which point she complied with BARZEE'S demands.

6. MITCHELL then committed a rape, attempted rape, forcible sexual abuse or attempted forcible sexual abuse against Elizabeth Smart. MITCHELL had previously threatened the use of a knife, and had previously threatened to harm or kill her family if she did not comply with his demands and directions. MITCHELL was aided and abetted throughout these acts by BARZEE.

7. After Elizabeth Smart was abducted, MITCHELL used a cable to restrain her. MITCHELL thereafter, on one or more occasions, committed a rape, attempted rape, forcible sexual abuse or attempted forcible sexual abuse against Elizabeth Smart. MITCHELL had previously threatened the use of a knife, and had previously threatened to harm or kill her family if she did not comply with his demands and directions. MITCHELL was aided and abetted throughout these acts by BARZEE.

8. From June 5, 2002, through and including March 12, 2003, BRIAN DAVID MITCHELL and WANDA EILEEN BARZEE held Elizabeth Smart against her will, and without consent and legal authority to do so, and restrained Elizabeth Smart and refused to allow her to leave, to make contact with others, or to contact her family.

9. From June 5, 2002, through and including October 8, 2002, BRIAN DAVID MITCHELL and WANDA EILEEN BARZEE held, detained and restrained Elizabeth Smart in a makeshift campsite in the mountains above Salt Lake City, Utah, in Salt Lake County, Utah, with little or no shelter; with no plumbing; with no water supply; and with little or no food, in circumstances posing grave risk of bodily injury to Elizabeth Smart.

10. Detective C. Nelson of the Salt Lake County Sheriff's Office reports that on or about July 24, 2002, at approximately 3:11 am, an unknown person cut, with a knife or other sharp instru-

ment, a first-floor screen window of a private residence located in Salt Lake County, Utah. The window belonged to the bedroom of a minor child.

11. The minor reported seeing something come through the cut screen. The person, in attempting to climb into the bedroom, awoke the minor child and her family, which caused the unknown person to flee.

12. On March 12, 2003, Defendant WANDA EILEEN BARZEE told Detective R. Moser and Special Agent S. Sorenson that she knew, agreed, assisted, aided and conspired with BRIAN DAVID MITCHELL to go [to] the same private residence in order to abduct a minor child over the age of 14 years and under the age of 18 years, to bring her to their camp in the mountains to be held against her will, without any legal authority to do so, and without the permission of the child's parents.

13. On March 12, 2003, BARZEE told Detective R. Moser and Special Agent S. Sorenson that MITCHELL was going to abduct the child in order to hold and detain her in their camp in the mountains above Salt Lake City, Utah, in Salt Lake County, Utah.

14. Your affiant states that he knows upon information and belief that the camp had little or no shelter; no plumbing; no water supply; and little or no food, in circumstances posing a grave risk of bodily injury to the child.

15. In October 2002, BRIAN DAVID MITCHELL and WANDA EILEEN BARZEE took Elizabeth from the state of Utah, through the state of Nevada, to the state of California, where they stayed until approximately March 5, 2003, when they began traveling back to Utah.

DETECTIVE MARK SHARMAN
Affiant[37]

the michael peterson case

BACKGROUND

Michael Peterson—not a relative of Scott Peterson—is a fifty-eight-year-old novelist and former journalist who was accused of murdering his business executive wife, Kathleen, forty-eight. She was found dead at the foot of a staircase in their million-dollar Durham, North Carolina, home on December 9, 2001. He claimed that she fell backward while ascending the stairs and struck her head on the doorframe—after a night of drinking wine and champagne and after taking a Valium tablet. His defense attorneys asserted that she then lay in a pool of blood—breathing and coughing. When she eventually tried to get up, she slipped on the blood and hit her head one or more times before bleeding to death.

Police investigators and prosecutors, however, saw her death very differently. Since pathologists found seven scalp lacerations and various body bruises that they believed suggested a beating, Michael was indicted for murder during a special session of a grand jury. The prosecution alleged she had been repeatedly struck by a blow poke—a fireplace tool. Their theory of a beating was bolstered sixteen months later when the body of another woman in Michael's life was exhumed. Eerily, she had died in Germany in 1985 from a fall down a staircase. Her death had been ruled by US Army and German authorities as accidental.

Nonetheless, Michael's subsequent murder trial had the prosecution not only trying to prove guilt beyond a reasonable doubt but also trying to prove that a murder had, in fact, been committed at all.

Another twist that would arise would be the defense's allegation that Michael's repeated newspaper columns, denouncing the competence of local police officials, set him up for the murder charge. In one column for the local *Herald-Sun*, Michael noted that the Durham Police Department had the worst rate of crime solving in North Carolina. In another, he wrote, "The chance of a criminal getting caught [here] is only slightly better than getting hit by lightning."[1] Michael's son Todd issued an early statement that the criminal case against his father was "an absolute sham" and that authorities were seeking to "quiet a harsh critic," not only as a *Herald-Sun* columnist, but also as a former city council and mayoral candidate.[2] This theme of a personal vendetta against Michael would be played over and over again, both in and out of the courtroom.

KEY PEOPLE

Michael Iver Peterson

The son of a career military officer, Michael Peterson was born in October 1943 and moved from place to place throughout his childhood. He graduated from Duke University in 1965 with a bachelor's degree in political science. While there, he was the editor of the student newspaper and fantasized about someday becoming, like Ernest Hemingway, a hard-drinking, hard-living novelist. Instead, he started law school, though he quickly dropped out and took a job at the US Department of Defense as part of a think tank. There, he did research on behalf of increased military intervention in Vietnam. The experience led to his enlistment in the Marine Corps. Soon he saw combat in the northern parts of South Vietnam. After the war, Michael became a government consultant, living overseas for eleven years. In 1985 he and his first wife, Patricia Sue, lived and worked in Graefenhausen, Germany. Patricia, a schoolteacher, was the mother of Michael's sons, Clayton and Todd. The Petersons were good friends and neighbors of a widowed US Department of Defense schoolteacher, Elizabeth Ratliff, and her daughters, Margaret and Martha.

In November of that year, Michael walked Ratliff and her daughters home after dinner at the Peterson home. He reportedly helped put the children to bed, and he took out the trash. When housekeeper Barbara Malagnino arrived at the Ratliff home the following morning, she found Elizabeth dead at the bottom of a staircase. Both German and US authorities investigated and concluded that Ratliff had suffered a brain hemorrhage and fell down the stairs. She was said to have complained of severe headaches for several days before the incident.

Ratliff was buried in Texas, and her young daughters went to live with the Petersons and their two sons. (Later, the daughters, college students at the time of their stepmother Kathleen's death in 2001, would publicly maintain that Michael had nothing to do with either tragedy.)

In the late 1980s, the family moved to North Carolina and, in 1991, purchased a thirty-one-year-old mansion on Cedar Street in Durham. Between 1983 and 1998 Michael published three novels based on his experiences living and traveling in the Far East: *The Immortal Dragon*, *A Time of War*, and *Charlie Two Shoes and the Marines of Love Company*.

Michael met Kathleen Atwater in the mid-1990s. She was a Nortel executive who had a teenaged daughter, Caitlin. Eventually, he divorced Patricia and, in 1997, married Kathleen. Most of the Peterson children had blamed Kathleen for the divorce, but they later grew close to her because they claimed that there was a loving connection between Kathleen and Michael that Patricia and Michael never had.

Michael's reputation spread throughout the Durham area because of his books, his community activism, and his regular columns penned for the *Herald-Sun* daily newspaper. In them, he often labeled the local law enforcement establishment as inept. A bid for mayor in 1999 was unsuccessful, owing, in part, to an admission that he'd received a Purple Heart as a result of a wartime car accident in Japan and not because of combat wounds in Vietnam.

Kathleen Peterson

Kathleen was born on February 21, 1953, in Greensboro, North Carolina. Nee Kathleen Hunt, she attended high school in Lancaster, Pennsylvania, and became the first female student accepted into the Duke University School of Engineering.

After graduation with both bachelor's and master's degrees, she worked as an executive for several companies including Baltimore Air-Coil-Pritchard, Merck, and finally Nortel Networks. In her work she traveled worldwide: Canada, Europe, Russia, Ukraine, Vietnam, and Hong Kong. Her first marriage to Fred Atwater, a physicist, produced one child, Caitlin. (Caitlin would later sue Michael for the wrongful death of her mother.) Kathleen married Michael in 1997.

Before her death, she continued to work as an executive at Nortel and was active in the Durham Arts Council, the American Dance Festival, and the Carolina Ballet.

Elizabeth Ratliff

The "other" casualty of a fall from a staircase in Michael's life was Elizabeth Ratliff. Elizabeth was forty-three when she died in 1985. She and Michael's first wife, Patricia, had been close friends for many years and had both taught elementary school in the 1980s for US Defense Department children at an air force base near Graefenhausen.

Michael, in turn, had been friends with Elizabeth's husband, Air Force Capt. George Ratliff Jr., who died during a military operation in 1983. The circumstances of his death were shrouded in secrecy. Two months later, Elizabeth wrote a will naming the Petersons guardians of her daughters, Margaret and Martha, in the event of her own death.

It was well known that Elizabeth had a bleeding disorder, and in 1985 authorities speculated that it had predisposed her to a brain hemorrhage prior to her fall down the stairs.

David Rudolf

Rudolf is one of North Carolina's most prominent and successful defense attorneys. He graduated from New York University Law School in 1974, worked for the Legal Aid Society, and taught at the University of North Carolina School of Law. He began private practice in Chapel Hill in 1982 and, within a decade, was listed in the legal referral guide *The Best Lawyers in America*. Strong-willed and passionate about his work, he is known to have skipped meals and sleep in the preparation of his cases.

One of his most heralded cases involved former professional football player Rae Carruth, who was acquitted of first-degree murder but found guilty of conspiracy and other charges. In defending Michael Peterson, Rudolf was assisted by Thomas Maher, a mild-mannered, astute law partner. His devotion to his cases and impressive work ethic added a further dimension to the defense team.

James Hardin

Durham County district attorney James Hardin Jr. was an assistant district attorney before his interim appointment and then election to the top post in 1994. From the beginning, naysayers questioned his chances of proving Peterson guilty of murder, citing Hardin's lack of trial experience. But he proved more than able. His military-style approach in cross-examinations proved to be effective in neutralizing expert testimony for the defense. After the trial, he was appointed as a judge.

Assistant district attorney Freda Black collaborated with Hardin in the prosecution of the case. She, too, was an excellent attorney and was always well prepared for battle.

Judge Orlando Hudson

The Honorable Orlando Hudson Jr. received his law degree from the University of North Carolina at Chapel Hill. He practiced law privately for two years and then served as an assistant public defender in Fayetteville, as assistant district attorney in Durham, and as a district court judge for five years. He became a superior court judge in 1989 and in 1995 was named North Carolina's senior resident judge for the Fourteenth Judicial District.

PRETRIAL FACTS

The police did not believe Michael's account of what happened on the night he found his wife unconscious at the bottom of the stairs. Their suspicions had been immediately aroused upon noticing the large quantity of blood at the scene.

He said that the two of them had been sitting out back by their swimming pool, drinking wine and champagne, as they celebrated a possible movie deal for one or more of his books. Shortly after midnight, Kathleen said that she had to participate in an early morning conference call, so she left to go to bed. According to him, he remained outside smoking cigarettes for an unspecified length of time. Then he cared for their dogs before returning to the house to find her body. The time line—from her leaving the pool area to the discovery of her body—was to become the subject of intense scrutiny and controversy.

Michael's urgent 911 call was received at 2:41 AM. He was breathing hard and sounded frantic:

Telephone Operator: 911, what's the emergency?
Michael Peterson: 1810 Cedar Street, please.
Telephone Operator: What's wrong?
Michael Peterson: My wife had an accident. She's still breathing.
Telephone Operator: What kind of accident?
Michael Peterson: She fell down the stairs—she's still breathing, please come.
Telephone Operator: Is she conscious?
Michael Peterson: What?
Telephone Operator: Is she conscious?
Michael Peterson: What? No, she's not conscious . . . please . . .
Telephone Operator: OK, how many stairs did she fall down?
Michael Peterson: How many stairs?
Telephone Operator: How many stairs?
Michael Peterson: Huh?
Telephone Operator: Calm down sir, calm down.
Michael Peterson: 15, 20, I don't know. Please get them here right away . . .
Telephone Operator: OK. Somebody's dispatching the ambulance . . .

Michael Peterson: It's all so . . . It's in Forest Hills, OK . . . please, please . . . [3]

Whereas in that call, Michael stated his wife was still breathing, he called back one minute later and said she was dead.

*   *   *

Fire department and EMS responders arrived at 2:48 AM. Kathleen was indeed dead. Some police officers and emergency medical personnel initially believed that she had tried to ascend the poorly lit rear staircase while wearing flip-flops; that she fell backward, struck her head, and then hemorrhaged to death. A terrible accident, they thought. But detectives thought otherwise. Too much blood for a mere fall: over the stairs, the walls, and Michael's clothing. Too many lacerations on her skull.

A police report written by Durham police Sgt. Terry Wilkins stated Michael was wearing a blue shirt and light-colored shorts and was covered in blood when he first encountered him in the foyer. "Mr. Peterson appeared to be confused and was walking in small circles, back and forth," the officer wrote.[4]

One of the first on the scene, paramedic James Rose later said, "It was very unusual for us to see that amount of blood for a fall." He said Michael was very upset and was unable to answer even basic questions, like his wife's date of birth. Rose added that Michael was crouched over his wife, sobbing.[5]

Medical examiner Kenneth Snell was called to investigate the scene. His first impression was that her death was caused by an accidental fall down the stairs. In handwritten notes, he relayed: "Upon arrival, the husband admitted to having put towels under the head. Blood had been wiped up partially in the stairs with paper towels. . . . Blood is present in the bottom of the stairwell and on the last few steps. Appears she hit her head on the step above the corner, then hit the floor in the corner of the stairs and then landed at the base of the stairs on her back. Blood splatter appears to support this scenario. . . . My finding suggests accident."[6] Nevertheless, he ordered an autopsy. He attended the procedure that began at noon that same day. Then in a three-line addendum to his notes, he wrote, "After completion of the autopsy exam and review of some photographs provided by Durham P.D. the injuries are not consistent with an accidental fall down the stairs."[7]

In the opinion of the lead pathologist who performed the autopsy, Dr. Deborah L. Radisch, Kathleen was most likely beaten to death. Her full report—released February 18, 2002—listed the following pathological diagnoses:

- Multiple lacerations and avulsions [tearing away of tissues], posterior scalp
- Multiple contusions [bruises], posterior scalp
- Subarachnoid [beneath one of the coverings of the brain] hemorrhage, slight to moderate
- Early acute ischemic neuronal necrosis [death of brain cells from lack of oxygen]
- Fracture with hemorrhage, superior cornu of left thyroid cartilage [upper part of the largest cartilage of the larynx]
- Contusions of back, posterior arms, wrists, and hands
- Multiple small abrasions and contusions, face

The recorded cause of death was blunt force trauma of the head. In her summary and interpretation, Dr. Radisch wrote, "A blood ethanol (alcohol) concentration . . . obtained at the time of the autopsy [was] .07%. Diazepam [Valium] was present in the concentration of 0.15 mg/L. No opiates or organic bases were detected in the same blood specimen. In my opinion, the cause of death in this case was due to severe concussive injury of the brain caused by multiple blunt force impacts of the head. Blood loss from the deep lacerations may have also played a role in her death. The number, severity, location and orientation of these injuries are inconsistent with a fall down stairs; instead they are indicative of multiple impacts received as a result of beating."[8]

Thus, gashes in the back of Kathleen's scalp—described as at least seven in number—were considered to have contributed to her death, either because of resultant brain injury or blood loss, or both. But, as I would bring up later, were they gashes caused by the application of an external force? Or could they have occurred as a result of an accidental fall during which she hit her head on the steps and on the side of the door molding? And more than once. A fall, not from the top of the stairs, plunging downward and forward, but from the lowest steps, as she began to climb them and—in sequence—lost her balance, fell backward, struck her head, bled heavily from her scalp, got up, slipped in her own pool of blood, fell again, and struck her head at least one more time. She then exsanguinated or "bled out." Under the latter scenario, each gash need not be associated with a distinct contact with a step; rather, such individual contacts could have given rise to multiple gashes, more like *splits*, as the scalp became compressed against the bony skull beneath it. These were questions and issues that would be debated before, during, and after the trial.

Eventually, considerable attention would focus on yet another of Dr. Radisch's diagnoses: "Early acute ischemic neuronal necrosis." Loosely interpreted, it means death of brain cells from lack of oxygen. California forensic pathologist Dr. John Cooper Jr. intimated that such a finding leads one to conclude that the decedent did not die immediately, that she remained alive perhaps for an hour or two after a beating. He explained that that kind of brain cell degeneration could occur only over some time; that is, while the heart continued to beat, feeding a cascade of cell breakdown. "You just don't see that kind of lack of oxygen to these neurons unless there's been a period of survival," he said. "The neuronal changes take several hours of blood flow and circulation to develop. They involve biochemical processes that shut down at death."[9]

Although only preliminary results of the autopsy had been made available at the time, prosecutor Jim Hardin moved swiftly. He announced that evidence at the crime scene prompted him to believe that "she [Kathleen] was beaten . . . and had struggled with Mike Peterson to a degree and that he had to bludgeon her on multiple occasions . . . [and] after that she basically bled to death."[10]

A week later, Michael was charged with her murder, and he, in turn, quickly hired prominent defense attorney David Rudolf. He and the defense team vehemently denied the charge and argued that even if Kathleen had been murdered, his client didn't do it. They pointed out that the Peterson home was rarely locked and that six months before an unknown intruder had entered it after midnight, getting away with a computer and a cellular phone. There had also been previous such incidents, and on six occasions someone (or some individuals) had broken into the cars in the driveway. Their inference was that if someone had struck Kathleen, it was far more likely to have been an intruder than Michael.

The accused novelist and his family issued statements that reflected their feelings. "I knew for a fact that there is no way in this world my father would ever have hurt Kathleen," said his son Todd.[11] Michael himself claimed his innocence and stressed the apparent depth of his loss: "Kathleen was my life. I've whispered her name in my heart a thousand times. She is there but I can't stop crying."[12] Even Kathleen's biological daughter, Caitlin, supported Michael after the grand jury decided to indict him and take the case to trial. "My mother and Mike had an absolutely loving relationship and there is no way that either would ever wish any sort of harm on the other one," she was quoted as saying.[13]

It was on December 20 that a grand jury decided Michael should be charged with murder and, on that same day, he was denied bond and jailed. Within a few weeks, two key developments emerged, both reinforcing the convictions of the prosecutors: (1) news of the Elizabeth Ratliff death in Germany surfaced, and (2) the police, in examining Michael's computer, found evidence of his apparent homosexual tendencies: male pornographic photos and e-mail exchanges with a male prostitute. Prosecutors thus assumed that Michael was bisexual. Several family members stated they knew about his sexual proclivities all along. But Caitlin did an about-face and publicly accused her stepfather of the murder. She insinuated that the subject of his unorthodox sexual appetite must have come up the night of her mother's death, that a violent argument ensued, and that he subsequently killed her.[14]

Assistant prosecutor Freda Black declared that the motive for the crime had suddenly become clear. "She would have been infuriated by learning that her husband, who she truly loved, was bisexual and having an extramarital relationship—not with another woman but with a man—which would have been humiliating and embarrassing to her. We believe that once she learned this information that an argument ensued and a homicide occurred."[15]

Within a day of Kathleen's death and extending into February, the case became a battle between the prosecution with its search warrants and the defense with its legal motions. One warrant, executed the day after the death, December 10, resulted in the Petersons' home being searched on December 11 and 12. In these and subsequent searches, the police examined the Peterson vehicles and seized personal belongings, including a paperweight, condoms, and other items, as well as records of all outgoing house and cell phone calls made in November and December; and—from the staircase area—moldings, a piece of wood, hair, and cedar samples from several steps. A warrant dated January 11 indicated that the authorities took samples of Michael's head and pubic hair, blood, and saliva. The applications for both searches indicated that there was a large amount of blood at the scene, some of which was on the front steps and door, and on Michael.

Meanwhile, the defense contended that the police used false and misleading affidavits to obtain the search warrants. In one of several court motions, attorneys Rudolf and Maher claimed that such tactics were unconstitutional and therefore any information gleaned from the searches should be thrown out. Moreover, the motion suggested that the police had an ulterior motive: payback for the columns that Michael had written which severely criticized them. Four other issues were addressed in the same motion:

- That Michael was covered with blood because he lovingly cradled his wife after the accident as she lay bleeding on the floor; that he was allowed to place towels under her head and held her body close, even after the police arrived.
- That blood near the front door could be explained by the coming and going of emergency and police personnel who had come in contact with the body.
- That police exceeded the scope of any warrants when they seized unidentified paperwork from the home.
- That the warrant had not established "probable cause" for police to examine Michael's vehicles.[16] ("Probable cause" is the presence of evidence that justifies a search and seizure or an arrest on the part of the police or a private citizen.)

In a separate motion, the defense accused the prosecution of treating its client differently from others by having convened a special grand jury that was "premature and totally unnecessary." Attorney Rudolf stated that it was extremely unusual for District Attorney Hardin to convene the grand jury before the autopsy report (on Kathleen) was completed. Even seasoned court officials agreed that the special session was probably unprecedented in Durham.[17] But Michael's lawyers prevented him from saying whether or not he thought he was being unfairly targeted by law enforcement officials. A longtime friend, however, didn't hesitate. Attorney and former US congressman Nick Galifianakis said, "I think one of the mysteries for him [Michael Peterson] and his neighbors is why was there some presumption of guilt at the very outset of this tragic accident? What were the real reasons for generating a special grand jury? Whatever happened to the presumption of innocence?"[18]

Still another defense motion covered a broad range of topics. In it, the assertion was made that the integrity of the death scene had not been maintained; that, in fact, it was "contaminated" when police officers permitted at least three people to roam around it. Specifically, it cited two people who were allowed to enter the house and approach the body. Moreover, it noted that another person, a Duke University medical intern, saw several individuals walk through the blood-filled hallway near the body. "The extent to which the scene was improperly maintained, and therefore contaminated, will obviously affect the reliability of any opinions reached by the state's investigators," the defense motion read. It continued: "The substantial defects in how the Durham Police handled the . . . scene clearly tends to negate any alleged 'proof' of Mr. Peterson's guilt . . . and to impeach the quality of the investigation conducted."[19]

The defense motion also covered the reactions of people interviewed by the police about possible tension or violent conduct between the Petersons; the responses of several who witnessed Michael's behavior on the night his wife died; and some comments made by his former wife, Patricia. The motion read that everyone who had been interviewed had provided evidence establishing that there was no motive for Michael to harm his wife and that there was no known history of fights or violence between them. It then went on to quote those who observed Michael at the death scene. According to officers who had recorded the observations: "[that Peterson] was extremely upset, that he had been shaking and sobbing, that his breath was rapid and shallow, and that he appeared to be in shock and could not even speak in whole, coherent sentences." The motion said, "All of these actions were entirely consistent with Mr. Peterson having found Kathleen's body at the foot of the stairs, and inconsistent with his having done anything to harm her."

Labeling the above interviews as exculpatory (or tending to clear him), the motion finally mentioned another such interview—this one with Patricia, Michael's previous wife. She told officers, according to the motion, that "Mike Peterson had never been violent towards her, that she never knew him to be violent towards anyone else, that he was not physically or psychologically abusive, and that he was not capable of having done harm to Kathleen, regardless of his state of mind." She further told the police that "Michael Peterson loved Kathleen, cherished his children, and had no motive for killing Kathleen," the motion said. "She described Mike and Kathleen as intertwined; they loved each other and needed each other, and were soul mates."[20]

Scott Peterson.

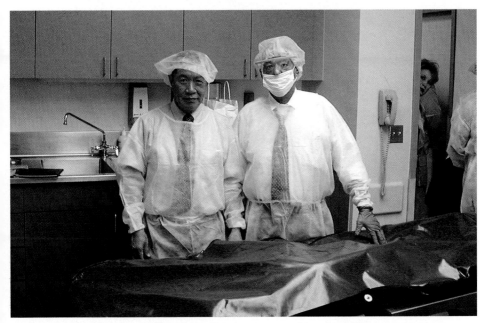

Dr. Lee and Dr. Cyril Wecht at the reautopsy of Laci and Conner Peterson.

All photos are the property of Dr. Lee.

Scott Peterson's boat. Attorney Mark Geragos in background.

The shore area where Laci Peterson's remains were found.

Dr. Lee examining the kitchen window screen of the Smart home at the point of entry.

Missing person poster of Elizabeth Smart.

A close-up view of the kitchen window at the Smart home showing a maximum opening of approximately eleven inches.

A chemically enhanced blood pattern from the Michael Peterson case showing a footprint. Note the additional blood drop near the heel area.

A variety of blood spatters in the landing area of the staircase at Michael and Kathleen Peterson's home.

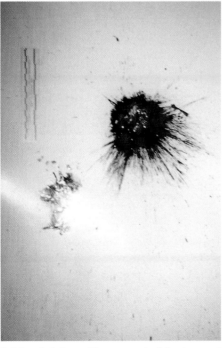

A bloodstain pattern created by impact force in the Michael Peterson case.

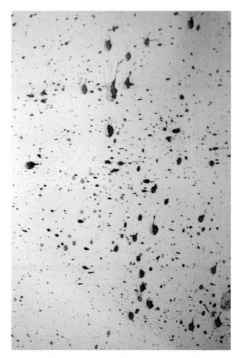

A bloodstain pattern created by coughing in the Michael Peterson case.

Dr. Lee conducting shell casing ejection pattern analysis in the Duntz case.

A spent shell casing.

Richard Duntz
being escorted to court.

A view of the family room at the Myeres' home showing the red-stained sofa, broken objects, and a baseball bat.

Bloodstains on the living-room wall and carpet at the Meyers crime scene.

Portrait of Janet Myers.

Michael spent the first third of this period in jail—from his indictment on December 20 to January 14. Simultaneous with the indictment was a disclosure that the prosecution would not seek the death penalty. After the three-week incarceration, he was released under an $850,000 secured bond. His collateral was his Cedar Street home, with a tax value of $1.2 million.

While in jail, he penned several articles titled *Jail Journals* in which he wrote about fellow inmates. After his release, and while awaiting trial, he continued to write as he launched into a new book about politics and corruption in a small southern town.[21]

On February 8, David Rudolf told the press that he had asked me to examine the Peterson staircase. "I don't think it's fair to say he'll be looking for anything in particular," Rudolf said. "He'll just be trying to get a sense of what, if anything, can be determined from the evidence that is there. This has always been a case where the forensic evidence is critical. We want the best qualified experts we can find to look for the stuff."[22]

I have known David for many years, having worked on several cases with him in the past and lectured at his bar association meetings. He can be extremely persuasive, and, after a long phone conversation, I agreed to take a look at the case—but without making any promises. I suggested that he contact some forensic pathologists to review the autopsy results. I also mentioned that there were two important issues to consider: (1) the manner and mechanism of the scalp wounds, and (2) the cause and mechanism of the large amount of blood spatter on the walls of the landing area.

Interrupting our attendance at a conference of the American Academy of Forensic Science, my able assistant, Tim Palmbach, and I flew to North Carolina and went to the death scene on Cedar Street to initiate our scientific investigation. We found the scene surprisingly well preserved. The staircase area had been sealed with plywood. Defense investigator Ron Guerette—one of the best in the business—assisted us in reestablishing the location of each piece of physical evidence. We noticed that a large amount of luminol had been sprayed on the walls, thereby causing some alterations and dissolving of bloodstains. In addition, we found numerous hairs and tissuelike material adherent to a metal chairlift, the molding of the lower door, the walls, and the staircase itself. This evidence had obviously not been collected. (The results of our scene investigation will be disclosed later.)

In October 2002 District Attorney Hardin informed the local media that he wanted to have the body of Elizabeth Ratliff exhumed for the purpose of a second autopsy. Nine days later, Michael was sued by his wife's estate. The lawsuit, filed by Kathleen's daughter, Caitlin Atwater, alleged that Michael Peterson was responsible for her mother's death.

Elizabeth's body was exhumed in Texas and transported to North Carolina. The second autopsy—by the same Dr. Deborah Radisch who performed Kathleen's autopsy—took place on April 28, 2003. She concluded that Elizabeth was the victim of a homicide, not a stroke as German and US military authorities had determined in 1985.

While on the subject of Elizabeth Ratliff's death, we should make several other relevant points:

- David Rudolf traveled to Germany to view the death scene and to talk with Patricia, Michael's first wife. She insisted that there had been no sexual relationship between Michael and Elizabeth; that there was very little blood at the scene; and that although Michael had been paid a small amount of insurance money after he'd assumed custody of the Ratliff girls, he used it to care for them.
- After the results of the second autopsy became known, German prosecutors tentatively reopened their investigation into the eighteen-year-old death.
- Rudolf attempted to exclude the "German case" from the trial *before* it was to begin during the summer of 2003. He said, "I think that the evidence about the death in Germany, if it comes in, will have a substantial impact, even subconsciously, on how the jurors evaluate the evidence in this case. Even though there's not a shred of evidence that Michael had anything to do with Elizabeth Ratliff's death."[23]
- A private hearing was held in which Judge Hudson was expected to rule on this matter, and, surprisingly, he refused to issue the ruling before the trial was to start. Michael was beside himself, questioning the decision. "It was just completely choreographed," he said. "This is Durham, it's unique, it's particular, it's dirty, it's corrupt, it's small. I don't think anybody knows this town better than I do," he was purportedly quoted as saying.[24]
- The night before the trial, nerves were taut, but Michael did his best to remain calm. "This case is no more and no longer about Kathleen," he stated. "The DA has to win, that's it. He doesn't care

how. And by the same token, my lawyers, they want to win. Truth is lost in all of this now. This has become a show."[25]

Months before, as each side formed its case, it became clear that the prosecution's case was a circumstantial one, with physical evidence playing only a supportive role. The wounds that Kathleen incurred and the copious amount of blood at the scene would, of course, be highlighted. So would Peterson's financial situation, which some believed was shaky at best, although the prosecution's views prior to the trial fell short of targeting money as a possible motive—that was for the time being, at least. Looming larger as a motive was the matter of Michael's sexual orientation.

Hardin, observers expected, would also play the Ratliff card during the trial—that is, that the deaths of Kathleen in the United States and Elizabeth in Germany were similar in nature; too similar, in fact, to be coincidental.

The defense would counter that the current case was weak and lacked a murder weapon, any eyewitnesses, or a compelling motive. It would call on forensic experts to dispute the prosecution's contention that its client wielded a blunt object to strike his wife repeatedly. More specifically, an analysis of the blood spatter in and about the staircase would be vital in disproving guilt beyond a reasonable doubt. Other key components of its case would be the relationship with his wife of less than five years, the anguish in his voice during the 911 call he made to summon help, and the claim that police and emergency officials allowed the death scene to become contaminated.

FORENSIC INVESTIGATION

From my Connecticut base, I made five trips to Durham in early 2002 to assist the defense in the forensic investigation. Most of my time there was spent at the death scene—on February 14 and May 17, 2002—but I also visited with the forensic evidence unit of the Durham Police Department and with the State Bureau of Investigation (SBI) forensic laboratory. Tim Palmbach and I poured over hundreds of photographs, documents, diagrams, and laboratory reports. In addition, we examined every piece of physical evidence. The following represents both our findings and my interpretation of them. Rather than differentiate between the information I gained during direct investigations of the Peterson home and what I observed in scene photographs, I have decided to present the following as a compilation of all the above. It would serve as the foundation of my trial testimony more than a year later.

It is important to make several general statements concerning the Peterson staircase. First, it is an enclosed, narrow structure, located at the middle of the house. It has eighteen steps in all. Throughout the investigation and subsequently during the trial, the top step was designated step #1, while the lowest was step #18. For purposes of orientation: when looking down the stairs, the wall straight ahead—at the bottom—is the *north* wall; the one to the right is the *east* wall; and the one to the left is the *west* wall. The latter wall contains the lower entrance to the staircase and is surrounded by wide multicornered molding. Near the bottom of the stairs, a large, heavy metal chairlift is attached to the east wall; the device had been used by the previous homeowners. This lift might have played some role in the victim's scalp injuries.

Second, there was a large amount of blood spatter and many bloodstains at the scene—in fact, more than ten thousand individual stains. Most of the blood was concentrated near the foot of the stairs: two hundred spots on step #18; five hundred spots on step #17; eleven hundred spots on step #16; and forty spots on step #15. The north wall itself had four thousand individual spots. Moreover, the east wall and chairlift had approximately three thousand; the west wall and door molding, about one thousand.

A third general statement pertains to my interpretation of the overall scene—it must be regarded as having some limitations. For example, since I didn't know what the scene looked like originally, I had to depend on photographs taken at the time. Also, the scene had been obviously altered by Michael Peterson, family members, and EMT personnel before the police arrived. Even *after* detectives arrived, the scene was not properly preserved. Alterations continued when family members, visitors, the medical examiner, and the police themselves milled around, as evidenced by eyewitnesses and by multiple shoeprints found there.

Fourth, the scene was a "dynamic" one; that is, great activity had taken place. This led to additional blood smears on the staircase. It also meant that little could be deduced about where Michael and his wife were when certain blood patterns were made, and practically nothing could be determined about the sequence of events in that confined space. From careful inspection of the bloodstain patterns, all one can say is that Kathleen was moving at one point or not moving at another point; that she was upright at a certain time,

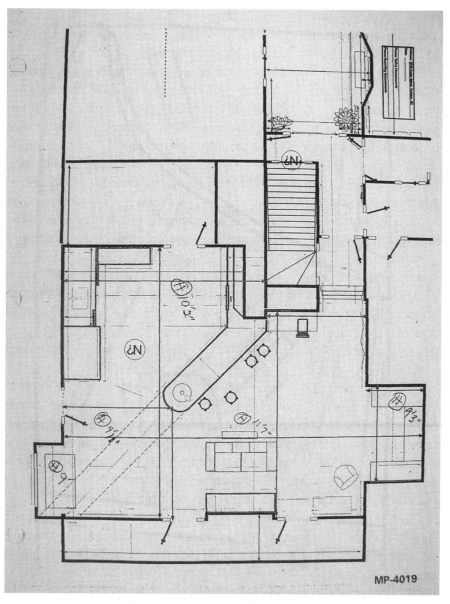

Scene sketch showing staircase and kitchen area.

sitting at another time, or lying down at still another. But, again, the sequence could not be definitely established. The same can be said of Michael's actions as he rendered first aid to his wife.

Fifth and finally, some of the bloodstained areas contained complex patterns in which there were drops, spatters, swipes, smears, and castoffs. Most of the spatter was of the medium-velocity type, a good portion of which was clearly the result of Kathleen's breathing out or coughing up blood. (I had observed blood in photos of her mouth.) Cast-off spatter could also have occurred by blood being flicked off fingers or hair, or by the shaking of the head. Furthermore, some areas had multiple deposits, that is, spatter on spatter, or spatter on smear.

Having just introduced a variety of technical terms, I shall offer a brief overview of bloodstain pattern analysis as applied to the reconstruction of *possible* crime scenes. Note the word "possible." A scene possessing blood spatters could, of course, be one in which a crime was committed, but it could also be one in which the characteristics of the blood might suggest that no crime had taken place at all. That is why, in this Peterson case, we have preferred to identify the stairwell area as a "death scene."

*   *   *

Bloodstain pattern analysis has been defined in several ways, but basically it is the evaluation of the static aftermath of bloodshed in attempting to determine the actions that created the bloodstains. The patterns may thus provide a window to the past. The totality of the findings—in conjunction with an assessment of the size, shape, and distribution patterns of the stains—can be used to reconstruct the event(s) that resulted in the bloodshed.

In some cases, bloodstain pattern analysis is even more useful than any serological or DNA information obtained from the blood. Among the most valuable components of a reconstruction are the following:

- direction of travel of the blood droplets
- distance of blood source to target surface
- angle of impact of blood droplets
- amount of blood deposits
- determination of blood trails, their direction, and the relative speed of motion

Overall view showing bloodstains in staircase area.

- nature of force creating the bloodshed
- nature of the object or weapon used (if any) to cause the bloodshed
- relative location of persons/objects near bloodshed
- sequencing of multiple events associated with the bloodshed
- interpretation of contact or transfer patterns
- estimation of elapsed time and volume of bloodshed

Forensic investigators must also determine the *type* of bloodstain patterns found at death scenes, such as low-velocity blood patterns, medium-velocity blood patterns, high-velocity blood patterns, and contact and transfer bloodstain patterns. However, we are only going to address the blood patterns relevant to this case.

Low-Velocity Blood Patterns

Without elaborating on "terminal velocities," "trigonometric relationships," "the physical and biochemical properties of blood," or other technical matters, suffice it to say that patterns produced by free-falling blood drops are influenced by the distance fallen, the target surface texture, the angle at which the drops strike the surface, the impact direction, and other factors. The drops are generally circular in shape, but they may be elliptical or oval; their edges may be smooth or rough; they may or may not have "tails"; and their diameter may vary in size—depending on the factors mentioned above.

Hard, nonporous surfaces will produce circular stain patterns that have smooth edges, whereas softer, porous surfaces will produce stains that are scalloped or have rough edges. As the angle of impact is made smaller or more acute, the bloodstain pattern will become more elongated. If a stain has a tail, it usually points in the direction of travel of the blood drop—in other words, in the same direction that a bleeding person is walking or running. An experienced investigator can even get a sense of the origin of a blood drop. This bears on the *directionality* of the bloodstain pattern, which, in turn, takes into account the direction of travel and the angle of impact.

Medium-Velocity Blood Patterns

Bloodstains that have been produced with more force than gravity and less than high-velocity force are called medium-velocity bloodstains. The force causes the blood drops to break into smaller-sized spatters of blood. *Medium-velocity spatter* has diameters of approximately 2 to 4 mm. The force associated with this type of impact spatter is greater than 25 feet/second and less than 100 feet/second. One type of medium-velocity spatter, distinct from others, occurs sometimes when blood from a bloody mouth or nose is sneezed out, or coughed up, or spit out. These drops usually contain a few air bubbles that burst upon impacting a surface, leaving deposits with "ghost" centers. Many of these blood patterns were present in this Peterson case.

Other patterns in this category are impact blood spatters, cast-off patterns, and projected patterns. Projected blood patterns are commonly associated with major injuries having open wounds and large amounts of blood projected on vertical surfaces—as in arterial spurts, for example. These patterns have sharp spinelike edges and frequently show movement or motion.

When an object or body part is used to inflict injury or makes contact with a sufficient amount of liquid blood, blood will transfer to the object or body part. The arc motion of the bloody object will produce a *cast-off pat-*

tern. The linear nature of the pattern, including repetitive changes in the individual blood drops, is distinctive to the trained eye. The shape changes are the result of differing impact angles throughout the arc motion. Any bloody object or body part that creates a flinging action, including moving hands, fingers, arms, legs, and hair, can produce cast-off patterns at a death scene. The same is true of a bloody scalp as the head moves abruptly in a snapping motion.

An *impact pattern* usually occurs when a force is applied or impacted upon a blood source, as in the case of a beating. But it is equally possible to see similar impact spatter when a person or an object falls onto a bloody surface.

Medium-velocity blood spatter is the most common type of bloodstain found at a crime scene. It could be produced by two types of energy source: (1) internal, such as in coughing, sneezing, and breathing by an injured person—or in the case of a person's major blood vessel being severed (e.g., arterial spray type pattern); and (2) external, such as cast-off spatter, as described above.

Contact and Transfer Bloodstain Patterns

This category of bloodstain patterns is replete with an array of additional terms that criminalists use to describe blood patterns: contact-transfer patterns, dispersion effects, blood smears, wipe and swipe patterns, secondary deposit stains, and shadow patterns. Some are self-explanatory; a few require comment. I noticed all at the Peterson death scene.

Contact-transfer patterns occur after blood adheres to an object or body part through direct contact and then gets transferred to a new location, either near or far. Such a pattern is in the shape of the object. For example, a bloody knife blade that is placed on a bedsheet will leave a direct contact pattern shaped like the knife blade. If patterns are created by the folding of receiving surfaces, then two similar bloody imprints may appear as a result of either contact with the same object or with a bloody image. Hence one sees a "butterfly" or mirror image of the original stain.

A second type of transfer pattern is produced by the dynamic motion of an object or surface having liquid blood on it. We speak of "wipe" and "swipe." A wipe pattern occurs when an object/surface contacts another surface having liquid blood on it, and the contact is made in a smear-type motion. An experienced bloodstain pattern analyst can tell the direction of wipe and the type of motion. A swipe pattern occurs when a bloody object/surface makes moving contact with a clean surface. Such motion leaves a bloody smear on the receiving surface. The most common example of this is a hair swipe pattern—the result of someone's bloody hair making moving contact with a surface.

The *presence* of blood spatter patterns often tells a tale, but the *absence* of bloodstain patterns can often be just as important. Sometimes there may have been an intermediate object between the origin of the blood and the impacted surface. The latter may be a vertical wall and the intermediate object may be a hand or an arm. The wall will then show a blood pattern containing a voided area corresponding roughly to the shape of the intermediate object. The object, in effect, has blocked and intercepted a portion of the traveling blood. Such a voided area is usually called a *shadow pattern*. Again, some of these appeared in the Peterson case. And now, to return to our investigation in Durham.

Description of Overall Scene

If I were to comment on every isolated bloodstain observed, I would, in a sense, be violating the very concept I advanced at the trial—that is, that one must take the *totality* of a crime or death scene into account before drawing any conclusions. This is not to say that certain clusters of stain or concentrations of stain do not yield valuable information. On the contrary—in this case, those on the north wall, on the northernmost door molding, and on step #16 were particularly telling, as we shall soon discover.

I have already pointed out the large amount of spatter I encountered. The majority of heavy spatter was observed on steps #16 to #18 and on the molding and walls above steps #17 and #18. This large amount is significant because it suggests multiple origins—from coughing, a moving head, moving hands, ricocheting, and so on. In other words, there was a great deal of activity at that scene. It was, in short, a dynamic scene. It was one in which Kathleen was probably dazed and writhing around. Many areas showed tissues and head hair adhering to them. As I have mentioned, there was spatter upon spatter, spatter upon smears, and, in addition, evidence that some spatter had dried and then received other spatter on top of it. This indicates that time had elapsed between the deposits of each layer of spatter. It is impossible to pinpoint exact times, but, taking into account the coagulation time of blood and other conditions at the scene, at least twenty to forty minutes would be an appropriate estimate. By contrast, if we were to set the timing in seconds, we could not have differentiated the patterns on top of each other. All things considered, my judgment is that the patterns were inconsistent with ones I have encountered at typical protracted beating scenes.

The spatter appeared to have multiple sources and multiple points of origin, with the majority projected from a low-to-high direction. Determining the *exact* points of origin in such a very small, confined space would be of little value. I can categorically state, however, that they came from within that space.

The metal chairlift had hair and approximately one thousand droplet stains on it. This means Kathleen's head might have struck it more than once. There were no overhand cast-off type blood patterns on the ceiling or high on the walls. This is an extremely important fact, for if there had been a beating that involved overhand action, one would have definitely seen cast-off type blood spatter on the ceiling. And there was none. Even a half swing or a side swing with a weapon such as a lengthy fireplace poker would have produced cast-off patterns on the walls and/or left some sign of damage there. Thus, the lack of such evidence is a clear indication that an overhand beating had not taken place.

It cannot be overemphasized that many of the blood drops were of the "ghost-center" variety, demonstrating that Kathleen must have been coughing up, spitting out, or expiring some quantities of blood. At the trial, prosecutors suggested that there was no blood in her mouth. In this regard, not only had I observed such blood when examining several close-up photographs, but also autopsy findings revealed evidence of blood in her lungs.

The north wall, the molding around the lower entrance, and the lower steps were of critical interest. First, the north wall at the base of the staircase:

- It had a conglomeration of spatter types. Most were of medium velocity caused by coughing, sneezing, movement, hair swipe, impact, and so on.
- The spatter came at the wall from multiple directions.
- Some were smears. Some had ghost centers.

- Some created downward flow patterns.
- There was considerable evidence of bloodstain upon bloodstain.
- There were eight to ten void or shadow patterns that most likely represented a hand or an arm intercepting blood being projected onto the wall. It could have been Kathleen's own hand or arm.

Next, the molding:

Various types of bloodstain were seen on the molding that surrounded the lower staircase entrance. These included dripping patterns and smear patterns—with adherent hairs and tissues. But of most significance were the contact-transfer patterns there. Kathleen was 62 inches tall. The uppermost tissue pattern was at a 61.5-inch-high level. Another bloodstained area was at a 43-inch level. A single bloody palm print was also present. The most likely interpretation is that she struck her head on the molding while in a upright position, then—likely disoriented—slid down and struck it again at the next level, and finally assumed a sitting position for a time. Her arriving at this latter position seems logical by virtue of the saturation of blood at her waist area. Following that, she might have risen, slipped on her own blood, and struck her head on one or more steps of the staircase and on the metal chairlift. This is the most logical explanation as far as sequence is concerned.

With regard to the steps, they, too, contained a variety of bloodstain patterns, including contact, dripping, cast-off, swipes, and diluted. The diluted stains were consistent with Kathleen's having involuntarily urinated at some point in the ordeal or with Michael's having placed a wet towel on the staircase. On the surface and riser of step #16 were two bloodstains that were crusty in nature. This indicates a longer period of contact. Off to the side of that step, on the east wall, was a hair cast-off pattern consistent with her head movement. Steps #14, 15, 17, and 18, along with their risers (the vertical faces between steps), also had contact bloodstains.

Kathleen's Clothing, Movement, and Scalp Photos

Tim and I examined death scene photographs taken by the police. In one, Kathleen's head rested on step #18 and her body was sprawled out into the hallway. There were three blood-soaked towels rolled up under her head. A pair of eyeglasses and several bloodstained paper towels lay on the step above. Some of the blood around her appeared wet while other blood appeared dry. There were bloodstains on the soles of her feet, indicating she had stood in her own blood at one point. Except for footwear, she was fully clothed in a jersey and sweatpants. There was a stationary transfer footprint on one of her pant legs; the print faced away from the body. All this supports my analysis that once her bleeding began, she stood up, and there followed one or more episodes of slipping, falling, and striking her head again. Indeed, she must have been in motion at various times during the incident. If this is reasonable, then it is just as logical to conclude that she had been injured for some time (perhaps twenty to forty minutes?) before she died.

Photographs of her scalp revealed several lacerations, variously described by the defense and the prosecution as either four or seven in number. My personal count is four or five because some of the lesions could have been caused by secondary splitting following the primary traumas.

Michael's Clothing

There was no spatter on the front of his shirt and no cast-off patterns on the back. This fact is inconsistent with a beating having taken place. Some medium-velocity spatter was observed on his khaki shorts. Some appeared diluted, perhaps the result of his having put wet towels under his wife's head and, in the process, contacting a portion of the shorts. There was no indication that he attempted to wash his shorts. Much significance would later be attached to a small amount of spatter found on the inside of his right shorts leg. This could be easily explained away. The shorts are baggy and Michael's legs are relatively thin. The drops could have been deposited while he was crouched down, trying to assist his wife. The spatter could have resulted from her moving, her coughing, or from blood bouncing off her hair as he lifted and even accidentally dropped her limp head.

Scene photographs showed Michael's tennis shoes and socks, a roll of paper towels, and a dark-colored shirt near Kathleen's outstretched left leg. His socks had spatter on their undersides, and his tennis shoes had multiple deposits with directionalities, but nowhere near the amount of blood spatter on the stairway and walls. The shoes should have had more spatter if they had been worn during a beating.

The conclusion to be drawn from the findings on Michael's shorts and tennis shoes is that they were consistent with postincident contact. When he

Close-up view of bloodstain patterns on door molding.

found his wife at the staircase, she was still breathing (as the 911 call recorded). Some of the blood spatter was deposited on his body and clothing. Some diluted bloodstains could have transferred to him when he placed wet towels under her head. Other transfer smears were more likely the result of his cradling her head. The point here is that all the bloodstains on his shoes and clothing had an entirely reasonable and logical explanation, one that was *not* consistent with the prosecution's assertion that they were due to a beating.

Cleanup Claim

The prosecution stated that void areas and dripping patterns on the north wall meant that Michael had attempted to clean off the blood there. My observations are at odds with that contention. It is important to compare photographs of the wall before and after the police's application of luminol. (The chemical luminol is a field test reagent used to detect the presence of blood.) Far more likely is that the dripping was the result of the luminol spraying, and that the void areas represent shadow patterns (as described above), or evidence of contact by a shoulder or other body part. Furthermore, the wall contained wipe and swipe patterns, which were probably produced by contact with her hair, clothing, the towels, or a combination of them. With respect to the towels, it was just as Michael had indicated in his statement to the police: that he had placed them under his wife's head.

Beyond the Staircase

There were secondary transfer patterns in the hallway adjacent to the stairwell, in the sitting room, in the kitchen, on the slate entrance walk to the house, and on the inside doorknob. These were consistent with various persons walking through the areas after Kathleen's body was discovered. No blood was found on used wine glasses in the kitchen's sink basin.

During this period, Tim and I frequently worked through the night with attorney Rudolf and defense investigators, trying to find real evidence that would provide a reason why Michael Peterson had murdered his wife. We found none.

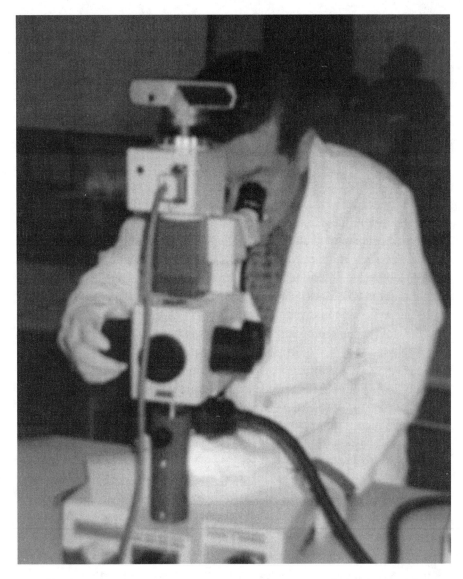

Dr. Lee conducting microscopic examination of physical evidence.

THE TRIAL

Finally, jury selection began on May 5, 2003, and lasted seven weeks. The three-month-long trial, which started on July 1, 2003, can be divided into thirds. The first two thirds were devoted to the prosecution's case against Michael Peterson, while the case for his defense and the rebuttal testimony covered the last third.

Opening Statements

The reverse was true, in terms of time, for opening statements. That is, District Attorney Hardin took thirty minutes to present his points, and defense attorney David Rudolf took three times as long, ninety minutes, to make his opening remarks.

Hardin claimed that Kathleen's death was not the result of an accidental fall, but that she had likely been struck with a fireplace poker, which had mysteriously disappeared. He said he would show that seven lacerations in her scalp could not have resulted from such a fall. He stressed that the case was about things not being as they appeared; it was about appearances and pretenses. For instance, he intended to prove that Kathleen's relationship to the defendant was not the storybook marriage that the defense had portrayed in the media and, moreover, that Michael might have had financial reasons for wanting his wife dead. He also told the jury that there was evidence someone had reformatted the hard drive of Michael's computer right after her death and reinstalled select files. Finally, Hardin indicated experts would be called to prove that the amount and location of blood were more consistent with a beating by a blunt object than with a fall.

Rudolf began his opening statement by playing a digital recording of Michael's frantic 911 call on the morning of his wife's death. The defendant could be heard muttering, sobbing, and breathing heavily. His lawyer said he would leave it to the jurors to decide whether or not his client was faking his emotional reaction.

Rudolf criticized the prosecution's handling of the case—that, from the beginning, they doggedly pursued Michael as a suspect. The attorney charged that (1) Michael was forced to miss his wife's wake while prosecutors executed a search warrant, and (2) they were single-minded in rushing to convene a special—and rare—grand jury just before Christmas 2001. That procedure, Rudolf held, produced the swift indictment that the prosecution sought, which meant Michael was incarcerated over the holidays. Rudolf said that it was *after* the indictment, not *before*, that the state's investigation moved into high gear. In fact, the state did not begin collecting the bulk of the Petersons' financial records until after jury selection began, May 5, 2003. Such records, the defense attorney asserted, would show that the Petersons' net worth was about $2 million and that Michael would have had to divide evenly a $1.8 million insurance policy with Kathleen's daughter, Caitlin Atwater. Hence, it would not all go to him.

Before the trial, the prosecution had constructed a $7,700 replica of the Peterson stairwell. In the opening statement, the defense attorney played a videotape of the tests that SBI Agt. Peter Deaver conducted in the mock stairwell using bloody sponges, a bloody wig, and a fireplace poker. This demonstration would itself be mocked during the trial.

Rudolf accused the Durham police of waging a vendetta against Michael over his newspaper columns that strongly criticized them. And, in what some court observers labeled a surprise tactic, Rudolf raised the issue of Elizabeth Ratliff's death in Germany, going to great lengths to demonstrate how her demise differed from Kathleen's. Hardin did not mention the subject during his opening comments. Presiding Judge Orlando Hudson had not yet ruled on the admissibility of that case as prosecution evidence.

While the state and the defense combatants were making their presentations, Michael's adopted children, Margaret and Martha, sat in the front row of the courtroom. They were joined by Michael's sons from his previous marriage, Todd and Clayton. All four stood steadfastly behind their father, proclaiming his innocence.

Kathleen's mother, two sisters, brother, and daughter, Caitlin, sat on the other side, firmly convinced that Michael was a killer.

Guilt Phase

In direct examinations and cross-examinations of prosecution witnesses, the majority of the time was spent on topics we have arbitrarily grouped into six principal categories:

- possible motive(s), if the death was a homicide and not an accident
- crime scene integrity
- blood spatter and other physical evidence
- the death in Germany eighteen years earlier
- stark differences in interpretation
- autopsy reports and testimony of medical examiners

Some of the topics appeared to be more pivotal than others; some produced conflicting and even confusing testimony; and most were marked by contentious interpretations by prosecution and defense attorneys. The jurors heard from financial experts, a firefighter, police officers, detectives, crime scene technicians, a forensic serologist, a DNA specialist, special agents from the State Bureau of Investigation, a forensic meteorologist, a forensic chemist, a neuropathologist, a US Army pathologist, two medical examiners, and many more. The meteorologist testified about cool weather conditions at the time that Michael, dressed in T-shirt and shorts, allegedly remained near the pool. Prosecutors called fifty witnesses and presented hundreds of photographs, documents, diagrams, other exhibits, the 911 recording, and the replica of the staircase to show how a beating had taken place.

Motive

The opening days focused on the Peterson family's financial condition, as assets, debts, and stock options were introduced into evidence. One side claimed that the family was in considerable debt and that Michael stood to gain financially from his wife's death. The other side ridiculed the claim, providing proof that the Petersons had a combined net worth of $1.4 million. Outside the courtroom, the buzz was that if the jury failed to buy monetary gain as the motive for murder, then the state would postulate another one: the homosexual pornography found on Michael's computer, together with eventual testimony from a male prostitute regarding a sexual liaison that was discussed but never consummated. The idea here is that Kathleen discovered the computer material and confronted her husband about it on the night of her death.

Crime Scene Integrity

It didn't take long for the defense to pounce on prosecution witnesses during cross-examinations, punctuating its premise that the police had committed serious blunders in handling the crime scene. Rudolf and his team aimed to show that police were befuddled from the start, beginning with an initial wrong assessment by the police that they were dealing with an accident in which a woman had gotten up from a wheelchair and fallen down the stairs. Because of this, they failed to keep people from contaminating the scene.

And because of that, all subsequent evidence was flawed, so that any conclusions regarding how Kathleen died would be meaningless. One police officer admitted that yellow police tape and other basic measures to ensure scene integrity were not put into place until thirty minutes after the arrival of the first respondents. Referring to a police log, Rudolf showed that personnel were going in and out of the home frequently, including senior commanders who had no duties requiring them to be inside. He went on in his criticism, bringing out breaches of police protocol. For example, a wine bottle had been tested for the presence of blood, making it impossible to dust for fingerprints, a procedure that should have been performed first. Another involved Hardin's argument that Michael beat his wife to death, removed his sneakers and socks, and left a blood trail of bare footprints throughout the kitchen. According to the police, the trail became visible when the chemical luminol was sprayed, but there was no documentation of it through photographs, nor was mention made of it in an initial forensic report. An extension of the argument was that Michael removed two wineglasses from a kitchen cabinet and poured wine down the sink, trying to create evidence that he and his wife had been drinking heavily. But this could not be corroborated by fingerprint analysis.

One crime scene technician, Dan George, was cross-examined for seven hours over three days. Salient points that came out of his testimony were the following:

- He noticed blood on a cordless telephone, but did not seize it into evidence.
- He did not seize Kathleen Peterson's clear plastic sandals because he did not see any blood on them.
- Michael Peterson's bloody shorts and shirts were put in the same evidence bag.
- Blood-soaked towels and paper towels found around the body were not taken into evidence.
- Few notes were taken, and single-paragraph narratives encapsulated hours worth of crime scene work.
- He found evidence of blood transfer and other scene contamination caused by police.[26]

A most embarrassing gaffe occurred when the prosecution tried to introduce into evidence a small piece of metal found on step #15. Hardin, with great formality, had an evidence technician identify an evidence bag, then the container within it. When the container was opened, nothing was in it. All things considered, the opening weeks of the trial were not favorable ones for the prosecution.

Blood Spatter and Other Physical Evidence

Despite the fact we have not yet arrived at any direct testimony for the defense, sufficient information within this category surfaced during cross-examinations that provided a balanced account of the physical evidence. Later, my own testimony will be outlined. (Of course, I have already given a report of my pretrial forensic investigation of this case.)

The prosecution called on SBI Agt. Peter Deaver as its expert on blood spatter analysis. Recall that it was his "mock stairwell test" that was referenced during the defense's opening statement. Although I believe Agent Deaver tried his best, I must part company with him on many of his conclusions, and especially on the scientific value of the "experiments" he conducted. The following were among his conclusions:

- That Kathleen Peterson was assaulted in the stairwell by someone outside the stairwell wielding a blunt object. Deaver cited a drop of blood on a wall nine feet above the floor outside the stairwell to support that finding. He concluded that this was consistent with a cast-off pattern.
- That the victim was struck at least three times and that her head may have struck the stairs when she fell more than once.
- Michael Peterson had to be standing, crouching, or sitting near a blood source—either his bleeding wife or a pool of her blood—when a great force was applied to the blood source. He concluded this as a result of the location and size of eight tiny drops of blood found inside Peterson's shorts, on the right rear leg. He testified that when a small amount of force is applied, large drops, or spatter, are created. A large amount of force breaks blood up into small specks, he explained.
- The blood smears found on the stairs are evidence that someone smeared blood in a failed effort to clean it up.
- Marks in blood were present on two of the steps. He concluded that the patterns appeared to have been made by something like a fireplace poker.[27]

But in cross-examination, attorney Rudolf tried to convince jurors that the blood spatter analyst made telling mistakes, misinterpreted many of his findings, and went way beyond the bounds of scientific analysis. Rudolf explained that anyone wielding something as long as a fireplace poker, and standing where Deaver suggested Michael had stood, would have hit the overhead molding on the doorframe leading into the stairwell, or the surrounding wall. But there was no visible damage or other evidence of that. The attorney noted that Michael is five feet nine inches tall and that the doorframe is about a foot higher. As to the few one-drop, so-called cast-off stains, Rudolf stated that they could have been made when a distraught husband had to be forcibly separated from the body of his dead wife, or when an EMT tried to administer first aid.

The videotaped tests that Deaver had conducted were shown to the jury. The agent said he had wanted to see what sorts of bloodstains would arise under differing scenarios. He dropped a blood-soaked Styrofoam head from twelve feet onto a poster board, smashed a Styrofoam head wearing a blood-soaked wig against steps in the replica of the stairwell, and stomped his foot in a pool of blood from standing and sitting positions. Rudolf scoffed at the whole idea, charging that the tests had no controls, no standards, and were not scientifically valid. He also pointed out that after Deaver had hit, beaten, smashed, and stomped on the blood-soaked wig and Styrofoam head at least thirty-eight times, the amount of blood spatter and the condition of the spatter were still not consistent with that found on the staircase.

Deaver maintained his calculations proved, among other things, that three separate blood patterns which he measured came from three distinct "points in space" above the steps and away from the walls. But Rudolf got him to admit that two nationally renowned bloodstain experts retained by the prosecution also disagreed with his conclusions.

Of Deaver's assertion that someone smeared blood in a failed attempt to clean it up, the defense attorney retorted that police photos taken on the same day revealed small differences in the bloodstains on the staircase—and he suggested that, indeed, someone may have tried to clean it up. He followed with: "Well, if it was cleaned up, it was cleaned up by police and not by Michael Peterson. That's the kind of thing that creates questions in the minds of the jurors."[28]

The German Case

Ending months of speculation, Judge Hudson finally ruled—two months into the trial—that the 1985 death of Elizabeth Ratliff in Germany could be introduced into evidence by the prosecution. This was a major blow to the defense. The German case dominated the trial over a ten-day period. Michael's lawyers supported the decision of German law enforcement and medical authorities that stated Ratliff had suffered a brain hemorrhage, but Hardin said it was the result of a beating and indicated that Michael was the last person to see his neighbor alive. The district attorney further implied that even if the defendant hadn't caused the death, he at least had knowledge of staircase falls. Some of Michael's supporters lambasted the prosecution for its oblique reference to him as a "serial staircase killer."

Several friends and relatives of Ratliff testified for the prosecution, all giving similar opinions that they had been suspicious of the final disposition of her case. Nonetheless, two items that appeared to add credence to the diagnosis of a cerebral hemorrhage were the established fact that Ratliff had a bleeding disorder not unlike hemophilia and that she reportedly complained of severe headaches in the days before her death. On the other hand, recent surgery prevented a German woman from attending the trial, but she provided a written statement indicating that she saw Michael running away from the Ratliff home on the night in question. The defense said that he was running because it was a chilly, late November evening.

Autopsy Reports and Testimony of Medical Examiners

Dr. Kenneth Snell, the medical examiner who initially concluded that Kathleen had died from an accidental fall, testified that he changed his opinion after getting a close-up look at her wounds at the morgue. He then called it a homicide from a beating. This was a second major blow to the defense. He stated that in his first examination at the death scene her hair was so matted with blood, he was unable to assess the real extent of the scalp injuries.

As noted earlier, Elizabeth Ratliff's body had been exhumed in April 2003. The same pathologist who had performed Kathleen's autopsy—Dr. Deborah Radisch—then performed the second autopsy on the exhumed body. Her announced intracranial findings, together with the belief that Ratliff's external head wounds were too numerous and deep to be explained by a fall, led her to judge the fatality a homicide. Attorney Rudolf declared the judgment to be in variance with the US Army pathologist who had conducted the original autopsy and with the prestigious Armed Forces Pathology Institute.

The next-to-last witness called by the prosecution—the forty-ninth—was Dr. Thomas Bouldin, a professor of pathology at the University of North Carolina. He testified that Kathleen probably lay bleeding from her head wounds for "several hours" before she died.[29] This opinion shored up the prosecution's contention that Michael had spent a substantial amount of time trying to clean up and to create a staged death scene—one that would be compatible with an accidental fall.

The last witness in the state's case—and the one considered the most damaging to the defense—was Dr. Radisch. She said that, although the cause of Kathleen's death was blunt trauma to the head, a broken cartilage in her neck suggested that someone tried to strangle her. In her examination of the body, Dr. Radisch informed jurors that the decedent:

- sustained seven distinct lacerations to the back of the head from separate impacts;
- may have fought off an assailant, based on apparent defensive wounds;
- suffered a fractured thyroid cartilage in her throat, which suggested an attempted strangulation; and
- did not have a fractured skull.[30]

Hardin asked his star witness whether a fireplace poker could have caused these injuries. She answered in the affirmative, after scrutinizing a duplicate of the poker that had been missing from the home. It was four feet long with a hollow shaft. "This item has weight to it," she said, "but it is not solid. This is metal but it is hollow metal and under the right circumstances, may have been sufficient to cause severe lacerations without leaving any skull fracture."[31] In earlier testimony, Kathleen's sister said she had given her sister a fireplace poker, or "blow poke," as a Christmas gift in 1984. It was not present when police examined the home on December 9, 2001, but was seen in family photos taken in 1998. Rudolf used home videos to prove that the missing poker was gone long before Kathleen's death.

Dr. Radisch also revealed that she had reviewed 289 deaths from falls in

North Carolina from 1991 to 2000, and she found that most victims had incurred only one or two lacerations to the scalp, not seven. Rudolf retaliated by asking why, in the more than 250 recorded beating deaths in North Carolina in the past decade, there was not one single incident involving multiple blows to the head that did not include skull fractures or brain injuries.[32] Rudolf also attempted to impeach her testimony, indicating that several nationally renowned forensic pathologists had disagreed with her conclusions.

Stark Differences in Interpretation

The case for the prosecution was riddled with many differences of opinion and interpretation among its own witnesses—the question of moist blood versus dried blood, for example. Some witnesses swore one way, others the opposite way. The prosecution said that dried or coagulated blood would indicate that the defendant waited some time before summoning help.

And during the state's questioning of these witnesses and the defense's cross-examinations, different versions arose with respect to: (1) whether or not Michael had been granted permission to embrace his deceased wife; (2) who was at the Peterson computer, surfing the Internet, only hours after Kathleen's death—was it Michael or was it Todd (Michael's son), who had arrived home from a party at the same time as the paramedic unit and firefighters entered?; (3) the real impact of Michael's repeated criticism of police authorities in his columns; (4) the meaning of specific findings on the north wall: cleanup, screw up, or luminol testing?; (5) weather factors in the early morning hours of December 9: was it too cold for Michael—in T-shirt and shorts—to remain outside for thirty to forty-five minutes, or not?

On the matter of alleged changes in Michael's hard drive, a *prosecution expert* was forced to admit that the computer's antivirus software automatically performed a function that made it only *look* as though someone had tried to sanitize the hard drive.

* * *

In contrast to the array of witnesses for the prosecution, only a handful took the stand for the defense: a total of nine over a nine-day period. The first was neuropathologist Dr. Jan Leestma, who buttressed the defense's theory that the lacerations in Kathleen's scalp, no matter how numerous, could still be accounted for by an accidental fall—two falls, in fact. "[The person] may be dizzy or slip or do something and do it again," he said, remarking that the double-fall scenario was "not a crazy idea." The expert branded the number of lacerations as a misreading of the number of actual impacts, informing the jury that a fall on a flat surface could produce a complex split or tear in the scalp that may look like several separate wounds, but it is really the product of a single impact.[33]

He sharply disagreed with the conclusions of Dr. Radisch as he presented skull diagrams, microscopic slides of brain cells, and data collected from more than 250 beating deaths in North Carolina. "Kathleen Peterson's injuries were the result of a fall, and not the result of a beating," he said. "I frankly am not left with any other conclusion that I am happy with." He specified that his "robust, reliable" conclusion was supported by the facts that Kathleen's injuries were:

- "not consistent with the linear lacerations of a cylindrical weapon (a fireplace poker [had] been suggested as the murder weapon);
- devoid of underlying injury (which would rule out a beating altogether); and
- not consistent with the beating-death data collected by the medical examiner."[34]

Dr. Leestma also criticized the state's analysis of Elizabeth Ratliff, stating that vascular anomalies in her brain were consistent with an aneurysm or spontaneous brain hemorrhage, not a beating.

In cross-examination, Hardin tried to shake the expert's version of the cause of death but was unsuccessful. The district attorney used terms like "coup" and "contra-coup brain injury" as described in Dr. Leestma's own textbook, but he was no match for the pathologist in a game of medical one-upmanship.

Testimony was interrupted when the jurors were invited to visit the Peterson home. During their hour there, they concentrated on exploring the stairwell, the kitchen, the sitting room where Michael was detained after police arrived, and the fireplace area where prosecutors had theorized Michael selected a fireplace poker as a murder weapon.

My two-day testimony for the defense began on Monday, September 14.

Much of what I said in the courtroom dealt with the scientific principles of forensic examinations, with bloodstain patterns, and with the danger of over-interpretation.

I also stressed that the death scene showed signs of alteration and that there was obvious evidence of much activity prior to scene documentation. These would inevitably lead to changes in some blood patterns; they became secondary altered or modified patterns. All this was a perfect illustration of the need for careful and complete documentation *prior* to alteration (e.g., by luminol, collection of evidence, or moving the body). I also underlined the importance of viewing the *totality* of a death or crime scene, and not simply looking at one isolated blood drop. I knew that it was trite to say, but I felt a reference to "seeing the forest, not just one tree" was especially apt.

I employed some techniques I've used at other trials to drive home several principles in blood spatter analysis and reconstruction: squirting red ink from an eyedropper onto a white poster board from a variety of heights and angles—to demonstrate how many types of bloodstain patterns can be formed and how blood drop diameters change with impact speed; slamming my ink-soaked fist onto another board to demonstrate impact spatter; and flicking the eyedropper at a board to show what real cast-off spatter looks like. When it came to the issue of coughing up blood, I traded red ink for watered down ketchup and food coloring that I put in my mouth and then expelled onto a board. As I said before, I feel certain that Kathleen was writhing in agony before she died. Some of the diluted bloodstains were not the result of Michael's attempt to clean up, but were the result of her urinating, sweating, and coughing up blood that coated the lower portion of the stairwell wall. I reiterated several times that the blood evidence as a whole was inconsistent with a death by beating.

I rebutted the claims of Agent Deaver and the demonstrations he had performed as shown in the videotape. I reminded the jury that the agent had used the word "experiments," but my feeling is that they were more like planned "tests" or one-sided demonstrations. They were, in fact, not experiments at all, for they depicted only one aspect of activity without taking into account all other variables. For example, Deaver hadn't considered coughing up blood as an alternative. In addition, no control experiments were conducted, nor had he considered the voided areas on the north wall as shadows. And props like a mannequin's head, a wig, and a sponge soaked with blood were far-fetched. Even more so was using thirty-eight blows in the demonstration! If I were pressed to pick one word to characterize his tests, it would be "misleading." In short, his tests did not replicate what actually happened, and they did not meet the standard of "scientific experiments."

I emphasized at least four other areas of disagreement with the prosecution's blood spatter expert: (1) He made much of "point of origin." This is of little or no value in this case because the stairwell is such a small and confined space; the origin was obviously within the space of the stairwell. (2) He homed in on one drop of blood on the ceiling and two drops on the wall, saying they represented castoff from a weapon. Not likely. There were far too few to call them a significant pattern indicating arcing blows by a weapon. They could have been produced by the flick of a finger or hand, for that matter. Or possibly Michael himself could have cast off the drops because he had been cradling his wife's head. Deaver also made an assumption that the drop on the ceiling had been created together with the two found on the wall—but where, then, was the blood spatter in between? (3) He said the void areas on the north wall were the result of attempted cleaning. Not so. If a dry towel had been used, it would have left a bloody residue. If a wet towel had been used, it would have left a diluted bloodstain and dripping pattern. (4) He suggested that Michael had tried to clean the front of his shorts. But telltale lines of demarcation were present, and these would have been obliterated in a cleaning or washing; that is, the cleaning would have smoothed out such lines. Furthermore, in consideration of the prosecution's claim that many hours had passed before Michael called 911, he should have done a better overall cleaning job and not left thousands of blood spatters behind.

I believe that I imparted what I intended to impart: that, although nobody can ever exclude everything, the patterns I observed in the Peterson house and the information I had been given by law enforcement and forensic authorities (including the autopsy findings)—all told me that Kathleen's death was more consistent with an accidental fall than with an intentional killing.

The next day, Dr. Faris Bandak, a biomedical research scientist, was called by the defense. "This is not a Hollywood tumbling fall down the steps," he said. "I would venture to say this is a ground-level fall." He plugged Kathleen's height and weight into some physics equations and theorized that she began walking up the stairs when she fell backward, striking her head on a ridged molding on the doorjamb. As she fell to the floor, he continued, her head perhaps grazed the north wall before impacting the edge of a step at least once. She next may have attempted to stand up, but she slipped and fell backward once more, again with potential multiple impacts.[35] His rendition largely dovetailed with that of the defense. The expert's testimony was accompanied by a fifteen-second computer animation of a female figure reeling backward and striking the doorjamb. When queried about whether or not Kathleen's injuries could have been sustained by being beaten in the head with a rodlike object, he answered that the biomedical evidence and the injuries were not consistent with that kind of force.

My associate, Timothy Palmbach, director of the forensic science program at the University of New Haven and former director of scientific services for the Connecticut State Police, told jurors that the investigation of the death scene was a study in errors. He has had extensive crime scene experience and was previously assigned to the Connecticut State Police Major Crime Squad. He made clear that maintaining the integrity of a potential crime scene is second only to the duty of first respondents to save lives. After a victim is declared dead, he said, the "priority area" around the body should be protected, the scene should be thoroughly documented, and family members should not be allowed to rush to the body. Some of the other issues Tim singled out were the following:

- Kathleen Peterson's shoes were not individually packaged, and could have been cross-contaminated.
- Her eyeglasses were not collected as evidence.
- Towels at the scene were not collected.
- Sandals at the scene were not collected.
- More photographs should have been taken of the scene, including close-ups of blood spatter evidence.[36]

The final day for the defense's case provided one of the more dramatic moments in the entire trial. Attorney Rudolf held up a hollow, brass fireplace poker that he said was found resting, undamaged and rusty, in the defendant's garage. Prior to showing it, he teased out this exchange with Det. Art Holland, lead officer in the case:

[Rudolf said,] "Did you ever ask us if we had located the blow poke?"
"No, I didn't," said Holland.

"Did you just assume that it was gone?" said Rudolf.

Holland paused, then replied, "Gone or put up somewhere."

Rudolf unveiled a blow poke from its plastic wrapping. "See that?" he asked Holland.

"Yes, sir," said the investigator.

"That's a blow poke, isn't it?"

Rudolf said that the tool had been located by the defense and did not appear to have been used as a weapon. Then he asked, "Have you ever given any thought to what would happen to an item like this if it were used to beat someone to death?"

"Probably be mangled up," said the investigator.

"See any dents in there? Even like a tiny indentation?" asked Rudolf.

"It doesn't appear to have any dents," said the investigator after thirty seconds of inspection.[37]

Rudolf underscored the fact that the blow poke was rusty and had accumulated dirt, cobwebs, and dead insects.

In a brief rebuttal phase, the state questioned six witnesses: a police detective, another of Kathleen's sisters, the custodian of the police department's property room, the chief medical examiner of North Carolina, and two injury biomechanics experts. One of the experts was found to have lied about his credentials as a university faculty member. None of these witnesses seemed to shed new light on the case. For the defense's part, however, attorney Rudolf managed to launch three last-minute salvos: (1) that the combination of alcohol, Valium, a muscle relaxant, and antihistamines in Kathleen's blood could have made her dizzy enough to fall down the stairs; (2) that the police had not begun DNA testing of the "missing" blow poke— the one allegedly found in the garage; and (3) that such a tool matched one that Kathleen's sister had given to another sibling in 1986.

Closing Arguments

The core of David Rudolf's three-and-a-half-hour closing argument was a list of ten reasons why the jury should have reasonable doubt about his client's guilt. He explained that the list was modeled after David Letterman's

Top Ten list, but that the jurors should feel free to add their own reasons. The list given was:

1. [An imagined] missing murder weapon isn't missing—and [the fireplace poker] wasn't [a murder weapon at all].
2. There is no credible motive—and you just don't decide to kill your wife for no reason.
3. Michael and Kathleen Peterson were happily married with no history of violence—and spousal abuse generally doesn't start with murder.
4. Michael Peterson's grief and shock were sincere—and no one who was there disagreed.
5. Kathleen Peterson's injuries are not consistent with a beating. No skull fractures + no other fractures + no traumatic brain injury = no beating.
6. [The state hired a nationally known expert to support Agent Deaver's claims, but that expert's conclusions were not what the prosecution wanted, so he was not called by the state as a witness]. The bloodstain evidence is not consistent with a beating . . . because:
   a. The lack of castoff on walls and ceilings defies the laws of physics.
   b. The spatter on the wall was not created by impacts to Kathleen's head.
   c. The small amount of blood on the sneakers and socks is inconsistent with a beating that created the amount of spatter on the walls.
   d. The lack of spatter on Michael Peterson's shirt, watch, and glasses is inconsistent with a beating that created the amount of spatter on the walls.
   e. The presence of spatter on the back of the shorts is impossible to explain as [being the] result of a beating.
   f. The dilution theory of the state makes no sense [; that is, that the void area was produced by a cleaning agent].
   g. The shoe print on Kathleen Peterson's pants faces away from her body.
   h. The void area is a "shadow" as explained by Dr. Lee—not [a] cleanup, [but covered by her own body parts].
7. Information and documentation from the scene [are] not reliable: Garbage in—garbage out.

8. The state relied on junk science and ignored the limitations of real forensic science.
9. The state has relied on emotion, guess, and conjecture.
10. The state's investigation suffered from "Tunnel Vision." Indictment first—evidence afterwards.[38]

Rudolf condemned the prosecution's misinterpretation of the physical evidence, the credibility of its expert witnesses, the links it had assigned to both stairway deaths, and the police investigation. He assailed the state's motives, saying that it had "trotted out" the "old standbys" of sex and money, when, in fact, the couple's five-year marriage was in fine shape, both financially and romantically. "No one, not even her two sisters, [testified] that Kathleen Peterson ever said a negative word about Michael Peterson or their relationship," he said. Referring to the sisters as soul mates, he asked, "How extraordinary is that?"[39]

On the matter of Kathleen's scalp lacerations, the defense attorney reminded the jury of evidence he had presented, which showed that the wounds did not match those found in 257 beating cases in North Carolina dating back for more than a decade.

Rudolf ended his closing argument the same way he began his opening statement three months earlier: he played the tape of Michael's whimpering 911 call.

*　　*　　*

The next day, the prosecution team of Jim Hardin and Freda Black took two hours for its closing arguments.

Attorney Black alluded to Michael's work as a novelist when she derided his claim that he was out by the pool when Kathleen was near death, calling it another fictional plot he was trying to sell. She weaved into that plot the defense's dramatic discovery of the "missing" blow poke—two days before it rested its case—and suggested it could have easily been obtained after the fact on eBay.

She also addressed the case of Elizabeth Ratliff's death in Germany and urged the jury to consider its similarities, "in the totality," to the Peterson case. "Do you really believe that lightning strikes twice in the same place?" she asked jurors. "Do you? This defendant knew the blueprint of how to make this look like an accidental fall. Because it had worked one time. And he tried to make it work again. But it didn't."[40]

District Attorney Hardin finished for the state. He gestured to a photograph of the bloodstained walls in the stairwell and said, "Ladies and gentlemen, these walls are talking. Kathleen Peterson is talking to us through these walls. She's screaming at us for truth and justice. . . . Thirty-eight injuries, ladies and gentlemen. How in the world can someone get 38 injuries over their face, back, head, hands, and wrists by falling down the stairs, even if there's two falls? That makes absolutely no sense." In softspoken terms, the prosecutor said the story was a complete fabrication. "It's counterintuitive. It doesn't fit right here in your gut. It's something that's made up."[41]

Deliberations and Verdict

After three months, sixty-five witnesses, and more than eight hundred pieces of evidence, jury deliberations finally began on Monday, October 5, 2003. The jury panel of eight women and four men considered the evidence for fifteen hours, over five days. The process was glitch-free except for an instance of juror replacement and a denial by Judge Hudson over a request to review a transcript of the prosecution's opening statement. He had previously informed the jury that such material did not constitute "evidence."

A verdict was reached on Friday, and, in Courtroom Number 1 on the fifth floor of the Durham County courthouse, the clerk read it aloud: "We the 12 members of the jury unanimously find the defendant to be guilty of first-degree murder, this the 10th day of October 2003."[42]

Cameras clicked; Michael's face blanched; prosecutors congratulated each other; defense attorneys shook their heads in disbelief; and members of the Peterson family sat momentarily stunned. The Ratliff sisters, whom Michael had raised from a young age, began to sob in the front row of the eighty-seat room.

Defense attorney Rudolf stated he would file an appeal. Judge Hudson asked Michael if he wanted to comment before receiving his mandatory sentence of life in prison without parole.

The novelist faced the gallery and, quietly, gently said, "I just want to say to my children, it's OK." He looked at each of his children and repeated the phrase.[43] Then he turned to the judge and heard, "The defendant is imprisoned in the North Carolina Department of Correction for the remainder of his natural life."[44]

Michael was handcuffed and led out of the courtroom. On the way, he again expressed words of comfort to his family: "It's all right," he said.

For nearly two years, the story of the author and the staircase had consumed the Triangle area of the Tar Heel State—and fascinated many others.

POSTSCRIPT

Many legal observers believe David Rudolf did an excellent job in trying to prove this to be an accidental death and not a homicide, but the prosecution won an entirely circumstantial case. On the surface, there is nothing wrong with that, for circumstantial evidence can be quite compelling. But if the *interpretation* of such evidence is flawed, then its validity suffers. Whether or not this occurred in Durham depends, to a large extent, on which side of the adversarial system of justice one sits.

Furthermore, in many circumstantial cases, some meaning must be squeezed out of every finite piece of scientific evidence. The trial can then turn into a "battle of experts." This might have happened here. Some observers believe the evidence presented to the jury panel was so complicated that they dismissed most of it and relied, rather, on the issues of bisexuality and the death in Germany. In fact, an appeal by the defense is expected to encompass these very issues. It is true that the prosecution won most of the legal skirmishes within the trial, such as those resulting in the presiding judge's allowing the Ratliff case to be explored and allowing the male prostitute to testify about his e-mail correspondence with Michael.

If we were to eliminate differences in interpretation, the value of this case—from a forensic point of view—rests with the injuries on Kathleen's head and the blood evidence in and about the narrow confines of the stairwell. The patterns there became a tutorial in blood spatter analysis and they drive home the precept that they must be evaluated as an entire mosaic—in their totality.

One final thought. It involves a question never posed in the investigation or trial, one that reduces, if not eliminates, the relevance of the death in Germany: Does anyone really believe Michael was so foolish that he did not realize a prosecution team would link the two stairway cases?

chapter 4

the duntz brothers case

I can tell you what has happened, how it happened, and when the events at a crime scene happened. I may even be able to tell you who was involved, but I cannot tell you why.

—Dr. Henry Lee

Salisbury, Connecticut, a bucolic community of three thousand people, is nestled in the state's extreme northwest corner. New York State forms its western border. This case deals with two major crimes—arson and murder—and with the bizarre tale of three look-alike brothers who were well known to area police: Richard, Ronald, and Roy Duntz.

Richard, the oldest at thirty-nine, had trouble with the law since his teenage years, compiling a rap sheet of more than twenty convictions, including time in prison. He was purported to be the biggest cocaine dealer in the area and was described as "the toughest guy in town."[1] Ronald and Roy were hardly strangers to criminal behavior either, but they were convicted of lesser crimes.

The three were descendents of tough, clannish miners who helped settle the town in the early eighteenth century. They were proud of their background, often jabbing a finger in the air—if not into one's shoulder—to emphasize that they were tough working-class people, unlike the wealthy New Yorkers who kept moving into town each year. The brothers, along with others having ties to Salisbury's earliest residents, were a closely knit group who tended to stick together in times of trouble.

FACTS OF THE CASE

At 1:00 AM on the night of August 5, 1985, firefighters received a call: the landmark Salisbury Town Hall was burning. The 235-year-old Greek Revival structure had no fire stops, so the respondents were no match for the relentless blaze that soon destroyed nearly everything in its path. The firefighters were able to remove some historical artifacts and as many of the town's records as they could, but, in the end, two centuries of carefully preserved history had gone up in flames.

The fire marshall and investigators soon considered the fire suspicious in origin, particularly after they noticed that a ground-level window screen had

Salisbury Town Hall fire scene.

been pulled away and put off to the side. They also recognized deep uneven burn patterns on the floorboards that indicated the probable use of some type of accelerant.

The townspeople reacted with a combination of fear and anger. They took it personally. This was their town; there was a palpable sense that every citizen there had been violated.

I was asked to review the scene and concluded that the uneven fire burn patterns on the floorboards indicated the fire had been deliberately set. Arson investigators subsequently collected some debris residue and submitted it for forensic analysis. When the charred debris was examined, our laboratory detected trace amounts of gasoline. Further analysis with a GC mass spectrometer confirmed our suspicion that the accelerant used was, in fact, gasoline.

*   *   *

The investigation of an arson fire can be a complex event, especially when the point of origin is not obvious. The ideal situation is for the investigator to arrive at the scene while the fire is going on. This will allow for the documentation of the characteristics of the fire as well as the recording of the crowd watching the fire. Once the fire has been suppressed, photographs should be taken of all aspects of the scene, especially of any and all suspicious signs. Other traditional documentation methods such as videotaping, sketches, and notes are also necessary. Recording of all undisturbed or normal conditions is mandatory. For example, heating apparatus and all electrical circuits should be inspected and documented to demonstrate whether they could have or did indeed contribute to the cause of the fire. *For safety concerns, nothing should be moved before the initial examination of a fire scene unless absolutely necessary.*

The main purpose of the scene examination is to discover the point of the fire's origin. Then the overall search should begin in areas away from that point, those that have little or no damage. Through observation of the level of destruction and the pattern of charring (e.g., low burn configurations or inverted "V" patterns), the fire path can be traced back to the point of origin. The following areas should be carefully studied and evaluated:

- *Exterior fire damage patterns*: Examination of the charring and smoke pattern on the exterior structure will indicate the direction in which the fire spread, whether or not it started externally, and will give clues as to the condition of the windows and doors.

- *Doors and windows burn patterns*: Deeper charring to one side of a door or window will indicate the direction of the fire and whether or not the door or window was open during the fire.
- *Fire burn patterns*: When fire envelops a wooden beam, it will round the edges away from the fire and create an alligator pattern on the charred surface. The intensity of a fire at a particular point will be reflected in the burn pattern. Other burn patterns that experienced investigators look for include inverted cone or "V" patterns, multiple-origin burn patterns, low burn configurations, trailer patterns (ones owing to trails of an accelerant laid by an arsonist), uneven smoke stain patterns, material melting patterns, and concrete spalling patterns (splitting off in chips).
- *Signs of accelerant use*: Arson fires are commonly started with some type of accelerant, most commonly a flammable liquid. The primary objective in the examination of fire debris collected from the point of origin area is laboratory analysis for the presence of any chemical accelerant.

Liquid accelerants generally fall into two major categories:

1. Petroleum distillates
   Straight-run products: Hydrocarbon mixtures that are produced during the distillation process with little further processing. Examples are lighter fluid, kerosene, and fuel oils.
   Processed products: Extra steps are necessary in the distillation process. Examples are gasoline, benzene, and toluene.

2. Nonpetroleum accelerants
   Examples are turpentine, alcohols, and mineral spirits.

- *Presence of ignition devices*: The presence of an accelerant at the point of origin shows only that the fire *could be* a case of arson. To link a suspect to an arson fire, investigators often search for the presence of ignition devices, such as matches, cigarettes, candles, timing devices, or explosives.
- *Other types of physical evidence*: A variety of containers that an

arsonist may have used to transport an accelerant might be found at the scene, such as bottles, cans, or boxes. Likewise, the arsonist may have left behind tools used to enter the structure or to help start the fire, assuming that the fire would destroy them. Thus, all samples of debris, soil, and other evidence must be properly collected and submitted to the laboratory for analysis.

Other crucial findings include imprint and impression evidence, such as fingerprints, footprints, tire tracks, and tool marks. In addition, various forms of biological evidence may be apparent, including blood, tissue, or saliva. DNA typing may help link any or all of these to a suspect.

*   *   *

Meanwhile, fire investigators combed the scene for clues. Police canvassed the town, looking for a suspect. But not for long, because they had the perfect suspect in mind: Roy Duntz. He had been a town employee and was recently fired from his job. Furthermore, someone reported seeing him with singed hair on his hands and face. Then another name surfaced, a friend of Roy's: Earl Morey. It was difficult for investigators to obtain precise details from anyone in town, but rumor had it that Earl and Roy had been seen drinking together on the night of the fire. Earl was confronted with the rumor but allegedly refused to cooperate—that is, until law enforcement officials said they intended to obtain a warrant to search his house for evidence and to collect potentially incriminating forensic material.[2] Earl soon relented, even after police turned down his unusual request that they roughen him up so that it would look as though a confession had been beaten out of him.[3] In a four-page statement to police, he said that he and Roy Duntz were driving home from a bar in a pickup truck when Roy suggested that they burn down Town Hall. Earl stated that he refused, and they proceeded to his home to drink more beer. According to Earl, Roy again suggested torching the building and went to his truck to get a two-gallon can of gasoline. Earl said that Roy was very drunk, but he drove him to the building and followed him around the back, all the while trying to talk him out of the plan. He watched, however, as Roy removed the screen, punched out the window, and emptied the can of gasoline into the room. Earl said that he got very scared, ran home, heard about the fire on his police scanner, returned to the building, and helped firefighters try to extinguish the blaze. Earl Morey, twenty-nine, said he had great affection for Salisbury and, after the incident, didn't know how to handle his guilt. He claimed *that* was the real reason—not the threat of a search warrant—for his decision to confess his connection to the incident and to finger Roy as the true arsonist.

Two weeks after the fire, Earl made a deal with the district attorney's office. He pleaded guilty to third-degree arson and was freed on bond. Roy was also free on bond, awaiting trial for first-degree arson. Then there was a stunning turn of events that once again shocked the town. Earl Morey was supposed to testify at Roy's arson trial on the morning of October 23, 1986. However, he didn't show up in court. In the meantime, a male body had been discovered about 7:00 AM by three Hartford women who had driven to a secluded spot to fish—on the banks of Long Pond, near the edge of town. The man had been shot to death. He was identified as Earl Morey. The decedent's brother Chris learned that the state police major crime squad had been called to investigate an untimely death, and he immediately surmised that (1) his brother had been murdered, and (2) Richard Duntz had pulled the trigger. Chris, perhaps in his grief, told authorities that Richard had been supplying Earl with cocaine—*for free*. Thus, he said, his brother was not only terrified by the suspected arsonist and likely murderer but also dependent on him. He would not hesitate to go anywhere—even to the banks of Long Pond in the early morning—to obtain his cocaine fix.

THE INVESTIGATION

On the day Earl Morey's body was discovered—October 23, 1986—I was giving a lecture on rape and sexual assault investigations at the Groton Submarine Base in Connecticut to naval investigators and area police. My pager went off at about 10:30 AM. The ringing persisted and I sensed something was terribly wrong. The caller turned out to be Lt. James Hiltz, the commanding officer of the Western District Major Crime Squad. He asked for my assistance in the Morey case.

The distance from Groton to Salisbury is only about 130 miles. However, since there is no direct highway linking them, it would have been a three- to four-hour drive by car. Flying, on the other hand, takes only forty minutes. Thus, a state police fixed-wing airplane picked me up at the Groton

Airport. Weather conditions were menacing: a strong thunderstorm was moving in from the coast. I can still feel the motion in that tiny plane; it was like a giant yo-yo. We landed on a strip of grass not far from the crime scene. State Police Sgt. Martin Ohradan and Det. Tim Palmbach briefed me on what had transpired up to that point. Connecticut's chief medical examiner, Dr. H. Wayne Carver, arrived. We began documenting and processing the scene.

My initial impression was that it was an "organized" crime scene. This usually indicates the crime was well planned: an execution. The body lay in a prone position facing Long Pond. A dirt road connected this location to the major rural road. Two sets of overlapping tire tracks were visible in the dirt road. We acted swiftly in making plaster casts of the tracks before the storm came. The lower set appeared to have been made by a heavier vehicle, a truck. Indeed, we later learned that a tow truck had pulled a car from the pond that very night, sometime before midnight. In checking with the towing company, we found that its records showed that the towing job occurred at 10:30 PM. Thus, since the truck's tire marks were *beneath* another set, we had the makings of a basic time line by analyzing the sequence of tire tracks. The upper set presented a pattern that indicated a U-turn had been made and, as it turned out, was consistent with the tires on the car which Earl Morey had driven before he was shot. And the time line suggested that this happened after 10:30 PM.

Two types of shoeprints were also found next to the body. One, having a wavy design, was consistent with that of the sole pattern of Earl's sneakers; the other had a special hexagonal design. Subsequently, at the laboratory, my assistant, Ken Zercie, discovered that a Korean company was the only one that manufactured such a sneaker with this particular sole pattern. The model name was Foot Joy. During a later search of Richard's apartment, investigators didn't find any Foot Joys, but they found the next best thing: a photograph of him wearing such a pair. This proved he had more than likely been at the scene, but it did not prove that he was the killer. Police detectives hit the streets, but, again, no one talked, fearing the same fate as Earl Morey's. It bears repeating that Richard Duntz was immensely feared in the community. Whenever his name came up, people shied away; they changed the subject; they said they didn't know him.

In inspecting the body, I could easily see that Earl had been shot three times. Compatible with that were three shell casings which had been ejected to the front right side of the body. Our opinion was that the shooter, there-

Close-up of sole pattern of Earl Morey's sneakers.

fore, stood *behind* the victim. All three bullets had passed through his body; we recovered two from the ground under the body. This meant that a third bullet had passed through his body and ended up in the pond or the woods beyond. In the lab, we verified our initial hunch—that the bullets came from a 9 mm Smith & Wesson handgun, model 459. Our firearms examiners, Bob Hathaway and Ed Jachimowicz, confirmed the finding.

Other important items turned up at the pond, in Earl's car, and in Richard's van and apartment:

- A packet of white powder was found on the dead body. Cocaine was suspected, but our toxicology expert, Dr. Richard Pinder, identified it as crushed aspirin.
- Earl's car was located in a parking lot in Cornwell, a Connecticut town ten miles from the crime scene. When we examined it, we detected some bloodstains on its left rear fender. The blood type matched Earl's. More about this later.
- Two sticks of Big Red chewing gum were found in Earl's pants

pocket. Several sticks were also found in Richard's van. We found that each wrapper's bar code allowed it to be traced back to a specific manufacturing plant, machine, and work shift. However, a match could not be made.

- Several blue synthetic nylon fibers were embedded in the sole of Earl's sneaker. They were consistent with fibers found in the carpet of Richard's van. This proved only that at some time the victim had to have been in the van.

At Richard's apartment, no murder weapon was found (nor was one found by police divers in the pond), but detectives came upon a spandex belt, one normally used for waist support. Still, they conjectured what it was used for in this case: to support and hide a gun at waist level. Through the aid of a special ALS forensic light source, the inner surface revealed the pattern of a handgun.

Connecticut State Police Major Crime Scene Detective Palmbach and others searched the van and discovered a small lightbulb and assorted coins resting on the front seat's console. We compared striation markings on the bulb with those of a housing in the roof of Earl's car. It was found that the lightbulb fit perfectly within the housing. Had Richard removed it so that the car's interior would not be illuminated when the door was opened? It made sense to investigators that if he were the murderer, he would want it that way; so he would remove the dome light and put it in his pocket. Then after a night of bar hopping, he would have emptied his pockets of change—and the bulb—and put them on the console.

A fishing vest was also found in the van. But it was no ordinary fishing vest, because, upon being subjected to microscopic examination, a rare but familiar sneaker sole pattern emerged. It was lifted from the vest with an electrostatic device that, in essence, lifts dust residue onto a metallic transfer film. The lift showed a partial footwear pattern. A second lift was made from the surface of the van's dashboard. A similar Foot Joy sole pattern was found. Furthermore, it exhibited the same hexagonal pattern found at the crime scene.

Detectives decided to become more aggressive and took an approach that they hoped would pay dividends. They knew that brother Ronald was also dealing cocaine. An undercover agent approached him for a buy. Unsuspecting, Ronald handed the agent a supply of the drug and was arrested on

Dr. Lee and Maj. Tim Palmbach examining suspect's van.

the spot. It worked. Facing a long prison term, Ronald told investigators that he had purchased a stolen 9 mm Smith & Wesson handgun and then sold it to Richard for two hundred dollars. A check of local burglary records showed that such a gun had been stolen in nearby Litchfield. Next the police contacted the original gun owner and asked if he had any bullets or shell casings associated with it. He led a detective to a wooded area over the state line into Millerton, New York, a site he had used for target practice. There, they found twelve casings lying on the ground. These spent casings were collected for later analysis at the forensic laboratory. The man pointed out a tree trunk that he and a friend had used for target practicing. Bullet holes were still visible on the trunk. Of course, the simplest way to retrieve the bullets that made the holes would have been to *dig* them out, but that might have damaged striation patterns made by the gun barrel's lands and grooves. A discussion ensued between investigators and laboratory scientists about the best way to preserve such evidence. They decided to cut away the section in question and ship it to the forensic lab. There, the spent bullets were retrieved without damaging them. (This same method was used in 2002 in the case of the Beltway Snipers in the Washington, DC, area. FBI and ATF agents removed a tree trunk from the yard of one of the killers—in Seattle, Washington—and sent it to the federal laboratory for examination.) At our Connecticut lab, firearms examiners Hathaway and Jachimowicz compared the bullets from the tree trunk with those at the crime scene. Their conclusion was that the same kind of gun was used for both the target practice and the murder.

Richard was questioned at length and denied any involvement in the crime, claiming that he wasn't even in town at the time. He said he was bar hopping in

Tree trunk from which bullets were extracted.

the northwest corner of the state when his van broke down and he called his brother Ronald for a ride home. It was between 12:30 and 1:00 AM. He said that the van was left in the parking lot of a restaurant in Torrington, twenty-five miles away. But the police were certain they had their man, and they were just as certain that more than a few town residents were concealing information that could be used against the suspect. People were simply too afraid to open up, except for one brave informant who revealed where Richard stashed his supply of cocaine: in the woods near one of Salisbury's private boarding schools. The informant also said that Richard was about to make a delivery of two one-eighth-ounce packets of the drug. Authorities had come to the conclusion that, as long as Richard continued to walk the streets, they would get nowhere in solving the murder. They believed that he had to be put behind bars. A state police SWAT team in camouflaged jump-suits was dispatched to stake out the area. Richard was caught red-handed with the cocaine and was arrested. He was given a six-and-a-half-year prison term for selling cocaine. Predictably, once he was imprisoned, individuals came forward to provide the kind of information that law enforcement offi-cials needed to link him to the murder case: one after another said that he had heard Richard threatening to kill Earl Morey. Incriminating evidence mounted, and eventually—three years after the killing—Richard was charged with Earl's murder.

* * *

The examination of firearms is one of the most important services provided by our forensic science laboratory. (In earlier days, this was referred to as ballistics analysis.) Generally, a firearms examiner provides services in the following areas: (1) weapon function and identification, (2) bullet compar-isons, (3) shell casing comparisons, (4) shell casing ejection patterns, and (5) muzzle-to-target distance determinations. But first, we need some defini-tions.

Bore: the interior surface of a firearm barrel.

Rifling: the parallel spiral lands and grooves in the bore. They produce a rotational spin on the bullet when the firearm is discharged. The spin sta-bilizes flight through the air after the bullet leaves the barrel. Almost all commercially made handguns have five or six lands and grooves.

Lands and grooves: the lands are the raised metal portions between the grooves, while the latter are the cut or depressed portions between the lands.

Twist: the direction in which grooves spiral, either clockwise (right) or coun-terclockwise (left). Most handguns have a right twist.

Now, on to those aspects of firearms examinations that are integral to this case:

1. *Weapon function and identification*: An examination of a firearm to determine its functionability, triggerpull, safety, and so on. The land

and groove impressions found on a bullet can determine whether or not a particular gun fired the bullet. The manufacturer's processing in machining the rifling in a barrel is unique to each barrel because of wear on the cutting tools, wear from previous firings, variations in the metal of the barrel, and other distinct factors. These influence the barrel in such a way that they leave specific marks on any fired projectile. The unique markings take the form of striations on the bullet that are caused by the lands and grooves of the barrel. The number, width, depth, and direction of twist of these lands and grooves are therefore unique class characteristics for weapons identification.

2. *Bullet comparisons*: If a weapon is seized, it could be test fired. Then the resultant known or control bullets are compared with those found at a crime scene or in a body. By determining a bullet's metallic composition, weight, size, shape, and manufacturer's markings, its so-called class characteristics can be established. On the other hand, individual characteristics require an examination of striation markings resulting from the pressure of the bullet on a specific gun's lands and grooves as it passed through the barrel. The matching of striations is performed by using a comparison microscope. Additional markings and changes can occur after a bullet leaves a barrel (post-muzzle markings). Examples are those striations made by a silencer (producing striations unique to the silencer), damage to the markings owing to the bullet's impacting an intermediate target (including the possibility of trace evidence attaching to the bullet's surface), and changes resulting from the bullet's striking a terminal target surface. These markings and changes are important not only for identification purposes but also in crime scene reconstructions.

3. *Shell casing comparisons*: Test firings and the comparison microscope also come into play here. Wear and tear of the firing mechanism and other mechanical parts of the gun produce individual markings on the shell casings. The origin of impressions is explicit in certain technical terms that are derived from various parts of the gun. Examples are firing-pin impressions, breechblock marks, and extractor and ejector marks. (The firing pin is released when a trigger is pulled. The breechblock is the rear part of a firearm barrel. Extractor and ejector refer to the mechanism by which a shell casing is withdrawn or thrown from an automatic or semiautomatic weapon.) Sometimes

other marks are present as a result of scraping, scratching, and pressure marks in automatic and repeating firearms. If no gun is found, the casings can be entered into a firearms search database system, such as NIBIN (National Integrated Ballistics Information Network), where they are compared with a database of spent shell casings. In this murder case, the weapon was never recovered. But by using the bullets found at the crime scene as the known (or control) bullets, and those recovered from the tree trunk as the unknown (or questioned) bullets, a match was made. And although this resulted in a type of *indirect* link, it had tremendous forensic value, for it established a connection between the suspect and the bullets.

4. *Shell casing ejection patterns*: Casings at a crime scene can be used for comparisons with a gun in order to determine if that particular type of weapon ejected them. The location of the shell casings at the scene may be useful in establishing the approximate location of the shooter. While a majority of semiautomatic and automatic firearms eject to the rear and right, experimentation must be conducted with the actual weapon used, or a similar make and model, to determine its ejection pattern. Several factors must be taken into account during test firings, since they may influence the pattern. These include the type of ammunition, the shooter's handhold and body position, whether the shooter was stationary or in motion when firing the shot, and the ground surface on which the ejected shells landed. Consideration must also be given to the possibility that the shell(s) may have been kicked or moved after being ejected.

5. *Muzzle-to-target distance determinations*: These were extremely important in this case. From the estimated distance, an experienced forensic investigator can answer questions such as: Was this a self-inflicted wound? Or an accident? Or a murder? What were the victim's and suspect's relative positions?

When a firearm is discharged, gases, soot, primer residue, and partially burned or unburned gunpowder are emitted. These substances are propelled forward with the bullet toward the target. Simultaneously, some are blown backward toward the shooter. These substances constitute the major components of gunshot residue (GSR). GSR collected from an individual may indicate that he or she could have (a) discharged a firearm, (b) handled a recently discharged one, or (c) been close to it when it was fired. In addition, GSR patterns found on and about an entrance wound are also valuable for muzzle-to-target distance determinations:

CONTACT WOUNDS: Soot deposits are seen around the entrance hole. Very little or no unburned powder will be found. In a contact wound, the muzzle (end of the barrel) is against the skin at the time of discharge.

CLOSE-RANGE WOUNDS: Residues are deposited around the bullet hole with black soot and smoke. The pattern is small and dense.

MEDIUM-RANGE WOUNDS: Scattered GSR is present without black soot deposits. The pattern spreads out as the distance increases.

DISTANCE WOUNDS: GSR is usually not found when the distance is greater than five feet.

Interpretations are also dependent on the type of gun used, the length of the barrel, the type of ammunition, the amount of load, whether or not an intermediate target was involved, and other factors.

In this case, we conducted several tests using a Smith & Wesson semiautomatic pistol and ammunition similar to those used in the murder. We found that the muzzle-to-target distance fell within the close-range category—approximately one and a half to three feet.

The investigation of shooting incidents requires not only an examination of firearms evidence such as bullets, shell casings, the gun, and GSR but also another critical step: *shooting reconstruction*. This pertains to the determination of the location of the shooter, the position of the victim, the bullet trajectory, and the distance between the gun barrel and the target. Other considerations are whether or not an intermediate target was involved and whether or not the scene was consistent with the alleged shooter's alibi.

CRIME SCENE ANALYSIS

On the day of the murder—October 23, 1986—I was with detectives from the Connecticut State Police Western District Major Crime Squad, combing the crime scene for clues. Subsequently, we issued a crime scene analysis report that summarized our observations.

Overall Scene

A male victim's body was located along the beach beside Long Pond. A dirt road led from the major road into the pond area. Various types of tire track marks were visible on the dirt road. The scene had been properly secured by Major Crime Squad personnel.

The victim was in a prone position with his face partially facing the ground. He lay on a grassy area near the dirt road. A tirelike track was seen adjacent to the left front of the victim's head. No bloodlike stains were noticed on the back portion of his pants or the back middle portion of his shirt. His hands were crossed in front of his chest. A large amount of blood-stains on the ground appeared to have originated from his wounds and had soaked into the ground. The stain appeared to be in a semicoagulated and gel-like state. Dirty bloodstains were on the victim's face. Blood and tissue-like material were stuck to his hair. Blood spatter was seen on his left hand and nostril area. Bullet holes were observed in the back portion of his shirt, near the collar region. Gunpowder-like residue appeared to have adhered to the collar region. In addition, hair fragments were seen in the same place. Medium-velocity impact-type blood spatter was observed on his hands. Such spatter was consistent with a breathing-related action in which blood is exhaled and projected onto the hands.

Soil-like material was found that had stuck to the undersurface of his sneakers. The sole design appeared to be wavy in configuration. The location of a soil smear on his right sneaker implied that some type of pivoting motion had been made. Sunglasses broken into two pieces were spotted in the grass. They were devoid of bloodstains, which indicated that they had probably been deposited on the ground before the blood was shed.

Three shell casings made of brass material were seen near the body, two in the grass and one on the dirt road. Bloodlike material was noticed on the underside of one casing.

A semicircular-shaped tire track was located a slight distance in front of the victim's foot. This signified that a vehicle had made a U-turn there. There were footprints and tire track impressions adjacent to the body. Some of them had a wavy type pattern, others a hexagonal type pattern. One of the latter was adjacent to the body.

Physical evidence collected from the victim's body was subsequently examined in our lab. The following was found.

The outer surfaces of Earl's sneakers contained red-colored stains that gave negative results when tested for the presence of blood. There were approximately three hundred spots of green paintlike material on the right sneaker. The pattern of soil smear found on the sneakers was most likely caused by a pivoting action against a soil surface. The absence of bloodstains on the sneakers suggests that the victim was shot and fell to the ground within a very short period of time after receiving his injury. Therefore, blood did not have a chance to be deposited on the sneakers.

Earl wore a blue plaid flannel shirt with a button-down collar. Bloodstains covered the collar region and left shoulder area. The bloodstains circling the collar were consistent with a typical transfer type pattern. Crusty bloodstains on the collar's inner surface appeared to have come from a direct contact with and transfer from his wounds. The back of the shirt contained about five hundred individual bloodlike stains at its upper portion. These were consistent with high-velocity impact-type spatter. They appeared to be between 0.5 mm and 2 mm in diameter, a finding typically associated with gunshot wounds.

Three holes were observed on the back portion of his shirt. Microscopic and macroscopic examination revealed that two of them were not consistent with bullet holes. Burn marks were detected on the edges of the two holes, suggesting that they were holes created by cigarette burns.

But examination of the third hole indicated it was produced by a bullet-like projectile; gunpowder residue was observed on the surrounding surface. The bullet appeared to have entered through the outer rear portion of the collar, penetrated it, and exited through its upper inner portion. The bullet then passed through his neck and exited at the front. Chemical tests for nitrates and nitrites were positive on the surrounding areas of the hole, confirming the presence of GSR. The GSR pattern on his shirt indicated that the shot was fired from a distance of about twenty inches.

The victim was wearing gray corduroy pants with a brown belt. No bloodstains were seen on the major surfaces or the cuff areas of the pants, but some were found on the lower right side of the zipper region. They were approximately one inch by one-half inch in diameter and were consistent with light contact smears. Microscopic and macroscopic examination of a nearby quarter-inch hole revealed that it was not a freshly made one. The left rear portion of the pants had a tear, about a one-and-a half-inch square. The direction of the tear was from the lower portion to the upper portion. On the left side of the pants, a mended area was observed. It measured two inches by one and a quarter inches. Green-colored paint smears were scattered about the outer surface of the pants. There were blood smears on the outer aspect of the left rear pocket and on the inner surface of both the left and right pockets; they were all consistent with a contact type transfer. It appeared that an individual and/or object with wet blood came in contact with the inside of the pockets, which resulted in the transfer.

His sweatshirt revealed green- and brown-colored stains on its front side. Chemical presumptive tests for blood proved negative, but instrumental analysis revealed components consistent with paint.

In addition, we examined Earl's car, a two-door, hard top Chevrolet Chevelle with Connecticut registration plates 677 EBM. It was then that we detected a group of most telling smears. Located on the left rear fender, they were reddish brown in color and could be best described as bloodstains made by hair swipes. The bloodstains were tested and found to be human in origin and type O, which was Earl's blood type. The stain covered an area of about twelve inches by twelve inches. The direction of the blood swipes was from the front of the vehicle toward the rear and from the top toward the bottom. This fact indicated that a bloody source with hair had come in contact with the car while the source was moving. I shall address the significance of this finding shortly.

It should be mentioned again that two 9 mm spent bullets had been recovered from beneath the victim's head during our search of the crime scene with detectives from the Western District Major Crime Squad.

Medical Examiner's Report and Autopsy Findings

Dr. H. Wayne Carver, Connecticut's chief medical examiner, was also present at the scene. He described what he saw:

> The deceased is an adult white male . . . in a semi-prone position with both arms folded underneath his chest. The left side of the face is visible; the right side is in contact with the ground. The body is dressed in a blue checked flannel shirt, gray corduroy . . . pants, brown belt, blue and white athletic style shoes and white socks. There is a slight downhill slant to the ground between the deceased and the pond and a large bloodstain issues from the head and passes

toward the [pond]. It is approximately 2 [feet] wide and 4 [feet] to 5 [feet] long. Within this, occasional thick bone fragments are discovered. There is a trail of blood passing from the nose to the ground and from the left ear canal to the ground. There is a wound to the left posterior head which is not completely visible due to caked blood. There are two circular defects on the posterior aspect of the shirt, one on the collar and one just below the collar. One of these partially overlies a blood covered wound which, within the limitations of the examination imposed by the fact that it is covered with blood, is consistent with a bullet wound. Grossly visible gunpowder residue patterns are not immediately obvious; however, rare shiny black granules are present on the back of the shirt. In the position in which the body is lying, the back of the left hand is directly in line and approximately 2 [inches] away from the nostrils. On the back of this hand is a fine blood spatter which has the appearance of a high-velocity spatter pattern. Rigor mortis and appropriate dependent livor mortis are present. [Livor mortis, which occurs after death, is a redish to purple discoloration of the skin owing to settling of blood in dependent areas of the body.] The corneas show very slight clouding.[4]

The following day, Dr. Carver performed an autopsy on the body. The most significant findings were two gunshot entry wounds at the back of the head and one at the back of the neck. Distinctive exit wounds were located in front, indicating that the bullets traveled from back to front. The anatomic diagnosis was "Multiple gunshot wounds to head and neck with injury to soft tissues of neck and brain." The listed cause of death was "Multiple gunshot wounds to head." The listed manner of death was "Homicide."

At Connecticut's toxicology laboratory, a sample of Earl's blood was screened for the presence of ethanol (alcohol) and other common volatile hydrocarbons. Ethanol was found at a concentration of 0.23 percent, a level greater than that allowed for legal driving. Samples of blood and urine were screened for the presence of cocaine and proved to be positive.

Shooting Reconstruction

On October 13, 1987, about a year after the murder, Dr. Carver, members of the Major Crime Squad, and forensic laboratory scientists Bob Mills, Ken Zercie, Bob O'Brien, and Deb Messina went with me to Salisbury's Long Pond to conduct a crime scene reconstruction. It was divided into four parts. First, the crime scene was reestablished according to the original sketches and major reference points. Key locations were pinpointed by referring to the original measurements that the Major Crime Squad detectives took when they processed the crime scene. In this manner, the position of every important object found at the scene was replicated. Second, the exact position of the body was determined and a mannequin was used to represent the victim. It was dressed in the actual outer clothing that Earl Morey was wearing when he was found dead. Yellow numbered markers were used to depict the locations of each piece of physical evidence that had been collected. Third, experiments were conducted using standard outdoor laboratory test-firing procedures. A 9 mm Smith & Wesson, Model 459 handgun, serial number A-625011, was test fired from various angles and under various conditions. Shell casing ejection patterns and gunshot residue patterns at various muzzle-to-target distances were recorded, and these data were used to establish the most likely circumstances of the shooting. The fourth and final part of the reconstruction involved a reenactment of the possible sequence of events. After placing Earl's vehicle in the location most consistent with the pattern evidence, the following events were reconstructed:

- Earl's body was found on a grassy area between a path and a dirt road near Long Pond in Salisbury, Connecticut.
- He had been shot three times in the area of the back of the head.
- Two 9 mm projectiles were recovered from the area under his head.
- Bullet locations were marked on the ground so as to coincide with the entry and exit tracks located on the mannequin's head. Steel rods were used to follow the trajectories of the bullets.
- The distance from the barrel of the weapon to the entry for wound number one was relatively close: under eight inches. For wound number two, the distance was estimated at about forty-two inches or more. This is because no gunshot residue was found around the

wound. And for wound number three, the distance was about twenty inches, based on the pattern of GPR on his shirt.

- Laboratory examination of Earl's vehicle revealed a blood smear consistent with a swipe-type pattern on the rear driver's-side fender. The location and direction of this smear strongly suggested that after the victim received his initial head injury, he fell toward the car, his bloody head hair making contact with the fender. The direction of the smear was from top to bottom and front to rear.
- Footwear impressions had been observed at the actual crime scene. Some were consistent with his sneakers while others had a hexagonal design. These impressions were reproduced on the ground in the approximate locations observed in original photographs. Their relative locations indicated that, at one point in time, two persons were in close proximity when the impressions were made.

Based on the examination of the crime scene; the laboratory analysis of physical evidence; a study of crime scene photographs, reports, and diagrams; and the reconstruction we were able to conclude the following:

- The crime scene location, adjacent to Long Pond in Salisbury, was consistent with a primary scene, which means the victim died there. The scene appeared to be of an organized and execution type.
- Earl was either transported or drove to this primary location prior to his death.
- On or about October 23, 1986, Earl was killed with a handgun consistent with a 9 mm semiautomatic pistol. Three discharged shell casings were recovered at the scene, indicating that he was shot at least three times at the location where his body was found.
- The bullet tracks, entry and exit wounds, and information of gunpowder-like particles suggested that three shots were fired in a sequential manner, which caused the three wounds. The first shot was fired at his head at close range—under eight inches. The second was fired at a distance greater than forty-two inches. The third was fired from a range of approximately twenty inches from Earl's head.
- The fact that two bullets were recovered from the ground suggested that two of the shots (the second and third) were fired after the victim was in a facedown, prone position on the ground.

- An individual wearing a type of footwear with a hexagonal sole design was in close proximity to Earl at the time he was still standing upright.
- At one point in time, a source of blood, consistent with Earl's blood type, came in contact with the rear driver's-side fender of his automobile. At the time of contact, the blood source was moving from top to bottom and front to back.
- Earl's vehicle may have departed from the general area of the body, leaving tire-type patterns while performing a U-turn. Photographs taken during the reenactment depicted these patterns. They were similar in appearance to those observed in photographs taken of the actual crime scene in 1986.

Crime scene reconstruction—a fact-gathering process—is an integral part of my work as a forensic scientist. It is the process of determining or eliminating the events and actions that may or may not have occurred at the crime scene through analysis of the crime scene patterns, the location and position of physical evidence, and the laboratory examination of that evidence. Although reconstruction is based partly on scientific experimentation and partly on past experiences, its steps and stages closely follow basic scientific principles, theory formation, and logical methodologies. The foundation of such reconstruction is established by following the basic principles used in the forensic examination of physical evidence at the crime scene and the laboratory.[5]

The developing fields of artificial intelligence and expert systems have created a new dimension in reconstruction. These systems provide forensic modeling, crime mapping, crime scene reasoning and logic, comparing and profiling of suspects, and other tools for decision making. Advances in computer hardware and software have added crime scene animation and three-dimensional scene sketching to the mix. It must be stressed, however, that crime scene investigation is not to be confused with what is portrayed on television shows. Real-life scene investigations are a team effort and involve logical and systematic procedures.

THE TRIAL

Seven men and five women were impaneled to decide Richard Duntz's fate in the old Superior Courthouse in Litchfield, Connecticut. The seven-week trial featured not only divergent claims by the prosecution and the defense but also a succession of unexpected witness accusations, counteraccusations, and frequent emotional outbursts by the defendant in open court. At one juncture, Richard, who had heart problems, was briefly hospitalized and prescribed extended rest and sedation, resulting in a one-week hiatus in the proceedings. By the trial's end, one hundred witnesses had testified.

According to the state, a trial officially starts with the selection of a jury—the voir dire—but in this case, Richard brazenly called it "railroading."

"I'm facing 60 years for a crime I didn't commit," he said, "and I'm not getting any help."[6] He complained that his defense was ill conceived and that the initial trial judge, Anne Dranginis, was biased against him because he had been prosecuted ten years earlier for sexual assault and because of the recent prison sentencing of him for drug dealing. Richard requested a replacement. Commenting on the performance of his defense lawyer, special public defender Louis Avitable, the defendant said that not enough defense witnesses had been rounded up, adding, "Personally, I like the man, but he had my case for seven months, and I didn't see him for seven months."[7] He again requested a replacement. Eventually he broke even on his requests: Judge Walter Pickett Jr. replaced Dranginis, but Avitable remained on the case—at least his office did—for Richard, by agreement, would be primarily represented by the defense attorney's associate, Denise Dishongh.

The opening sessions revealed nothing unanticipated. The state contended that the defendant murdered Earl Morey to prevent him from testifying that Richard's brother Roy had burned down the town hall the year before. The defense proclaimed its client's innocence and further suggested that the police's motive for arresting him in the first place stemmed from a lawsuit that Richard and his wife, Susan, had filed two days after the murder. In the million-dollar suit against the state police, they questioned the methods of the dozen officers who spent ten hours searching his apartment for clues and evidence. Specifically, Richard stated that he was not allowed to leave the premises or to contact a lawyer and that he was thrown against a wall when the officers entered. Throughout the proceedings, Dishongh tried repeatedly to convince the jury that Roy, the defendant's brother, had the strongest reason for killing Morey, the only witness to the fire.

We pick up the trial near the end of the first week: On January 23, 1990, the state's chief medical examiner, Dr. H. Wayne Carver, was on the stand for three hours. He stated that the bullet that felled Morey three years earlier was fired from eight to twenty-four inches behind him and was followed by two slugs that ended his life in a matter of minutes. Under questioning by prosecutor Frank Maco, the doctor outlined how he arrived at the firing distance and the bullet sequence. The first wound—just below the base of the skull—was surrounded by small scrapes and gunpowder particles that led him to believe the pistol had been discharged from within two feet. But the lack of soot from gun smoke around the wound indicated that the weapon was fired from no closer than eight inches.

There was a large scrape around a wound near the center of the skull. This was evidence, according to Dr. Carver, that the victim's face touched the ground when the bullet—the second one fired—entered the body. By analyzing the pattern made by cracks in the skull, he determined that the bullet hitting Morey close to the top of the head came last. His conclusion was that Morey was standing when hit by the first shot, and he was on the ground when the last two shots were fired.

On this same day of testimony, defense counsel Dishongh referred to the issue of motive. She claimed that Richard's brother Roy, who was then serving time for torching the town hall, had more motivation to kill Morey than her client did.

The next day, a state police detective testified that the two bullets found under the body could have come from a gun owned by Richard Duntz. The chain of custody for the stolen gun was traced for the jury. He also delineated the locations of Morey's car, which was allegedly used by the killer to flee the crime scene. The vehicle, later found ten miles away in the parking lot of the Cornwall Electric Company, belonged to Morey's brother Howard. Police had said Earl borrowed it the night of the slaying and drove Richard to Long Pond in anticipation of obtaining some cocaine. The detective said that blood typing results from the forensic lab showed that the blood found on the car's bumper was similar to that of the defendant.

Lt. James Hiltz, commander of the Western District Major Crime Squad, took the stand on January 24 and again the following week. He testified that after Morey fingered Roy as the arsonist, Morey was so afraid of retribution that he asked police to "slap him around so he would look like he was beat up" by interrogators.[8]

Hiltz elaborated on the statement Richard gave police about his whereabouts on the night of the murder: that he had been bar hopping in and around Salisbury and ended up at the White Hart Inn. He left there between 12:30 and 1:00 AM, he said, and, on the way home to Unionville, his van broke down in Torrington. He called his brother Ronald, who picked him up and drove him home. Subsequent testimony by a Torrington police officer contradicted that time line. He indicated that during two patrols near the parking area at about 2:30 AM and at 3:30 AM, there were no vehicles in the lot the first time, but Richard's van was there the second time.

Hiltz said that at one point in the statement he asked Richard if he had killed Morey. "And his whole attitude changed," the commander said. "He was calm up to [then]. His bathrobe was open and I could virtually see his heart beating."[9]

In additional testimony, Hiltz stated that he hadn't considered Ronald or Roy as suspects because, among other things, they had no history of violence, whereas Richard's long criminal record included at least five convictions for assault. Moreover, Hiltz said, when Morey spoke about the arson case, he expressed fear of retaliation from the defendant, not from the other two brothers.

The appearance of the commanding officer prompted several nasty outbursts by the defendant, who was seated at the defense table. When Hiltz said that Richard was free to leave his apartment during the search in 1986, Richard erupted. "You're a f—— liar, Hiltz!" he screamed. "I can see why they got you on the force. I wouldn't let you in my doghouse, let alone my home." When the commander was leaving the courtroom, Richard stiffened, stared intently at him, and sneered, "I'll see you later. I love you, Hiltz."[10] At another point when Hiltz was on the stand, he stated that some people interviewed during the murder investigation had expressed fear of Richard and a lack of confidence in the state police. "Yeah, especially when you tell them I'm going to kill them," the defendant exclaimed. "Why don't you tell the truth? You've been lying all along." At still another time, when the prosecutor said there was no evidence directly linking Roy Duntz to the Morey murder, Richard shouted from the table, "You don't have any evidence to directly link me to the murder either, but you put me here."[11] Surprisingly, Judge Pickett never cited the defendant for contempt of court for his repeated outbursts.

In the third week of the trial, the following transpired:

- Earl's brother Chris testified that his brother said to him the night before his death: "If you find me dead . . . Richie Duntz did it and Roy

Duntz knows all about it. Tell the cops everything you know."[12] Chris also identified the broken pair of sunglasses found at the murder scene as his brother's.

- Lieutenant Hiltz said Roy Duntz's hands were tested for gunpowder residue around four hours after the body was found and that the tests proved negative.
- Hiltz stated that Foot Joy sneaker imprints found at the crime scene and in Richard Duntz's van were relevant to the homicide.
- Bryant James Allen of Tampa, Florida, testified that he once resided in Torrington and that he sold a stolen Smith & Wesson 9 mm pistol to Richard's brother Ronald. Police had testified the previous week that Ronald indicated he had sold the gun to Richard for two hundred dollars. Under cross-examination by Dishongh, Allen admitted that he was testifying with the understanding that Torrington court charges of gun theft, criminal possession of a weapon, and failure to make a court appearance would be withdrawn. He was asked if the charge for failure to appear was related to the 9 mm pistol, and he replied, "I don't know. I've been arrested so many times, I forget."[13]
- A friend of Richard's denied that Richard instructed her to destroy family photos of him in white, low-cut sneakers, like the ones allegedly worn by Earl's killer. But she also stated that her estranged husband tore up some photos after the murder, possibly at Richard's request. It was brought out that State Police Det. David Carey had interviewed her two years ago. When asked for photos of Richard, she asked Detective Carey to return with a search warrant, so it would not look like she freely gave them to him. He obliged and confiscated some negatives. Carey described her as fearing for her life, like many other witnesses. For that reason, he called the case "the most bizarre investigation I ever had to do" in his twenty years with the state police. "I never had so many people so afraid about what they saw, what they heard and what they knew," he said.[14] Later, her husband denied that he acted upon Richard's request when he tore up the photos—rather, that he did so to avoid getting involved in the case.

I was called to court to testify during the fourth week of the trial—on February 2—and indicated we had found three strands of blue nylon fibers on the sole of Morey's sneaker. Laboratory analysis revealed that they were microscopically similar to fibers from a carpet sample taken from the front floor of Richard's van. The fibers were also compared with carpet samples from Morey's and Roy Duntz's cars, and no match was found. I further testified that blood spatters and a blood smear on Morey's car, along with the blood, tire tracks, and footprints at the crime scene, had led me to conclude that such a car had been at the scene and that Morey was standing next to the car when the first shot was fired. I interpreted the smear as one that was made by Morey's hair as he received his head wound. He swirled and fell against the car after the first shot, and I stated that the blood type indicated that the blood smears matched his blood. My analysis of gunpowder particle patterns and soot deposits led to my conclusion that the first shot was fired from less than eight inches away. The rest of my testimony was based on our laboratory reports issued earlier.

After the trial, many court observers thought that the key part of my testimony involved my reconstruction of the crime scene. It was accompanied by reference to sixty-one colored slides that I took during my crime scene investigation. Here is my reconstruction.

Morey and the killer arrive at Long Pond at approximately 2:00 AM. Morey, the driver, is under the influence of alcohol and cocaine. He drives the car within about ten or fifteen yards of the pond. The tires on the driver's side rest on a border of grass and sand. Those on the passenger's side rest on the hard track of sand, over which many vehicles have traveled during the previous summer. Morey gets out of the driver's-side door. He stands facing the rear of the car, its left door and left rear fender to his left. The killer gets out of the passenger's side, hurries around the front of the car, leaving a few distinctive sneaker sole prints with a hexagonal design similar to that used on Foot Joy sneakers. The killer stands behind Morey with a 9 mm semiautomatic pistol in his right hand, holding it about eight inches from the back of Morey's head. He fires. Morey apparently has his head inclined forward slightly, consistent with his activity at the time. The bullet exits his forehead, spattering high-velocity blood drops, "like spraying Windex," on the left rear side of the car. This bullet probably ends up in the pond. It is never found. The victim slumps forward and falls to the ground. On the way, his head hair (with blood on it) makes contact with the left rear fender, leaving a swipe-type pattern of blood. This blood smear turns out to be type O, the same as Morey's. The killer fires another shot at Morey's head, this time from about forty-two inches away. The bullet strikes within about an inch of the first one. He steps closer and fires a third time—from about twenty inches above Morey's head—striking his neck. (The three shell casings are ejected out onto the grass and are found during our crime scene search later in the day. The second and third slugs are found under Morey's head, about two inches down in the blood-soaked soil.) The killer hops in the car, makes a sharp U-turn, and speeds away.

I emphasized that, in the vast majority of my criminal cases, "I can tell you what has happened, how it happened, and when the events at a crime scene happened. I may even be able to tell you who was involved, but I cannot tell you why."

For the rest of February, the prosecution tried to bolster its claim that the defendant murdered Morey to keep him from testifying that his brother Roy Duntz had burned down town hall. Among the state's nearly one hundred witnesses during that time were the following:

- A Duntz family friend who said that Richard came to his home and, with his host's approval, helped himself to a half dozen bullets that were scattered on his bar. Under cross-examination, he stated that some of them were 9 mm in caliber. Morey was killed two months later.
- Richard's nephew, the son of Roy, sixteen at the time, said he was awakened on the night of the murder by the movements and voices of his father and someone else who sounded like his uncle Richard. He heard the latter say, "Give me something that looks like coke," as they apparently headed for the bathroom.[15] This fit in with the testimony of a state toxicologist who said that white powder found in a cocaine packet in the victim's pocket was actually ground aspirin. Richard was accused of using the counterfeit drug to lure Morey to Long Pond.
- Morey's cousin claimed that she spotted Richard's van parked outside a nearby bar when she last saw her cousin on the night of the murder. It was also during her testimony, and that of another woman, that Richard stormed to the back of the courthouse screaming, "You're an idiot, man!" and "You're a lying bitch!" He was rushed to a hospital but released back to the trial two hours later. The cousin returned to the stand to tell jurors she had heard Richard threaten Morey.

"Earl said he didn't want Richie to get mad at him or anything, but said, 'I heard you were gonna kill me.'" "[Then] Richie said, 'No, but I'll tell you one thing. If you testify against my brother Roy, I'm going to blow your . . . brains out.'"

- The other woman followed with her own version of what she had heard Richard say: "He said, 'Let me tell you something. I killed that kid. He was a . . . nobody.'"[16]
- The statements by the original owner of the gun allegedly used to kill Morey supported previous testimony regarding the changing ownership of the gun.
- Two male cousins of the victim stated Richard approached them at the Lakeville Café and told them, "I haven't got anything against you guys, but if Earl doesn't shut his mouth, I'm gonna shut it for him."[17]
- In testimony laced with obscenities and open-court accusations, Ronald said Richard admitted to him that he had killed Morey. From his chair at the defense table, Richard accused his brother of making a deal with the state to avoid going to prison on narcotics charges. Ronald countered with an admission that he decided to tell the prosecution the truth after reading in the newspaper that the defense was trying to pin the crime on his other brother, Roy. Richard blurted out, "This guy's going to face 20 years. Anybody'd say what you want him to say."

"Then why are you blaming Roy?" Ronald shot back. "I'm not blaming Roy!" Richard replied, his face flushed.[18]

Judge Pickett admonished Richard for his outbursts, suggesting that the defendant was helping the state convict him.

Ronald, still on the stand, then guided the jury through the events surrounding the killing, as he remembered them: Richard phoned him on the night of the murder, asking for a ride home because his van broke down in Torrington.

They drove toward Richard's home in Unionville, and, on the way, Richard asked him to stop along the Farmington River so he could dispose of a pair of sneakers. Richard got out of the car carrying two white sneakers and walked down an embankment toward the river. He returned empty-handed. The witness said Richard then told him that he had shot Morey in the back of the head beside Long Pond in Salisbury. Ronald said his brother instructed him to tell anyone who asked that he had picked him up between midnight and 12:30 AM, although the time was actually closer to 3:00 AM.

The defense asked Ronald why he lied at a pretrial hearing and continued lying about what had happened until recently. He answered that he wanted to protect his brother and, at the same time, not implicate himself because he had once owned the gun.

- The defendant's other brother, Roy, the prosecution's last witness, testified that Richard was the killer. "It hurts me to sit here and put my brother in jail for the rest of his life," he said calmly, "but I can't let him do it to me when I'm not guilty. He had a well-thought-out scheme to put the murder on me. . . . I'm telling the truth. Nothing he says bothers me."[19] In fact, he said, Richard had a number of schemes to beat the murder charge against him. One was a convoluted plan in which all three brothers would pin the crime on each other: Roy would blame Ronald; Ronald would blame Richard; Richard would blame Roy. The idea was to create sufficient doubt in the minds of the jurors to get Richard acquitted. Another scheme was to have Roy take the rap since he was already in prison for the arson conviction. If Roy agreed, Richard promised to get someone to marry him so he could have conjugal visits in prison.

On the second day of Roy's testimony, the story took a strange turn. He and his lawyer, John Williams, insisted that Earl Morey's death actually *hurt* Roy's chances of beating the rap for setting the town hall fire. So any claims that he was the murderer were absurd. A few months after the fire, Williams had taped an interview with Earl in which Earl said neither he nor Roy had any connection with the incident. The attorney played a transcript of that taped interview for the jury to hear. Williams said that Morey, under police pressure, had lied about who torched the building—that the police told him he would go to prison for twenty-five years if he didn't identify the arsonist or arsonists. Williams said that Roy needed Morey to swear to that in court— and now, Morey was dead. If Roy was telling the truth, this was a shocking development, particularly in terms of Richard's purported motives for the murder—to silence the man who fingered Roy.

To this point in the trial, everything had appeared straightforward: Richard would be convicted of first-degree murder; the bully who had held sway over a community through threats and intimidation would be imprisoned. With the revelation of the taped interview, however, some doubt crept into the picture. Momentum suddenly shifted away from the prosecution. In gambling parlance, what had seemed like a sure bet for the state now became an even-money uncertainty.

Finally, the main witness for the defense was Richard Duntz himself. But before him, three convicts testified on his behalf. Each vouched for Richard's innocence, yet their words, let alone their credentials, hardly set the stage for a favorable light on the defendant's upcoming appearance. One was a burglar who also served time for manslaughter, larceny, and selling narcotics; the second was a man serving time for petty larceny and risk of injury to a minor; and the third was an individual who had been convicted of eighteen burglaries in the past ten years.

When Richard Duntz took the stand, the trial came full circle. "I had nothing to do with the death of Earl Morey," he declared. "I always liked Earl and the Moreys. He never did anything to me."[20] During cross-examination, the defendant and state's attorney Maco tangled several times, their exchanges reverberating throughout the courtroom. Maco threw a new twist into the trial by announcing that protecting brother Roy was only a side motive for the slaying. Maco said Richard also wanted to send a message to residents of the Northwest Corner, letting them know what happens to people who defy him and cooperate with the police. Richard asserted that most of the state's witnesses were the same "liars" who convicted Roy of arson. He went on to accuse once-loyal allies, such as brother Roy and brother Ronald, of testifying against him because the state threatened them with extended prison terms for crimes they'd committed.

In closing arguments on March 5, 1990, lawyers for each side painted a picture: on the one hand, of a calculating killer who wanted to cement his place as the area's premier drug dealer, and on the other hand, of an innocent man who was taking the rap for a murder that his brother had a more pressing motive to commit.

The state postulated that, while the fire was at the heart of the shooting, the defendant was motivated more by a desire to make an example of Morey for talking to police, than by his brotherly love for Roy.

The defense conceded that Richard was a convicted drug trafficker, but that selling drugs was not the issue in the case. Dishongh held that the state settled on the drug connection as a last resort when it realized that Roy Duntz had a much better motive for silencing Morey.

The jury deliberated less than three days and, on March 7, found Richard guilty of murder in the first degree. Six weeks later, he was sentenced to sixty years in prison, but the Connecticut Supreme Court threw out the conviction on a legal technicality. Before a second trial began, Richard decided to plead guilty of manslaughter in exchange for a sentence of fifteen years. Then, a little more than two years into the sentence, he died of a heart attack.

POSTSCRIPT

This was a case about a career criminal who believed that, through drug dealing and the fear he instilled in his customers and others, he had a solid lock on northwestern Connecticut.

In the years since the fire, Salisbury Town Hall has been rebuilt and looks nearly the same as the original.

Roy Duntz, after serving fourteen years for arson, is back in Salisbury. Apparently most townspeople believe he has paid his dues.

The region is calmer now. The tyrannical Richard Duntz is but a memory. The science of forensic investigation contributed to the testimony of witnesses in reconstructing the crime and putting him behind bars. Richard Duntz had thought that his little empire placed him above the law. But he was wrong.

chapter 5

the myers/fontanille case

. . . there was a bat, a knife, a gun, and a lot of violence.
—Homicide detective Martin Childs, February 24, 1984

W e travel now to New Orleans, Louisiana—the city so ravaged by Hurricane Katrina in 2005—for a criminal case as strange as any that area has ever encountered. It was a case in which two murder suspects accused each other of the crime and gave identical accounts of what had happened. A case in which we learn whether or not forensic science was able to unlock the real sequence of events. And a case with a wellspring of sordid secrets shared by many: conspiracy to commit double murder, and rumors of wife swapping, kinky sex, homosexuality, and sex clubs.

BACKGROUND

In the midseventies, two young men, Kerry Myers and Bill Fontanille, met while attending Archbishop Shaw High School in Marrero, Louisiana. After graduation, they went off to different colleges. Kerry transferred from Louisiana State University to Nicholls State College, and it was there that he met Janet Cannon. After graduation, the two men moved back to their old area, Jefferson Parish—a fast-growing community—on the west bank of the

Mississippi River. Their friendship grew stronger and, in June 1979, Bill took part in Kerry and Janet's wedding party.

Four years later, Bill's world began to unravel. He lost his job; his wife, Susan, left him; and he became withdrawn. He had frequent attacks of rage: punching holes into the walls of his home, breaking windows, and trashing appliances. For a few months, he spent no time with most of his old friends, who had lost track of him. Around Christmastime, he picked up his son, Matthew, during a visitation arrangement and failed to return him to Susan at the specified time. After several anxious hours for the mother, the boy was returned safely to her.

Then on Tuesday, February 21, 1984, Bill appeared at the Myerses' home on Litchwood Lane. He spoke to Kerry of his failed marriage. Kerry reciprocated, revealing tales of his own unhappy and volatile relationship with Janet.

FACTS AND INVESTIGATION

This baffling case required three trials, two of which were unique in ways we'll examine later. The following account deals with facts derived from an intense and protracted investigation—from the time of the crime up to and including the *first* trial.

Exactly what happened in that Litchwood Lane home two days later, on Thursday, February 23, 1984, may never be fully understood. It depends on which story you believe: Kerry's or Bill's. Beautiful Janet Myers had been savagely beaten to death with a baseball bat. Both men were at the blood-spattered scene during the murder—that much has been firmly established. But which one wielded the weapon? Or had they taken turns? Was it part of a conspiracy—one in which Bill's wife, Susan, may have also been targeted for death? Later, the men's official and public statements were oddly similar, save for each one pointing the finger at the other. And Bill freely admitted that he and Janet, his best friend's wife, had had sex the day before the murder.

But first, let's start with the 911 emergency call from Kerry Myers to the Communications Center of the Jefferson Parish Sheriff's Office at 1:40 AM on February 24. It was a rambling call that would later be described as suspicious, overly dramatic—possibly staged.[1] In it, Kerry claimed that someone had broken into his home and tried to kill him; that he had stabbed the intruder, who then fled. The following are excerpts from the conversation between him, a dispatch trainer, and Operator 73:

Myers: . . . I'm scared! I need to pick up my gun in case he comes back. . . . Oh! Get 'em here quick! I'm scared to death!

Dispatch trainer: All right, and tell me exactly what happened . . .

Myers: I came home at 3:30 this afternoon. I know the man. He's been despondent over his wife and [*inaudible*] . . . his wife and the kid, they left him. I walked in the door. He had my wife tied up! And he ambushed me with a baseball bat! I think my arm's broke! And he beat me over the head with the bat—and everything in my house he could find—and I been struggling with him—and trying to calm him and talk to him—and I just had an opportunity where he had a— then he tried to come at me with a knife—I took the knife away— and got an opportunity to—to—and just got him outa the house. And I stabbed him! He's got a—he's wounded!

Dispatch trainer: Just calm down.

Myers: —don't know if he may come back!

Dispatch trainer: Okay, your doors are locked, huh?

Myers: . . . [*inaudible*] mad. Oh God! I got two small children— and one of them's stuck—one of them's [six] weeks old! And hasn't even eaten since two o'clock.

Dispatch trainer: Are your children all right, sir?

Myers: I think so! My wife's tied—he says my wife is tied up and wouldn't let me go in the room and see her! I need to go and see about my wife.

Dispatch trainer: Okay.

Myers: Okay, hold on.

OP 73: Sir, did you check on your wife?

Myers: (*In background*) Oh, God! God! Oh my God—oh God—oh God! Janet! Oh my God!

OP 73: Get on the phone.

Myers: (*Still in background*) Oh, my God! I think he—*ohhh!*

OP 73: Get on the phone!

Myers: (*Back on phone*) I think he killed my wife![2]

Kerry went on to identify the intruder as Bill Fontanille and to give Bill's age, description, the make of his car, and other detailed information—perhaps *too* detailed for a man who had just discovered that his wife was bludgeoned to death.

At 2:43 AM—at least eight hours after the crime—police arrived to find not only Janet's lifeless body in the living room but also the couple's two-and-a-half-year-old son, Ryan, in the master bedroom. He lay comatose from head injuries. And, in another bedroom, they discovered the Myerses' six-week-old daughter, Sarah, unharmed and sitting in a portable baby seat. EMT personnel and crime scene investigators arrived shortly thereafter.

Janet lay on her back. Her face was bashed in. Medical examiners and detectives noted that the body was cool to the touch, that generalized rigor mortis was present, and that there was no postmortem lividity. (As noted earlier, postmortem lividity, also called "livor mortis," refers to a reddish, purplish blue discoloration of the skin owing to settling of red blood cells in the lowest parts of the body after death.) She wore a multicolored pullover shirt and blue gym shorts over maroon leotards. A spot of blood was detected on one of her white sneakers. Large amounts of blood spatter were found on the wall above the victim's head and blood was pooled beneath her head, saturating the carpet there. A piece of a broken ivy plant was seen below and around her neck. Blood spatters were observed over a wide area of the living room's east wall.

Detectives noted several drops of blood on the foyer floor and a large number of bloodstains in the den. There, two water glasses lay on the floor adjacent to a sofa. Many items were scattered about, including keys, broken dishes, a cup, a lampshade, and an ashtray. Reddish bloodlike stains, hairs, and a large clump of reddish material were observed on the sofa. The room also contained bloody footprints, smears, and spatters. It looked like a major battlefield.

A bloody baseball bat was propped against the sofa. A loaded shotgun had been lifted from the crook of Kerry's injured arm by the first officer on the scene. It was seized as evidence, along with smashed glassware, a table lamp, and an assortment of other shattered objects. Also seized was a bloody kitchen knife found on the kitchen counter. In the processing of the crime scene, nearly 140 photographs were taken.

Paramedics took Kerry and Ryan to West Jefferson Hospital. The child was put on the critical list. His father's injuries included a shattered left forearm; bruises over the left eye and forehead; lacerations on the right side of the head and hairline that required sutures; scratches and lacerations on the right forearm, elbow, and wrist; and puncture wounds of the lower abdomen.

Meanwhile, Bill Fontanille had gone to his parents' home. When his parents saw the extent of his injuries, they all went immediately to the closest hospital, Jo Ellen Smith Hospital, not the one that Kerry and Ryan were taken to. A preliminary evaluation by emergency room nurses indicated that Bill's clothes were bloody and that he was still bleeding from at least five stab wounds to the upper right chest and back. Eventually, Bill would require a blood transfusion.

A police officer on duty at the hospital later commented: "[Bill] was walking under his own power, and was calm. He wasn't gasping for breath. No sentence fragments. No hyperventilation. Never did he rant or rave that whole morning. I've seen a lot of scared [patients] in my years, but he was not one of them. . . . [He repeated several times], 'I've been stabbed. My best friend stabbed me. He killed his wife and baby and is going to blame it on me.'" The officer stated that, after the last repetition, Bill added, "He's going to tell you we had a plan to kill both our wives but he didn't think I'd go through with it."[3]

Sgt. Robert Masson, a seasoned homicide detective in the Jefferson Parish Sheriff's Office Homicide Unit, took a statement from Bill Fontanille, beginning at 2:50 AM, Saturday, February 25, 1984. Two key parts of it were as follows:

First part:

Masson: Why did you go to his house [on Thursday, the day of the murder]?
Fontanille: I had gone over there to pick up a baseball bat that I had been using as a cane. I had left it there the previous night.
Masson: Why did you leave the baseball bat at his house?
Fontanille: I had gone over to his house Wednesday night. We were gonna go play basketball together and I arrived at his home at about 7:30. I left the bat there. Two other friends picked us up. When they brought us back to Kerry's house I just got in my car and left, and just left the bat in his house.

Masson: How many times were you at Kerry's house on Wednesday?
Fontanille: Twice.
Masson: What time did you get there the first time?
Fontanille: Around 1:00 PM in the afternoon.
Masson: How long did you stay?
Fontanille: Stayed till about 5:00.
Masson: Was anyone there when you got there?
Fontanille: Janet was there and the two children.
Masson: What time did Kerry get home?
Fontanille: He came home about 3:30, between 3:30 and 4:00 I guess, stayed for about 45 minutes, went back to the office. And then I left before he came back again.
Masson: What took place between you and Janet?
Fontanille: We sat down. We were talking about my separation from my wife and she became very comforting to me. And I suppose I was very appreciative of that. And we ended up in, well, I'm gonna say, we didn't go to bed. We made love in the baby's room. We were looking out the window while we were doing what we did.
Masson: Why were you looking out the window?
Fontanille: We were afraid Kerry might come home. On Wednesdays she says that she's never sure what time he'll come home.[4]

Second part:
This part is quoted at length because it became crucial evidence at the trials. Kerry Myers's later statement was virtually identical to this one by Bill, save for its beginning. Prosecutors labeled the statements mirror images of each another.

Masson: What time did you get over to the Myers house on Thursday?
Fontanille: Between 3:30 and 4:00, probably closer to 4:00.
Masson: Where did you park your car?
Fontanille: I parked it down the block. . . .
Masson: Why did you park down the block?
Fontanille: I didn't want to park my car in front of the house and have Kerry drive by. I wasn't sure if he expected that Janet and I had

done what we did and I didn't want to cause any trouble. I figured if I parked my car down the block, I'd just go in, get my bat and leave. And if he did just drive by without stopping he wouldn't, he wouldn't stop he'd just drive by but if he saw my car then he might suspect something. I parked my car. When I walked to the house Kerry was there already. So I figured what the heck that he can't expect anything. So I knocked on the door and went in.

Masson: Explain what happened when you got inside the residence.

Fontanille: Kerry opened the door for me. I guess I took two or three steps and then he hit me from the rear. At the time it seemed like I was stabbed twenty times in the back. It, it's three wounds back there. I guess some of them were just punches. I ran into the room where they keep their television set. Leaning against the love seat was the baseball bat. I picked it up. Kerry came into the room and we looked at each other. I said, "Kerry, why are you doing this to me. I don't understand." I was, I was hysterical. I thought I was dying. He just said, "I'm doing what I've got to do." Said, "I'm doing what I've got to do." He came at me again with the knife and I started swinging the baseball bat. I don't know how many times I hit him. I know I did hit him in the arm with the baseball bat 'cause he later said I broke his arm. I lost control of the bat while we were struggling 'cause I was more concerned with keeping that knife away from me than anything else. We struggled around. I was picking up anything I could find, cup, an ashtray, anything, little glass objects that I was hitting with it. Finally, we both fell to the floor. . . . He kept telling me I didn't understand, just to be quiet while he thought things out. We stayed in that position I guess for 45 minutes or so. I kept saying, "Kerry, I think I'm dying." So finally he told me if we got up he wouldn't hurt me any more, he'd just let me go. So he got up. He sat on the sofa and I sat on the floor. And we sat there again for an hour without saying a word. Then he turned the [TV] set on. We watched television from around 7:00 till 11:00, 11:30, I don't know. . . . I was still, still thought I was in a lot of trouble physically. . . . I said, "Kerry, I got to go to the bathroom very bad." I got up and he got up behind me and I was walking toward the hall and he lunged at me again with the knife and we started struggling. We struggled down the hall. I was stabbed twice more, and apparently he was stabbed too. . . . We came to rest at the end of the hall toward the bathroom . . . each of us having control of the knife. . . . Then he started talking about problems that I don't know anything about and that I would never know. So I started telling him about my problems, how I'm separated from my wife, how I might lose the house that I just bought. I haven't seen my son since December, which shook him up quite a bit . . . and we were gonna wait in the hall, each of us holding the knife so we couldn't do any more damage to each other. . . . I guess we were there in the hallway for two hours when I, when I felt his grip on the knife was loosening up. And when it did I took off down the hall. I guess I had taken three or four steps and I heard him coming behind me. I went out the front door. He followed me and shouted something out the front door that, I couldn't make out what it was. I was running too hard. I was too scared. I never did see Janet or the children although I did hear the infant, the little girl crying in one of the rooms. Also, when we were laying back there he was looking under the door into his bedroom, said that Ryan was in there. He didn't want Ryan to come out and see what had happened. He asked that, when he asked me, when he saw Ryan move if I would hold the door and not let Ryan out, just hold the door where he couldn't get out. There was a couple of times when he asked me to do that. That's pretty much what I remember, sir.[5]

Three weeks later, on March 14, 1984, Sergeant Masson took an official statement from Kerry Myers. In part, it read as follows:

Masson: Okay, why don't you describe what happened when you got home Thursday. About what time did you get home?
Myers: I got home approximately 3:30, 3:45.
Masson: Did you see Bill's car?
Myers: No.
Masson: What happened when you got into the house?
Myers: As I walked into the house, I unlocked the door. The door was locked. I unlocked the door and walked in, more or less not paying attention to anything. I had reached around to turn and close the door behind me and take my keys out of the door. And as I did I

took a step in. As I did that, took a step in, I heard my name being screamed and Bill jumped out of the living room area with a baseball bat, swinging at me.

Masson: What happened from that point?

Myers: He took a couple of swings. I raised my arms up to try, try to block the swings and deflected at least one or both of them partially 'cause the swings were at my head. And one of them, both of them I believe hit my arms and deflected into my shoulder or possibly into my head. And broke my left arm on one of the first initial swings. As that happened, the first thing I did was stumble into the open area of the den, stumble back into the den where he continued to come at me with the bat and take a couple of swings. . . . And as that happened he wrapped one of the arms around my neck and started grabbing things off the counter, a candle lamp and a coffee mug and a glass candle holder or vase, candle vase. I don't know. And my table lamp, and everything he seemed like he could reach his hands on and try to smash it over my head, and as he continued to squeeze me around the neck. And I was screaming at him, "What are you doing? What are you trying to do?" And he kept saying, "Everybody's trying to get me. You out to get me." . . . And I started screaming at him, "I don't want to, I don't want to hurt you. I don't want to do anything but I'm gonna bleed to death. You gotta stop. You're gonna kill me." . . . And I kept asking if my family was alright because I knew my wife and my children were home. I was hearing some moans coming from the living room. And I kept asking if my wife was okay. And he kept saying she was fine, he had tied her up, that he didn't hurt her. And I asked him about my kids. And he said they were fine and they were both [in] the rooms, and my little girl was in her room sleeping and my little boy was in the room and he closed the door and told him not to come out, and he probably, and he said he probably fell asleep, you know, that he was frightened and he probably fell asleep. . . . And then . . . as it got dark he said he wanted to watch a particular program . . . *Magnum P.I.* . . . . And it was dark. And the only light on in the house was the [TV] which was on the whole time. . . . And he said he was going to leave. And he said he wanted to go to the bathroom before he left. . . . As I got up, he made me walk in front of him. He grabbed me by the

shoulder, which made me jump suddenly the way he grabbed me
. . . and as I turned he tried to stab me with a knife in the back. And
we started struggling again . . . and that's where he partially injured
me by puncturing in my pubic area. And I grabbed his arm, and we
struggled into the hall and we both fell down on the floor, which he
fell down on top of me. And I grabbed the knife with both of my
hands on the blade. He had the handle. And I had it by the blade. I
was squeezing it but I also, I had also as we fell down I had fell on
top of the knife with my body covering it. With that and plus me
holding onto it, he couldn't pull the knife out and he, he, we struggled for a while like that as he kept trying to pull the knife away
from me. And I kept screaming at him. He was trying to kill me
again and I wasn't letting go of the knife. And finally he, I don't
know if he got tired or whatever, he just kept saying, "I won't pull if
you won't pull but, you know, again I gotta calm down and I gotta
think, and I gotta think of a plan." . . .
Masson: How long did this, this encounter with Bill take place?
Myers: What?
Masson: How long did it last, this second encounter in the hall?
Myers: Maybe two to three hours that I, you know, two to three
hours at least. He seemed to be able to tell time from the [TV]. And
the only time I remember that he heard something on the [TV] and
he said, "Oh, it must be about 11:00." And it seemed like it wasn't
too long because he was thinking about how long he would have to
wait before he left the house to go over to his wife's house. And the
nearest thing I can think from there, the time as it elapsed was two,
possibly three hours.[6]

What was most significant and, in some cases, not necessarily explicit in
the statements of both men was the following:

• They arrived at the house somewhere between 3:30 and 4:00 PM.
• Each accused the other of attacking him.
• During the struggling, they stopped periodically to rest and to drink
  water.
• They took breaks to watch television programs, even *The Johnny
  Carson Show.*

When Myers asked Fontanille what happened, Fontanille said, "You don't want to know."

When Fontanille asked the same question, Myers said, "You don't want to know," and then he stabbed Fontanille.

Neither man mentioned seeing Janet's body on the living-room floor.[7]

As police compared notes and scrutinized the men's stories, they grew increasingly suspicious of Bill Fontanille, so he became the prime suspect. They had major questions. For example:

- Why did Bill park his car two blocks away on the day of the murder, but not during any of his preceding visits?
- The rooms in the house were small. Why didn't either man see Janet's body during their scuffles?
- Why did Bill, who believed he was critically injured, drive directly past a hospital to visit his parents?

Authorities juggled answers to these and other questions, critiqued inconsistencies in official interviews of both men, and tried to piece together a chronology of events leading up to Janet's cold-blooded beating and its aftermath. They interviewed family members and close friends. They listened to crime scene analysts and bloodstain pattern experts give varied interpretations. They waited patiently for forensic laboratory results, only to be told that they were "inconclusive." There was even an inconsistency in a statement given by a Litchwood neighbor who initially said she saw a man with a bat in front of the Myers house on the afternoon of the murder. Three days later, she changed the time to the preceding day. Then Bill changed his own statement about the bat. That he had *not* left it at the house on Wednesday night—that it was the next afternoon, early, at about 1:00. He claimed that he stayed for an hour or two, left without the bat, and returned at 4:00 to retrieve it. Detectives were skeptical and felt their suspect was changing his time line to dovetail with the neighbor's account.

Other factors also buttressed the detectives' suspicion: (1) When told someone had seen him with his bat outside the house on Thursday, the twenty-fourth, Bill appeared unrealistically calm. (2) He said he had had sex with Janet even though she had given birth only weeks before. (3) A longtime friend described Bill as a very good pathological liar. (4) His estranged wife, Susan, stated he had had frequent outbursts of rage, would quit jobs abruptly, and tried to commit suicide on five occasions. (5) On February 24, his choice of words for two police officers was the same as he had given to others before: "[Kerry's] going to tell you we had a plan to kill both our wives, but he didn't think I'd go through with it." Later one detective commented: "When I heard that, I knew something was out in left field. Why is he telling me this?" The other officer said, "Damn strange statement, without a doubt." The officer's implication was that suspects don't usually implicate themselves during an official statement made against another person.[8]

Then on February 26, three days after the murder, the *Times-Picayune* carried a front-page headline: "Family Friend Is Booked in Beating Death." Underneath, the lead to the story was:

> While her family prepared to bury 25-year-old Janet Myers, and her husband and child remained hospitalized, Jefferson Parish authorities Saturday arrested the best man at their wedding and booked him with murder.[9]

But did they have the right man? Some detectives and a prosecutor believed that Bill Fontanille had been telling the truth. Sergeant Masson and others believed otherwise.[10] By and large, the general public didn't know what or whom to believe.

There were those who subscribed to one of two possible scenarios: First, a man comes home from work and finds his wife and best friend in a compromising position. A violent argument ensues. The husband beats Janet to a pulp and, in the process, their child gets in the way and is accidentally injured. The men have a prolonged fight. The friend runs off. Or, second, a man visits his friends who are husband and wife. The husband had been lying in wait because he suspects a sexual liaison between his wife and the friend. A violent argument ensues . . . and so on. The stories are practically the same—only they blame each other.

However, some individuals—both in and out of law enforcement—were pushing a conspiracy theory: that the whole thing was staged—that Bill and Kerry had devised this uncanny plan to eliminate both wife Janet and wife Susan.

Yet another theory surfaced. It included the angle of homosexuality. Defense attorney Pat Fanning recalled: " . . . when you first see those pictures of [Janet] like that? . . . it's like, 'We've got psychosexual murder at least, whether it's [homosexual] or not.' See, when you get these sorts of crimes of passion that are aberrations on the part of the people . . . for people to get that aroused, I mean, that kind of fire in the belly is only brought out by sexual activity. . . . This case reminded me of cases I've seen in the past. . . . Gays, lesbians . . . when they have it in for each other? I mean, they do some bad things. They cut each other up, body parts and stuff. I mean, they do those kinds of things. And when I saw what was done here, I said, 'Some [son of a] bitch was *really* mad. We've got a passionate endeavor here.'"[11] I should add here that spurned lovers of all sexual orientations have committed some very horrific murders.

There were several significant developments over the course of the next few days:

- The chief of detectives announced that Bill Fontanille had not been under the influence of drugs or alcohol on the day of the murder.
- No one described either Kerry or Bill as despondent during Janet's wake or funeral.

On Thursday, March 1, the *Times-Picayune* ran a story (which Kerry Myers's backers called unfair):

Kerry Myers, whose wife was bludgeoned to death in their Harvey home last week, is a suspect in her slaying although there is no conclusive evidence of his involvement, a prosecutor said Wednesday. Authorities said they expect to get the results Thursday of laboratory tests to determine if Mrs. Myers' hair and blood are on the clothing of her husband or Fontanille. That could help answer some of the questions in the bizarre case, they said. "The investigation is still open," Chief of Detectives Eugene Fields said. "We are keeping an eye on Kerry Myers."[12]

The Jefferson crime lab released blood grouping test results:

- Janet had type A blood.
- Kerry Myers has type O blood.
- William Fontanille has type B blood.
- Ryan Myers has type A blood.

However, the conclusions associated with these findings confounded nearly everyone connected with the case. It had been expected that the type and quantity of blood found in the house would certainly have shed some light on who was lying and who was telling the truth. But there were discrepancies regarding whose blood was on whom; in short, the serology reports, as previously mentioned, came back as totally inconclusive.

Developments did continue, but at a slow pace. Grand juries were called but, at first, couldn't reach definite decisions. Finally one did, and in May 1986—more than two years after the murder—Bill Fontanille was indicted for first-degree murder. The trial was held six months later. The *Times-Picayune* described the outcome:

A mistrial was declared in William A. Fontanille's murder trial Saturday, leaving unanswered the 2-year-old question of who killed Janet Myers. Following five hours and forty minutes of deliberations . . . the jury declared itself hopelessly deadlocked with six members voting for a first-degree murder conviction and six for acquittal.[13]

There followed a four-year hiatus comprising legal maneuverings, more grand jury sessions, and trial dates set and then postponed. As Mardi Gras seasons came and went, people in greater New Orleans—from the average person on the street to those in the criminal justice establishment—remained both mystified and uneasy about the case. The titillating questions of wife swapping, kinky sex, and sex clubs—which permeated much of the talk prior to the first trial—seemed to fizzle. This is not to say that the subjects didn't pop up now and again, but none of it could be verified by law enforcement authorities.

At the beginning of this period, early 1987, I received a call from the investigative team of the Jefferson Parish Sheriff's Office, and, after a lengthy conversation, I knew I had to fly to Louisiana to study the actual crime scene.

Over the years, I've visited and lectured in New Orleans and in Jefferson Parish several times. During one of the visits, I met the legendary sheriff Harry Lee. He stands six feet two, weighs in at about three hundred pounds, and looks like a typical Cajun cowboy. (His walk, talk, style, and size are definitely not typical of a person of Chinese ancestry!) A former assistant United States attorney and a judge, he has been the Jefferson Parish sheriff for the last twenty years or so. His heart is as big as his body, and he truly cares for people, especially for the victims of crime. He is known to allocate whatever manpower, funding, and resources might be necessary to solve a major crime—and the Janet Myers murder was no exception. When he had phoned me, he said, "Cousin, we need your help in solving this strange homicide case." We are not related, but, after having met, we learned that we share many interests and beliefs about truth and justice. We also love to eat, especially good Cajun seafood. Consequently, we now refer to each other as "cousin."

The sheriff dispatched one of his top investigators, Lt. Vince Lamia, and others to consult with me in Connecticut. Vince and I had met before. He is an excellent homicide detective with years of experience. Large binders of crime reports, crime scene photographs, autopsy reports and photos, crime lab reports, and forensic consultant reports followed.

I must pause here to say that many mystery writers, news reporters, and movie producers believe I have a special ability to absorb all investigative reports and forensic facts in a particular case and, in a matter of minutes, to arrive at clues that solve the case. Some even think that I possess a special set of eyes that can easily locate clues at a crime scene. The fact is that I have neither a special intellect nor special eyes to visualize clues. But I will admit to using a heavy dose of the most important tools in criminal investigations: logic, science, keeping an open mind, and reliance on a team approach.

To this point in the Myers/Fontanille case, we have an almost identical version of a story told by two men. Either both of them are telling the truth, or they both are liars and have carefully rehearsed their stories. Of the case's three eyewitnesses, two are too young to give the real story, and Janet has been silenced. Only scientific evidence might be able to speak for her. Only a forensic scientist—through the examination of evidence—might be able to interpret the silent language left behind at the scene.

Some clothing seized from the victim and the suspects was forwarded to the Connecticut State Police Forensic Laboratory. The baseball bat, knife, and various other items collected from the crime scene were also submitted. In addition, as a show of appreciation, the offices of the Jefferson Parish district attorney and sheriff shipped two hundred pounds of crawfish by air to Connecticut. My personal assistant and friend, Sgt. Robert Mills, drove to the airport to pick up the little creatures—and we had a crawfish party at the lab. What a feast! The next morning, two-thirds of our staff phoned in sick.

And one-third came to work with upset stomachs. Apparently, some Connecticut Yankees cannot tolerate good Cajun seafood.

For two solid weeks, I worked every night and weekend on the case. (During the day, I still had to work on Connecticut cases.) My right-hand assistant, Elaine Pagliaro, was especially involved and helpful.

In June 1987 I flew to New Orleans to attend a pretrial meeting with the prosecutor and several detectives. We also visited the crime scene to reconstruct what had happened on the day of Janet's murder. The house had remained intact, but, of course, the bloodstains had all been washed away by the current owners. I stood in the center of the small living room and looked at the east wall. I could hear Janet crying out for help, and I could picture blood spatters projected onto the wall and the ceiling. Her body was so close to the foyer—why hadn't those two men heard her cry or seen her blood?

Later, in the district attorney's office, I met W. J. LeBlanc and Howat Peters, two prosecutors in the case. They are very knowledgeable on forensic evidence and bloodstain patterns, and our brain waves quickly linked. That night we gathered at Howat's home for more boiled crawfish. I truly enjoyed their southern hospitality.

I also met Paul Connick, then the top assistant to the chief prosecutor. Paul, a handsome, sharp attorney, has since been elected to the post of chief prosecutor of Jefferson Parish. We have worked many cases together and have developed a strong bond over the past two decades. He, like Sheriff Harry Lee, is not only a leader in Louisiana's law enforcement establishment but also a pillar in the criminal justice system of our entire nation.

The four-year hiatus ended in March 1990 when *both* Fontanille and Myers went on trial for Janet's killing. It was an unusual double trial in which a full jury panel would decide the fate of Bill Fontanille, while only the presiding judge would decide on the verdict for Kerry Myers. Confident that he'd be deemed innocent, Myers had agreed to such an option.

It may be helpful to step back for a moment and review some key dates:

Janet murdered: February 1984
Bill Fontanille indicted: May 1986
Mistrial declared: November 1986
I agreed to review case: early 1987
Reconstruction of the crime scene: June 1987
My official report: September 1987
Double trial begins: March 1990

FORENSIC CONSIDERATIONS

I daresay that, in a career spanning six thousand to seven thousand major criminal cases, I have never had one quite like this: one in which two suspects—each blaming the other—give the same story as it applies to the events surrounding a vicious murder. The only difference, as we've seen, is the story's beginning and ending. In this regard, the essential questions are: Whose version is the real one? And, could the facts and truth be found in the crime scene and the forensic evidence?

By carefully studying materials provided by Jefferson Parish police and laboratory officials, and through my own extensive investigation of the Myerses' home, my assessment of the crime scene was that it was a *complicated* and *disorganized* one—complicated in that it involved five different areas; disorganized in that much activity had taken place throughout those areas (there was evidence of movement from one location to another). Taken together, they signified widespread action. A third—and key—fact was that the rooms in this compact home were exceedingly small, leading one to wonder how two young adults could grapple with each other extensively, yet not see Janet's body in the living room nor hear her voice. At least each man *said* that he hadn't.

But I'm getting ahead of myself. Let's return to early 1987 when officials from the district attorney's office flew from New Orleans to my Connecticut State Police office. Despite an unwieldy workload, I had agreed to meet with them, discuss the case, and examine some of the physical evidence. They presented me with more evidence: Myers's shoes, his dress slacks, a dishtowel and a handkerchief recovered from the kitchen, a baseball cap found in the hallway, and part of a shattered ashtray. They had been led to believe that these items contained blood that matched Fontanille's type. But my testing results revealed that the bloodstains were actually consistent with Myers's type. And there were other discrepancies that surfaced during our two days of meetings and laboratory testing:

- Whereas they had determined the handkerchief had Janet's or Ryan's type A blood on it, we found it also had a mucus stain that was similar to Myers's type.
- Whereas they had found blood types B and O on the dishtowel, we found a mixture of A, B, and O types.

View showing front entrance of the Myerses' residence.

- Whereas their typing of blood on the cap was inconclusive, we found it contained both A and B types.
- Whereas the stains on the ashtray glass had been labeled as inconclusive in typing, we found it to be type A.

(To reiterate: Janet Myers had type A blood; her son, Ryan, also had type A; her husband, Kerry, had type O; and Bill Fontanille had type B.)

The reddish material found in the broken dish and on the love seat was not blood, but was red Jell-O.

In analyzing the crime scene, I relied on both an abundance of fine photographs taken by crime scene investigators and my own personal observations at the scene.

Entrance area: There were no blood drops on a concrete walkway to the front entrance, but on a brick wall adjacent to that area was a contact transfer–type pattern—about three inches in diameter. This suggested that a liquid blood source contacted that surface, causing the transfer. It was a direct transfer, that is, not of the blood spatter, or smear, or dripping variety—rather, it was a direct contact, transfer bloodstain.

Foyer: Numerous contact smears and blood droplets were scattered about. A Mardi Gras poster lay on the floor; it had no stains. Stains on the tile floor were no doubt the result of transfer blood from someone's shoes. In addition, there were some dripping-type stains there, plus blood smears on a glass cabinet near the far wall of the foyer. I believed that the cabinet had been pushed away from its original location, possibly by an injured person (or persons) who was dripping blood. A blood smear pattern was seen near the lock mechanism on the inside of the front door. The pattern had a "motion" appearance to it, meaning someone had touched that area, possibly moving a bloody hand over the door's surface.

Living room: This all-important area contained the victim's body. There was little doubt in my mind that the entire residence was a *primary* crime scene; that is, Janet's murder took place in that scene, not somewhere beyond the residence. She had been struck repeatedly with a blunt object, consistent with the baseball bat. However, the incident may have started in another room and ended up at her final location in the living room. Bloodstains on her sneakers suggested that at some time during the beating, she was in an upright position. An overturned plant stand with her blood transfer pattern indicated a defensive gesture on her part. A large quantity of blood was on

Overall view showing blood patterns on the living-room wall.

Close-up view of the baseball bat with bloodstains in the family room.

the carpet beneath and around the body. Her bloodstains were spread across more than twelve feet of the living room's east wall. We could infer that her palm and fingers touched the wall during the incident, as evidenced by bloody finger and hand marks within the bloodstains. I was able to reconstruct, with reasonable scientific certainty, that her fingers slid down the wall as she fell to the floor. Moreover, she probably fell from a right to left direction, which is consistent with the eventual body location. As already mentioned, Janet was hit repeatedly—the cast-off blood patterns tell us that. She most likely twisted her head from side to side during the process, as revealed by many fine-line brush-pattern stains on the inner aspect of her forearms and on the baseboard behind her head. Also, a special type of medium-velocity pattern on the wall indicated that her blood had been projected upward; that is, the blood source was at a lower point. This is known as an "arterial spurt" type of pattern: one produced by blood under pressure and, in this case, forced upward onto the wall behind the victim. In putting all this blood evidence together—blood spatter patterns, blood imprint patterns, and arterial bleeding patterns—I concluded that Janet had received some minor injuries *prior* to her falling down, for the patterns were well defined and were detected *on top of* the handprint. One could not miss the many trails of minute spatter on the walls, floors, and furniture. There were between twenty-five hundred and three thousand individual spatters on the walls alone. The trails could be seen winding from room to room.

Kitchen: There was a blood transfer pattern on the wall phone. There was also evidence that someone had been cleaning up in that area: blood smears on the dish towel and handkerchief, red-colored liquid in a plastic cup, and a diluted bloodstain on the counter. But my findings there were at odds with what both men had reported. They claimed to have entered the kitchen *after* having been injured; however, I found no blood drops on the kitchen floor or in the hallway leading to it—which would have substantiated their claims.

Family room: Large amounts of blood smears and blood droplets were seen here. The furniture pieces in disarray and the broken glassware support the idea that major fighting took place in this area. The bloodstained bat was leaning, barrel down, against an askew love seat.

Master bedroom: I believe that the beating began in this room as evidenced by the bloodstain patterns which I scrutinized—patterns of extensive bloodshed and vomited material on the carpeted floor. It was here, also, that the seriously injured Ryan was found. (Ryan, I am relieved to say, later completely recovered.)

Clothing: Close inspection of wearing apparel provided additional forensic information. Representative were Myers's dress slacks and Fontanille's blue jeans. At first glance, no bloodstains were apparent on Myers's gray slacks. But with the use of special lighting, definite stains were observed. Fontanille's blue jeans, on the other hand, displayed obvious stains such as a large brushing pattern on the back portion. This indicated back-and-forth contact with liquid blood. There were large numbers of blood spatter on both legs—from the tiniest spot requiring magnification to larger ones visible to the naked eye—more than one thousand in all. The patterns suggested frontward, sideward, backward, upward, and downward directionalities. Two things occurred to me while I examined the jeans: (1) Either Fontanille was swinging the bat, or (2) he had to have been in close proximity to Myers who was swinging the bat. Actually, three things: They could have taken turns swinging the bat. The point is that the jeans were covered with medium-velocity stains, and such stains would not have traveled six to eight feet across a room.

Variety of blood patterns found on Fontanille's blue jeans.

Random conclusions:

- The man wielding the bat the most had to be left-handed because the cast-off blood patterns were left-handed. Kerry Myers is left-handed.
- There was considerable spatter upon spatter. This indicates a time lag—more than one beating episode, possibly three or more.
- In my view, Myers's stab wounds were too shallow to have been inflicted with any degree of anger. I believe the men fought some, but they also took time out to plan. In other words, together, they decided to stage an explanation of what had taken place.

I stated in the quotation introducing the Duntz Brothers case that I can help reconstruct crime scene events, but I cannot always tell you who, and cannot tell you why. And that applies to this case, as well. Finally, it should be pointed out that some of the contents of the above section constituted the framework of my testimony later.

DOUBLE TRIAL

The unusual trial of both Kerry Myers and William Fontanille got underway on Wednesday, March 28, 1990, four years after the first trial of Fontanille alone, and six years after Janet's murder. The judicial principals were the following:

- Presiding judge: the Honorable Ernest V. Richards, Judge, Twenty-fourth Judicial District, State of Louisiana
- For the prosecution: attorneys W. J. LeBlanc and Howat Peters
- For the defense: attorney Wiley Beevers representing Myers, and attorney Nick Noriea representing Fontanille

As my friend Joseph Bosco explained in his book: "Before the first witness [was] even called . . . the complications inherent [in] the judge being the trier of fact on one defendant [Myers] while, simultaneously, the jury is the trier of fact on a codefendant [Fontanille] [began] to present themselves."[14] The complications became apparent in the decision of opposing sides presenting opening statements, the order of cross-examinations, as well as other procedural matters. For example, (1) the state had an opening statement, as did the defense attorney for Fontanille, but the attorney for Myers waived the opportunity; and (2) immediately after the first witness was called to the stand, the judge had to ask the state whether the witness was one in the Fontanille case or in the Myers case. This set an awkward tone for the entire double trial, for the issue would continue to be not so much *what* a witness would testify to, but *to whom* the witness was testifying: the judge, the jury, or both.

The actual opening statement by the state was no less awkward. Prosecutor LeBlanc presented both scenarios, that is, ones encompassing the version of events as given by each defendant. He mentioned that the evidence would show that there were copious amounts of blood on the clothes that the defendants and the victim had worn; that there were three distinct blood types involved: Myers's O, Fontanille's B, and Janet's A. He termed it a fortuitous circumstance, a serologist's dream. He indicated that the jury would learn that Janet's blood was on every piece of Fontanille's exposed clothing and that the judge would learn that her blood was on Myers's pants and handkerchief. LeBlanc ended with: "You're going to see photographs where Janet was found, you're going to see where Ryan was found. You're going to see where Sarah was found. You're going to see where the famous ten-hour fight took place—and you're going to see where it's one *gigantic plot*."[15]

Then it was the defense's turn. Attorney Noriea stressed that Fontanille's story was more compatible with the physical evidence than Myers's and that, at the very least, there was reasonable doubt of his client's guilt. The attorney also approached the subject from the opposite direction, stressing that some evidence hadn't been properly tested, preserved, photographed, or otherwise documented. But if it had been, he declared, his client would easily be found innocent.

Most of the testimony itself was old news, given by a predictable list of friends and relatives of the defendants, along with representatives from the medical, legal, forensic, and law enforcement professions.

Dr. Richard Tracy, who had performed the autopsy, presented his findings in graphic and—to some—unnerving detail. He gave as the immediate cause of death an air embolism to the heart, causing coronary arrest. He explained that Janet's large gaping wounds exposed large severed veins which, in turn, allowed air to enter the bloodstream.

My own testimony filled the greater part of two days in the eleven-day trial. At the state's request, I delineated the components of blood spatter analysis, defining terms such as medium-velocity blood spatter, angle of impact, terminal velocity, blood trail, impact spatter, satellite spatter, smears, swipes and wipes, diluted blood patterns, imprint patterns, and others. I followed with my partial reconstruction of the crime scene (essentially covering the material noted here under "Forensic Considerations").

The verdicts were met with the usual gasps from the usual corners and with stone silence from the defendants:

Kerry Myers: guilty of murder in the second degree. Sentence imposed: life in prison without the possibility of parole.

William Fontanille: guilty of manslaughter. Sentence imposed: mandatory twenty-one years in prison.

POSTSCRIPT

Bill Fontanielle was paroled on November 14, 2000. Kerry Myers is still in prison. Despite his incarceration, Myers remarried.

What this case illustrates is that blood evidence—once searched for, recovered, and properly identified—can tell a story all its own, one that may often be more tenable than any told by defendants, witnesses, or even police authorities.

As for the crucial triad of *motive*, *opportunity*, and *means*, the latter two presented no problem. But for *motive*, the number of possibilities was extensive. Forensic psychiatrist Dr. Aris Cox offered an intriguing interpretation after he had been informed of marital infidelity in Kerry Myers's early background—that Kerry had caught his mother with another man and that Kerry was most likely an illegitimate child. Moreover, he may have been keenly aware of this possibility. The doctor speculated: Could this brutal New Orleans killing be the direct result of history having repeated itself? That is, could Kerry have thought that Ryan or baby Sarah was not his own? And then, the psychiatrist's stunning conclusion: "Before, we could never account for that *amount* of rage, instant hatred—but this had been festering and growing for twenty years . . . every time he smashed that bat into her face, he was also smashing it into his mother's."[16]

I had no reason to quibble with the verdicts. In a sense, Fontanille was drawn into the decision because he had lied about Janet's being dead, or even about her body's lying on the living-room floor. These alone spell complicity, in my judgment. As for Myers's, I was not surprised at the determination that he was the "bat man." Janet's blood and the medium-velocity impact spatter were, after all, on his left shoe, his lower left pant leg, his left thigh area, and his left shirt-pocket area. And what about the cast-off patterns from the bloody bat? They were found on the left shoulder region of his shirt. These findings were consistent with a left-handed person swinging an object like a baseball bat. Recall, Myers is left-handed. There were large amounts of blood spatter patterns on Fontanille, yes, but few consistent with a bat swinging up and down.

In the end, it all seemed to fit.

epilogue

Our first task in writing this book was in deciding which cases to include. There were many to choose from, even if we limited ourselves to those famous ones in which I (Dr. Lee) had been personally involved as a forensic scientist. I have assisted law enforcement agencies around the world—investigating approximately seven thousand cases—in a career spanning forty-plus years. One of our criteria was to select cases that occurred on American soil, and that also represent different geographical locations in our country. Thus we have crimes committed in California, Utah, North Carolina, Louisiana, and Connecticut. We picked three cases that took place at the very beginning of the twenty-first century: Scott Peterson, Elizabeth Smart, and Michael Peterson. This was quite unintentional; yet, as it turns out, it allows us now to reflect on the range of domestic, social, and criminal justice issues in these most recent years—and on a new relationship between the media and the public.

Each of these cases is distinctive, offering its own instruction—historical, investigative, and scientific. Taken together, information gleaned from them may help thwart much human tragedy in the years to come.

The tenor of these recent times was such that authorities consider it remarkable for the above-cited cases (and others like them) to have dominated TV talk shows and news reports to the extent they did. The period was, after all, marked by the turn of a new century, the terrorist attacks of 9/11, the election and reelection of a United States president, wars in Afghanistan and Iraq, the capture of Saddam Hussein, the killer tsunami that crushed or washed away an untold number of lives in South Asia, and our own killer hurricanes in Louisiana and Mississippi. But time and time again, stories of less international consequence made their way onto the front pages and airwaves and the Internet, stories about individual acts of violence: murders, shark attacks, child abductions. One summer, the media claimed that shark attacks were on the rise; a year later, it was child abductions' turn. Yet, in both instances, the incidence had, in fact, decreased. It was the *volume of news coverage* that had increased. And so it was with murders.

We must all strive for looking for the truth. Our fascination with these kinds of cases perhaps derives from our curiosity about what we humans are capable of. Though murders and abductions may not be as rampant as some in the media would have you believe, we still need to solve these cases because the families and society need answers. Today we can use the most advanced tools in forensic science at our disposal to assist police detectives in finding the clues and following the leads.

Throughout the book, victims and perpetrators have been at center stage, while off to the side were loved ones who must accept their own special grief. It is a grief that I have seen far too often, not only at the time of a crime, during our investigation, and throughout the trial, but also for years later. I have always tried to maintain the neutrality and objectivity of a forensic scientist, but the anguish of such families has touched me over the years—so much so that I have toyed with the idea of writing a book about it. Its scope and weighty importance deserve one. We shall see.

This is our third book as coauthors. Many have inquired about our technique. We always respond: "I talk, he listens. He talks, I listen. He writes, I edit. I write, he edits. Then we confer and combine." It has worked well for us. We hope that it has for you, too.

Dr. Henry C. Lee
Jerry Labriola, MD

notes

CHAPTER ONE. THE SCOTT PETERSON CASE

1. *People*, December 13, 2004, p. 65.
2. Dr. Henry Lee and Dr. Jerry Labriola, *Famous Crimes Revisited* (New York: Berkley Books, 2004), pp. 228–30.
3. Henry C. Lee, Timothy Palmbach, and Marilyn T. Miller, *Henry Lee's Crime Scene Handbook* (San Diego: Academic Press, 2001), p. 135.
4. Amber Frey, *Witness: For the Prosecution of Scott Peterson* (New York: Regan Books, 2005), p. 176.
5. *People*, October 11, 2004, p. 67.
6. Michael Fleeman, *Laci* (New York: St. Martin's Press, 2003), p. 23.
7. Missing Person Supplement, Modesto Police Department, January 7, 2003.
8. Frey, *Witness: For the Prosecution of Scott Peterson*, pp. 104, 107, 124, 128.
9. Ibid., p. 107.
10. Ibid., p. 124.
11. Ibid., p. 128.
12. Lee and Labriola, *Famous Crimes Revisited*, p. 98.
13. Frey, *Witness: For the Prosecution of Scott Peterson*, p. 185.
14. Lee, Palmbach, and Miller, *Henry Lee's Crime Scene Handbook*, pp. 247–48.

15. Fleeman, *Laci*, p. 94.
16. Ibid., p. 109.
17. Ibid., p. 113.
18. KTVU, San Francisco, January 29, 2003.
19. Fleeman, *Laci*, p. 114.
20. Ibid.
21. Ibid., pp. 123, 125.
22. *Larry King Live*, CNN, February 19, 2003.
23. Ibid., April 18, 2003.
24. Associated Press, April 22, 2003.
25. Lee and Labriola, *Famous Crimes Revisited*, p. 58.
26. CourtTV.com, June 1, 2003.
27. Ibid.
28. Ibid., June 18, 2003.
29. Ibid., October 28, 2003.
30. *People*, October 11, 2004, p. 68.
31. ABC News, October 7, 2004.
32. Ibid.
33. Ibid.
34. Ibid.
35. CourtTV.com, October 22, 2004.
36. Ibid., November 11, 2004.
37. Ibid.
38. Ibid.
39. Ibid., November 12, 2004.
40. Ibid., November 13, 2004.
41. *On the Record*, FOX News, December 16, 2004.
42. Associated Press, December 14, 2004.
43. *All Info about Crime,* December 15, 2004.
44. ABC News, December 14, 2004.
45. Ibid.
46. *All Info about Crime*, December 15, 2004.

CHAPTER TWO. THE ELIZABETH SMART CASE

1. Associated Press, July 16, 2002.
2. Editorial, *Waterbury Republican-American*, July 20, 2002.
3. Ed Smart and Lois Smart, *Bringing Elizabeth Home* (New York: Doubleday, 2003), pp. 8–9.
4. Dr. Henry Lee and Dr. Jerry Labriola, *Famous Crimes Revisited* (New York: Berkley Books, 2004), p. 113.
5. *Salt Lake Tribune*, June 13, 2002.
6. Maggie Haberman and Jeane MacIntosh, *Held Captive* (New York: Avon Books, 2003), p. 165.
7. Smart and Smart, *Bringing Elizabeth Home*, pp.103–104.
8. Ibid., p.117.
9. Haberman and MacIntosh, *Held Captive*, p. 148.
10. Ibid.
11. Ibid., pp. 152–53.
12. Ibid., p. 157.
13. Ibid., pp. 181–82.
14. KSL Television and Radio, Salt Lake City, March 14, 2003.
15. Associated Press, March 18, 2003.
16. Smart and Smart, *Bringing Elizabeth Home*, pp. 98–99.
17. Crime Scene Reconstruction Report, February 11, 2003.
18. Ibid.
19. Tom Smart and Lee Benson, *In Plain Sight* (Chicago: Chicago Review Press, 2005), p. 373.
20. *Salt Lake Tribune*, September 1, 2002.
21. Smart and Smart, *Bringing Elizabeth Home*, p. 129.
22. Ibid., p. 134.
23. Associated Press, November 15, 2002.
24. Ibid.
25. Ibid.
26. Smart and Benson, *In Plain Sight*, dust jacket.
27. Associated Press, November 15, 2002.
28. *Larry King Live*, CNN, December 23, 2002.
29. Smart and Benson, *In Plain Sight*, p. 275.
30. Ibid., p. 329.
31. KSL Television and Radio, Salt Lake City, March 16, 2003.

32. Haberman and MacIntosh, *Held Captive*, p. 303.

33. Ibid., p. 305.

34. KSL Television and Radio, Salt Lake City, March 13, 2003.

35. Ibid.

36. Associated Press, March 18, 2003.

37. The Smoking Gun, http://www.thesmokinggun.com, March 18, 2003.

CHAPTER THREE. THE MICHAEL PETERSON CASE

1. CourtTV.com, July 1, 2003.

2. *Herald-Sun* [Durham, NC], January 15, 2002.

3. "The Staircase—Crime Scene or Accident," *CBC Newsworld*, January 16, 2005.

4. CourtTV.com, June 29, 2003.

5. Ibid., July 2, 2003.

6. *Herald-Sun*, February 19, 2002.

7. Ibid.

8. Report of Autopsy Examination, Office of Chief Medical Examiner, Chapel Hill, NC. Autopsy number B01-2384.

9. *Herald-Sun*, February 21, 2002.

10. "The Staircase—Crime Scene or Accident," *CBC Newsworld*, January 16, 2005.

11. Ibid.

12. Ibid.

13. Ibid.

14. "The Staircase—Crime Scene or Accident," *CBC Newsworld*, January 16, 2005.

15. Ibid.

16. *Herald-Sun*, March 5, 2002.

17. Ibid., February 22, 2002.

18. Ibid., February 8, 2002.

19. Ibid., January 12, 2002.

20. Ibid.

21. *Herald-Sun*, January 16, 2002.

22. Ibid., February 9, 2002.

23. "The Staircase—Crime Scene or Accident," *CBC Newsworld*, January 18, 2005.

24. Ibid.

25. Ibid.

26. CourtTV.com, July 23, 2003.

27. Ibid., August 18, 2003.

28. "The Staircase—A Weak Case?" *CBC Newsworld*, January 19, 2005.

29. CourtTV.com, September 2, 2003.

30. Ibid., September 4, 2003.

31. Ibid.

32. "The Staircase—A Weak Case?" *CBC Newsworld*, January 19, 2005.

33. CourtTV.com, September 8, 2003.

34. Ibid.

35. Ibid., September 17, 2003.

36. Ibid., September 23, 2003.

37. Ibid.

38. Ibid., October 2, 2003.

39. Ibid.

40. Ibid., October 3, 2003.

41. Ibid.

42. *News & Observer* [Raleigh, NC], October 11, 2003.

43. CourtTV.com, October 10, 2003.

44. Ibid.

CHAPTER FOUR. THE DUNTZ BROTHERS CASE

1. *Trace Evidence: The Case Files of Dr. Henry Lee*, Court TV, December 31, 2004.

2. Ibid.

3. *Waterbury Republican*, January 26, 1990.

4. Report of Investigation, State of Connecticut, Office of Chief Medical Examiner, M.E. Case No. L-86-457, October 23, 1986.

5. Henry C. Lee, Timothy Palmbach, and Marilyn T. Miller, *Henry Lee's Crime Scene Handbook* (San Diego: Academic Press, 2001), p. 272.

6. *Waterbury Republican*, January 3, 1990.

7. Ibid.

8. Ibid., January 26, 1990.

9. Ibid.

10. *Lakeville Journal*, February 1, 1990.

11. Ibid.

12. Ibid.

13. Ibid.

14. *Waterbury Republican*, February 2, 1990.

15. Ibid., February 7, 1990.

16. Ibid., February 21, 1990.

17. Ibid., February 10, 1990.

18. Ibid., February 8, 1990.

19. Ibid., February 22, 1990.

20. Ibid., March 3, 1990.

CHAPTER FIVE. THE MYERS/FONTANILLE CASE

1. Joseph Bosco, *Blood Will Tell* (New York: William Morris, 1993), p. 87.

2. Record of Jefferson Parish Sheriff's Office, Communications Division, Radio Room, 1:40 AM, February 24, 1984.

3. Bosco, *Blood Will Tell*, pp. 34, 45.

4. Record of Jefferson Parish Sheriff's Office, Detective Bureau, February 25, 1984.

5. Ibid.

6. Ibid., March 14, 1984.

7. Ibid.

8. Bosco, *Blood Will Tell*, p. 45.

9. [New Orleans] *Times-Picayune*, February 26, 1984.

10. Bosco, *Blood Will Tell*, pp. 62, 122.

11. Ibid., p. 70.

12. *Times-Picayune*, March 1, 1984.

13. Ibid., November 2, 1986.

14. Ibid., p. 397.

15. Ibid., p. 400.

16. Ibid., p. 512.

bibliography

Baden, Michael M., and Marion Roach. *Dead Reckoning*. New York: Touchstone, 2001.

Bosco, Joseph. *Blood Will Tell*. New York: William Morrow and Company, 1993.

Di Maio, Vincent J. M., and Suzanna E. Dana. *Forensic Pathology*. Austin: LandesBioscience, 1998.

Eckert, William G., and Stuart H. James. *Interpretation of Bloodstain Evidence at Crime Scenes*. New York: Elsevier, 1989.

Erzinglioglu, Zakaria. *Forensics True Crime Scene Investigations*. New York: Barnes & Noble Books, 2000.

Fanning, Dianne. *Written in Blood*. New York: St. Martin's Press, 2005.

Farley, Mark A., and James J. Harrington. *Forensic DNA Technology*. Boca Raton, FL: CRC Press, 1990.

Fischer, Barry. *Techniques of Crime Scene Investigations*. Boca Raton, FL: CRC Press, 1992.

Fleeman, Michael. *Laci*. New York: St. Martin's Press, 2003.

Frey, Amber. *Witness: For the Prosecution of Scott Peterson*. New York: Regan Books, 2005.

Geberth, Vernon J. *Practical Homicide Investigation*. Boca Raton, FL: CRC Press, 1996.

Giannelli, Paul C., and Edward J. Imwinkelried. *Scientific Evidence*. Charlottesville, VA: Michie Company, 1993.

Haberman, Maggie, and Jeane MacIntosh. *Held Captive*. New York: Avon Books, 2003.

Jones, Aphrodite. *A Perfect Husband*. New York: Pinnacle Books, 2004.

Lee, Henry C., and Robert E. Gaensslen, eds. *Advances in Fingerprint Technology*. Boca Raton, FL: CRC Press, 1991.

Lee, Henry C., and Jerry Labriola. *Famous Crimes Revisited*. Avon, CT: Strong Books, 2001.

Lee, Henry C., with Thomas W. O'Neil. *Cracking Cases*. Amherst, NY: Prometheus Books, 2002.

———. *Cracking More Cases*. Amherst, NY: Prometheus Books, 2004.

Lee, Henry C., Timothy Palmbach, and Marilyn T. Miller. *Henry Lee's Crime Scene Handbook*. San Diego: Academic Press, 2001.

MacDonell, Herbert L. *Bloodstain Patterns*. Corning, NY: Laboratory of Forensic Science, 1993.

Marriner, Brian. *On Death's Bloody Trail*. New York: St. Martin's Press, 1991.

Osterburgh, James W., and Richard H. Ward. *Criminal Investigation*. Cincinnati: Anderson Publishing Company, 1996.

Ridley, Matt. *Genome*. New York: HarperCollins, 2000.

Ragle, Larry. *Crime Scene*. New York: Avon Books, 1995.

Smart, Ed, and Lois Smart. *Bringing Elizabeth Home*. New York: Doubleday, 2003.

Smart, Tom, and Lee Benson. *In Plain Sight*. Chicago: Chicago Review Press, 2005.

Wecht, Cyril, and Mark Curriden, with Angela Powell. *Tales from the Morgue*. Amherst, NY: Prometheus Books, 2005.

Wecht, Cyril, and Greg Saitz, with Mark Curriden. *Mortal Evidence*. Amherst, NY: Prometheus Books, 2003.

Zonderman, Jon. *Beyond the Crime Lab*. New York: John Wiley & Sons, 1990.

index